Hotel Management and Hospitality Enterprises

Hotel Management and Hospitality Enterprises

JITENDRA K. SHARMA

KANISHKA PUBLISHERS, DISTRIBUTORS
NEW DELHI-110 002

KANISHKA PUBLISHERS, DISTRIBUTORS
4697/5-21A, Ansari Road, Daryaganj
New Delhi -110 002
Phones : 2327 0497, 2328 8285
Fax : 011-2328 8285
E-mail : kanishka_publishing@yahoo.co.in

Hotel Management and Hospitality Enterprises

First Edition-2006
Second Edition-2015
ISBN: 978-81-7391-820-1

PRINTED IN INDIA

Published by Madan Sachdeva for Kanishka Publishers, Distributors, 4697/5-21A, Ansari Road, Daryaganj, New Delhi-110 002, Typeset by Sunshine Graphics, Delhi, and Printed at Rajdhani Printers, Delhi.

Preface

Today, hospitality industry, including hospitality enterprises, comprise much more that traditional businesses and services of providing accommodation, serving prepared food and beverages and making arrangements necessary for guest's entertainment. New areas, such as hotel chains, brand management, product management, services quality management, enterprise management, managing marketing and accounting services, etc. Maintaining brand image involves upholding set of beliefs consumers hold about a particular brand. Similarly, today product is understood as anything that can be offered to a market for attention, acquisition, use or consumption that might satisfy a guest's wants or needs. It induces physical objects, services persons, places, organizations and ideas. The idea that consumers will favour products that offer the most of quality, performance and features, and that is why, the hospitality enterprises today devote their energy to make continuous products improvements. They help to convert the product idea into a workable product that enhances customer's satisfaction. This book "Hotel Management and Hospitality Enterprises" provide an introduction to all such aforementioned issues, besides giving an overview of contemporary hotel business worldwide in various categories, such as, hotel, motel, restaurant etc. The various associated management and governance issues involved with hotel industry and hospitality enterprises are dealt in detail, with special focus on brand management and product management. The most vital sector of marketing has been covered in detail, including market positioning , market targeting, marketing information system and marketing management. Focus has been there on the analysed planning, implementation and control of programmes designed to create, build and maintain beneficial exchanges with target buyers for the purpose of achieving organizational objectives, especially of hotels and hospitality enterprises. Full details have been provided about various marketing services agencies involved globally in these sectors, thus helping these enterprises to target and promote their products to the right markets. This also underlines the fact that in hotel and hospitality industries, as in most other ones, achieving organizational goals depends on determining the needs and wants of target markets and delivering desired satisfactions more effectively and efficiently than competitors. This necessitates today an integrated structure of people, equipment and procedures to gather, sort, analyse, evaluate and distribute the needed, timely and accurate information to marketing decision-markers. The hotel and hospitality enterprises in this book provide to the sector with systematic design collection, analysis and reporting of date and findings relevant to a specific marketing situation facing a hotel company in particulars and hospitality industry, in general.

This book provides its readers with detailed description about the "International Hotel and Restaurant Association" and the best practices suggested for environmental conservation.

It helps to provide an environmental management perspective to hotel industries in India and abroad in which the concerned form to takes aggressive actions to affect the public and forces in its marketing environment rather than simply watching and reaching to it. This book also provides readers with an exhaustive perspective on modern trends and practices in contemporary hotel industry world-wide, besides the various measures required for its continuous improvement in terms of service quality. A detailed World Trade Organisation and IH&RA classification of global hotel industry, along with its basis, is provided in a systematic way.

This book gives an extensive coverage, in form of various case studies, to major global hospitality enterprises and organizations related to guest management and hotel management. An extensive bibliography has been provided which will be helpful in future research in these areas of study. This book, therefore, serves a dual purpose of being a text book and a reference book, at the same time.

Jitendra K. Sharma

Contents

1

Introduction to Hotel Business and Brand Management

HOTEL

A hotel is an establishment that provides lodging on a short-term basis. Hotels often provide a number of additional guest services such as a restaurant, a swimming pool, child care. Some hotels have conference services and encourage groups to hold conventions and meetings at their location.

The word derives from the French hotel, which originally refers to a French version of a townhouse, not a place offering accommodation (in contemporary usage, hotel also has the meaning of "hotel"). The French spelling (with the circumflex) was once also used in English, but is now rare.

Hotels differ from motels in that most motels have drive-up, exterior entrances to the rooms, while hotels tend to have halls with interior entrances to the rooms.

The cost and quality of hotels are usually relatively indicative of the range and type of services available. Due to the enormous increase in tourism worldwide, during the last decades of the 20th century common standards, especially those of smaller establishments, have improved considerably. For the sake of greater comparability, various rating systems have been introduced, with the one to five stars classification being the most commonly used.

"Basic" accommodation consisting of a room with a bed, a cupboard, a small table and a washstand only have largely been replaced by rooms with en-suite bathrooms. Other features many travelers do not want to do without today are a TV, a telephone, an alarm clock, a small refrigerator (usually referred to as "mini-bar") containing snacks and drinks (to be paid for on departure), and tea and coffee making facilities (cups, spoons, an electric kettle and sachets containing instant coffee, tea bags, sugar, and creamer).

However, in Japan is an opposite example, that of the capsule hotel, where facilities and room space have been drastically reduced.

Apart from family-run or individual hotels, there are also national and worldwide hotel chains.

Hotels in Fiction

Hotels have often been chosen by authors as the setting of their literary works, *e.g.* The Hotel New Hampshire. It is especially true of crime fiction (Agatha Christie's Evil Under the Sun, A Caribbean Mystery, At Bertram's Hotel; Cyril Hare's Suicide Excepted) and farces. Hotels also feature prominently in films (Grand Hotel, Room Service, Plaza Suite), television series (Fawlty Towers, Hotelier), and songs, *e.g.*, "Hotel California."

Other Usage

In Australia, the word "hotel" often refers to a public house, a drinking establishment which does not necessarily, provide accommodations. In India, the word may also refer to a restaurant, since earlier the best restaurants were always situated next to a good hotel.

MOTEL

The word **motel** originates from the Motel Inn of San Luis Obispo, first built in 1925 by Arthur Heinemann. Entering dictionaries after World War II, the motel (aka the motor hotel) referred initially to a single building of connected rooms whose doors face a parking lot and/or common area, and their creation was the outcome of the creation of the United States highway system which predated the interstate highway system and allowed easy cross-country travel.

Unlike their predecessors, auto camps and tourist courts, motels quickly adopted a homogenized appearance. Typically one would find an 'I' or 'L' or 'U' shaped structure that included rooms, an attached manager's office, and perhaps a small dinner. Even so, postwar motels often featured eye-catching neon signs which employed pop culture themes that ranged from Western imagery of cowboys and Indians to contemporary images of spaceships and atomic symbols.

The modern motel began in the 1920s as mom-and-pop motor courts on the outskirts of a town. They attracted the first road warriors as they crossed the U.S. in their new automobiles. They usually had a grouping of small cabins and their anonymity made them ideal trysting places (or the "hot trade" in industry lingo). Even the famous outlaws Bonnie and Clyde were frequent guests, using motels as hideouts. The motel's potential for breeding lust and larceny alarmed then FBI chief J. Edgar Hoover, who attacked motels and auto camps in an article he penned called "Camps of Crime", which ran in the February 1940 issue of American Magazine.

Motels differed from hotels in their emphasis on largely anonymous interactions between owners and occupants, their location along highways (as opposed to urban cores), and their orientation to the outside (in contrast to hotels whose doors typically face a hallway).

With the 1950s introduction of Kemmons Wilson's Holiday Inn, the 'mom and pop' motels of that era went into decline. Eventually, the emergence of the interstate highway system, along with other factors, led to a blurring of the motel and the hotel. Today, family owned motels with as few as five rooms may still be found along older highways, but their lifespans appear to be short. The quality and standards of every independent motel differ so it is always wise to cruise around for good motel before setting in a room.

In seedy areas, motels also tend to be located near strip clubs, for the purpose of engaging in sexual activity. Motels are often places of prostitution and drug crime. Motels are also often inhabited by down-and-out and low-income people as well.

The largest and the more well-known budget motel chain is Motel 6. It has numerous locations throughout the United States and southern Ontario, Canada.

In the United States, many, but certainly not all, motels and other lodging establishments (especially small and medium-sized ones) nowadays are owned and operated by immigrants from India – particularly Gujarats, many of whom are surnamed Patel, which as a result has become a slang synonym of sorts for "motel" in some localities. According to an article in USA Today, more than 17,000 motels and hotels in the U.S. are owned by Asian Indian entrepreneurs.

Some other well-known motel chains include:

- Days Inn
- Super 8
- Travelodge

RESTAURANT

A **restaurant** is an establishment that serves prepared food and beverages to be consumed on the premises. The term covers a multiplicity of venues and a diversity of cuisine styles.

Restaurants are sometimes a feature of a larger complex, typically a hotel, where the dining amenities are provided for the convenience of the residents and, of course, for the hotel to maximize their potential revenue. Such restaurants are often also open to non-residents.

Kinds of Restaurants

- There exist many possible organizations for restaurants, depending on local customs and the formality and price of the meal:
  - one sits down, a waiter comes to take one's order, and later brings the food; one pays after finishing eating
  - one collects food from a counter and pays, then sits down and starts eating (self-service restaurant); sub-varieties:
    - one collects ready portions
    - one serves oneself from containers
    - one is served at the counter
  - a special procedure is that one first pays at the cash desk, collects a ticket and then goes to the food counter, where one gets the food in exchange for the ticket
  - one orders at the counter, after preparation the food is brought to one's table; paying may be on ordering or after eating.

Depending on local customs and the establishment, restaurants may or may not serve alcoholic beverages. Often, laws governing the sale of alcohol prohibit restaurants from selling alcohol without a meal (which would be an activity for a bar, often with more severe restrictions).

Restaurants range from unpretentious lunching or dining places catering to people working nearby, with simple food served in simple settings at low prices, to expensive establishments serving refined food and wines in a formal setting. In the former case, clients are not expected to wear formal attire. In the latter case, clients generally wear formal clothing, though this varies between cultures.

Restaurants often specialize in certain types of food. For example, there are seafood restaurants, vegetarian restaurants or ethnic restaurants. Generally speaking, restaurants selling "local" food are simply called restaurants, while restaurants selling food of foreign origin are called accordingly (Chinese restaurant, French restaurant, etc.).

Restaurant Guides

Restaurant guides list the best places to eat. One of the most famous of these, in Western Europe, is the Michelin series of guides which accord from 1 to 3 stars to restaurants they perceive to be of high culinary merit. Restaurants with stars in the Michelin guide are formal, expensive establishments; in general the more stars awarded, the higher will be the prices. In the United States, the Mobil Travel Guides and the American Automobile. Association rate restaurants on a similar 1 to 5 star (Mobil) or Diamond (AAA) scale. Three, four, and five star ratings are roughly to the Michelin one, two, and three star ratings while one and two star ratings typically indicate good casual restaurants. The popular Zagat Survey compiles individual's comments about restaurants.

Nearly all major American newspapers employ restaurant critics and publish online dining guides for the cities they serve. Unlike their European counterparts, American newspaper restaurant critics typically visit dining establishments anonymously and return several times so as to sample the entire menu. Newspaper restaurant guides, therefore, tend to provide the most thorough coverage of various cities' dining options.

Economics

In economics, restaurants are the end of the supply chain in the foodservice industry. There is usually too much competition in most cities since barriers to entry are relatively low, which means that for most restaurants, it is hard to make a profit. In most First World industrialized countries, restaurants are heavily regulated to ensure the health and safety of the customers.

The typical restaurant owner faces many obstacles to success, including raising initial capital, finding competent and skilled labour, maintaining consistent and excellent food quality, maintaining high standards of safely, and the constant hassle of minimizing potential liability for any food poisoning or accidents that may occur. This is why restaurants seem to come and go all the time.

Specific Kinds

In France, a brasserie is a café doubling as a restaurant with a relaxed setting, which serves single dishes and other meals. A bistro is a familiar name for a café serving simple meals in an unpretentious settings, at moderate prices, especially in Paris; because of their popularity, bistros have become increasingly tourist spots.

A special restaurant is the dining car in old-style long-distance trains. To passengers travelling long distances it offers more luxury than eating brought-along food in the train, while it saves time compared with eating in towns along the way. Also, compared with other restaurants, the ever changing views of the countryside enhance the pleasure of the dinner. Dining cars have become increasingly rarer, often replaced by bar cars selling some snacks and pre-packaged meals.

BRAND MANAGEMENT

Brand management is the application of marketing techniques to a specific product, product line, or brand. It seeks to increase the product's perceived value to the customer and thereby increase brand franchise and brand equity. Marketers see a brand as an implied promise that the level of quality people have come to expect from a brand will continue with present and future purchases of the same product. This may increase sales by making a comparison with competing products more favourable. It may also enable the manufacturer to charge more for the product. The value of the brand is determined by the amount of profit it generates for the manufacturer. This results from a combination of increased sales and increased price.

A good **brand name** should:

- be legally protectable
- be easy to pronounce
- be easy to remember
- be easy to recognize
- attract attention
- suggest product benefits (*e.g.*, Easy off) or suggest usage

- suggest the company or product image
- distinguish the product's positioning relative to the competition.

A **premium brand** typically costs more than other products. An **economy brand** is a brand targeted to a high price elasticity market segment. A **fighting brand** is a brand created specifically to counter a competitive threat. When a company's name is used as a product brand name, this is referred to as corporate branding. When one brand name is used for several related products, this is referred to as family branding. When all a company's products are given different brand names, this is referred to as individual branding. When a company uses the brand equity associated with an existing brand name to introduce a new product or product line, this is referred to as **Brand Leveraging**. When large retailers buy products in bulk from manufacturers and put their own brand name on them, this is called private branding. Private brands can be differentiated from **manufacturers' brands** (also referred to as **National Brands**). When two or more brands work together to market their products, this is referred to as **Co-Branding**. When a company sells the rights to use a brand name to another company for use on a non-competing product or in another geographical area, this is referred to as **brand licensing**.

Brand rationalization refers to reducing the number of brands marketed by a company. Companies tend to create more brands and product variations within a brand than economies of scale suggest they should. Frequently they will create a specific product or brand for each market that they target. They also do this to gain precious retain shelf space (and also reduce the amount of shelf space allocated to competing brands). But this can be a very inefficient strategy so a company may decide to rationalize their portfolio of brands from time to time. They may also decide to **rationalize their brand portfolio as part of an overall corporate downsizing. There are several problems associated with setting** objectives for a brand or product category.

- Many brand managers limit themselves to setting financial objectives. They ignore strategic objectives because they feel this is the responsibility of senior management.
- **Most product level or brand managers limit themselves to setting short term objectives because their compensation packages are designed to reward short term behaviour.**

Short term objectives should been seen as milestones towards long term objectives.

- Often product level managers are not given enough information to construct strategic objectives.
- It is sometimes difficult to translate corporate level objectives into brand or product level objectives into brand or product level objectives. Changes in shareholders equity are easy for a company to calculate. It is not so easy to calculate the change in shareholders equity that can be attributed to a product or category. More complex metrics like changes in the net present value of shareholders equity are even more difficult for the product manager to assess.
- In a diversified company, the objectives of some brands may conflict with those of other brands. Or worse, corporate objectives may conflict with the specific needs of your brand. This is particularly true in regards to the trade-off between stability and riskiness. Corporate objectives must be broad enough that brands with high risk products are not constrained by objectives set with cash cow's in mind. The brand manager also needs to know senior managements harvesting strategy. If corporate management intends to invest in brand equity and take a long term position in the market (*i.e.*, penetration and growth strategy), it would be a mistake for the product manager to use short term cash flow objecives (*i.e.*, price skimming strategy). Only when these conflicts and tradeoffs are made explicit, is it possible for all levels of objectives to fit together in a coherent and mutually supportive manner.
- Many brand managers set objectives that optimize the performance of their unit rather than optimize overall corporate performance. This is particularly true where compensation is based primarily on unit performance. Managers tend to ignore potential synergies and inter unit joint processes.

Brand

A brand takes the form of a symbolic construct created by a marketer to represent a collection of information about a product or group of products. This symbolic construct typically consists of a name, identifying mark, logo, visual images or symbols, or mental concepts which distinguishes the product or service. A brand often carries connotations of a product's "promise", the product or service's point of difference among its competitors which makes it special and unique. Marketers attempt through a brand to give a product a "personality" or an "image". Thus, they hope to "brand", or burn, the image into the consumer's mind; that is, associate the image with the product's quality. Because of this, a brand can form an important element of an advertising theme: it serves as a quick way to show and tell consumers what a supplier has offered to the market.

Well known products acquire **brand recognition**. When a brand has accumulated a mass of positive sentiment among consumers, marketers say that its owner has acquired brand equity or **brand franchise. Brand equity** measures the brands value to the marketer. It is an assessment of the investment a company has made in a brand. Brand franchise measure the effect of this investment on the target market. When enough brand equity is created that the brand has the ability to draw buyers (even without further advertising), it is said to have brand franchise. A **brand name** comprises that part of a brand consisting of words or letters that humans can verbalize. A brand name that has acquired legal protection becomes a trademark.

Branding has become part of pop culture. Numerous products have a brand identity: from common table salt to designer clothes. Non-commercially, branding can also apply to the marketing of entities which supply ideas or promises rather than goods and services—such as political parties or religious organizations.

Consumers as a group may look on the brand as an important aspect of a product, and it can also add value to a product or service. It carries the reputation of a product or company. A branded laundry detergent may sell twice as much product as a store-brand detergent. Although the two products may resemble each other closely in almost every other respect, people have learned to regard the branded product as superior. In some cases they believe that because it costs more if offers better quality. Advertising spokespersons have also became part of some brands.

History

Brands originated with the 19th century advent of packaged goods. Industrialization moved the production of many household items, such as soap, from local communities to centralized factories. These factories, cursed with mass-produced goods, needed to sell their products in a wider market, to a customer base familiar only with local goods. It quickly became apparent that a generic package of soap had difficulty competing with familiar, local products. The packaged goods manufacturers needed to convince the market that the public could place just as much trust the non-local product.

Many brands of that era, such as Uncle Ben's rice and Kellogg's breakfast cereal furnish illustrations of the problem. The manufacturers wanted their products to appear and feel as familiar as the local farmers' produce. From there, with the help of advertising, manufacturers quickly learned to associate other kinds of brand values, such as youthfulness, fun or luxury, with their products. This kickstarted the practice we now know as "branding."

Examples of Prominent Brand Names

The 2001 ranking of the 100 most valuable brands worldwide by Business Week magazine contained 62 American, 30 European, and six Japanese brands.

United States

- Apple (computer)
- Boeing (aerospace)
- Coca-Cola (soft drink)
- Columbia Records (recorded sound—since 1988 owned by Sony)
- Ford Motor Company (automobiles)
- Hershey's (chocolate)
- McDonald's (fast food restaurant)
- Microsoft (software)
- Panasonic (electronics)
- The Gap (clothing)

European

- BP (petrol-UK)
- BRIO (toys—Sweden)
- Cadbury (chocolate—UK)
- Ferrari (automobile—Italy)
- Ikea (furniture—Sweden)
- Lego (toys—Denmark)
- Mercedes-Benz (automobile—Germany)

- Nestle (food—Switzerland)
- Nokia (cell phones—Finland)
- Orangina (soft drink)

Japanese

- Canon
- Honda
- National
- Nintendo
- Sony
- Toyota

Australian

- Myer (department store)
- Qantas (airline)
- Rip Curl (surf/clothing)
- Telstra (telecommunications)
- Woolworth's (store chain)

Criticisms of Branding

Criticism has been leveled against the concept and implementation of brands, much of it associated with the "antiglobalization" movement. One of the better known criticisms of branding is found in Naomi Klein's book, No Logo. The book claims that corporations' brands serve as structures for corporations to hide behind, and that such global problems as sweatshop labour and environmental degradation have been permitted and exacerbated by branding.

Criticism of branding also comes from within corporations, with some employees becoming frustrated by being limited by overall brand strategies that restrict what they can say, how they say it, and what pantone colour to say it in. Some shareholders also have concerns about the amount of money invested in branding.

Brand Equity

Brand equity is the value built-up in a brand. The value of a company's brand equity can be calculated by comparing the expected future revenue from the branded product with the expected future revenue from an equivalent non-branded product. This calculation is at best an approximation. This value can comprise both tangible attributes (*e.g.* TWICE the cleaning power or HALF the fat) and intangible, emotional attributes (*e.g.* The brand for people with style and good taste).

It can be positive or negative. Positive brand equity is created by a history of effective promotion and consistently meeting or exceeding customer expectations. Negative brand equity is usually the result of bad management.

Positive brand equity can be a significant barrier to entry for prospective competitors. The greater a company's brand equity, the greater the probability that the company will use a family branding strategy rather than an individual branding strategy. This is because family branding allows them to leverage off the equity accumulated in the core brand. This makes new product introductions less risky and less expensive.

Individual Branding

Individual branding is the marketing strategy of giving each product in a product portfolio its own unique brand name. This is contrasted with family branding in which the products in a product line are given the same brand name. The advantage of individual branding is that each product has an image and identity that is unique. This facilitates the positioning process.

PRODUCT MANAGEMENT

In marketing, a **product** is anything that can be offered to a market that might satisfy a want or need. However it is much more than just a physical object. It is the complete bundle of benefits or satisfactions that buyers perceive they will obtain if they purchase the product. It is the sum of all physical, psychological, symbolic, and service attributes.

A product is similar to a good. In accounting, goods are physical objects that are available in the marketplace. This differentiates them from a service, which is a non-material product.

Three Aspects

There are three aspects to any product or service:

1. Core Benefits
   - in-use benefits
   - psychological benefits (*e.g.*, self-image enhancement, hope, status, self worth)

- problem reduction benefits (*e.g.*, safety, convenience)

2. Tangible Product or Service
   - product attributes and features
   - quality
   - styling
   - packaging protection and label information
   - brand name
3. Augmented Product or Service
   - warranty
   - installation
   - delivery
   - credit availability
   - after-sale service and maintenance

Classifying Products

Product management involves developing strategies and tactics that will increase product demand (referred to as primary demand) over the products life cycle.

One useful technique in understanding a product is the **Aspinwall Classification System**. It classifies and rates products based on five variables:

- replacement rate – how frequently is the product repurchased
- gross margin – how much profit is obtained from each product (average selling price less average unit cost)
- buyer goad adjustment – how flexible are the buyers' purchasing habits in regards to this product
- duration of product satisfaction – how long will the product produce benefits for the user
- duration of buyer search behaviour – how long will they shop for the product

Types of Products

There are several types of products:

- consumer product – used by end users
- industrial products – used in the production of other goods
- convenience goods – purchased frequently and with minimal effort
- impulse goods – purchase stimulated by immediate sensory cues

- emergency goods – goods required immediately
- shopping goods – some comparison with other goods
- specialty goods – extensive comparisons with other goods and a lengthy information search
- unsought goods – *e.g.*, cemetery plots, insurance
- perishable goods – goods that will deteriate quickly even without use
- durable goods – goods that survive multiple use occasions
- non-durable goods – goods that are used up in one occasion
- capital goods – installations, equipment, and buildings
- parts and materials – goods that go into a finished product
- supplies and services – goods that facilitate production
- commodities – undifferentiated goods (*e.g.*, wheat, gold, sugar)
- by-products – a product that results from the manufacture of another product

Product Management

Product management is one of the four areas of marketing. The other three parts of the marketing mix are pricing, and distribution. Product management deals with questions like:

- What products to produce and sell
- What new products to add
- What existing products to discontinue
- How long will it take for a product to penetrate the market
- How many products to have in the product line
- How to balance a product portfolio
- Whether to use a product differentiation strategy
- What is the best product positioning
- What brand name to use
- Whether to use individual branding or family branding
- Whether to use product bundling or product lining
- What logo to use
- Product Life Cycle considerations
- Planned obsolescence considerations

MARKETING

Marketing is the craft of linking the producers (or potential producers) of a product or service with customers, both existing and potential. Some form of marketing arises naturally in all capitalist societies but is not limited to capitalist societies. Marketing techniques are also applied in politics, religion, personal affairs, and many other aspects of life.

Marketing methods are informed by many of the social sciences, particularly psychology, sociology, and economics. Marketing research underpins these activities. Through advertising, it is also related to many of the creative arts.

Overview

In popular usage, the term 'marketing' refers to the promotion of products, especially advertising and branding. However, in professional usage the term has a wider meaning. It can be divided into four sections, often called the "Four Ps," only one of which is promotion. They are:

- *Product*—The product management aspect of marketing deals with the specifications of the actual good or service, and how it relates to the end user's needs and wants.
- *Pricing*—This refers to the process of setting a price for a product, including discounts.
- *Promotion*—This includes advertising, sales promotion, publicity, and personal selling, and refers to the various methods of promoting the product, brand, or company.
- *Place* or distribution refers to how the product gets to the customer; for example, point of sale placement or retailing.

These four elements are often referred to as the marketing mix. A marketer will use these variables to craft a marketing plan. For a marketing plan to be successful, the mix of the four "p's" must reflect the wants and desires of the consumers in the target market. Trying to convince a market segment to buy something they do not want is extremely expensive and seldom successful. Marketers depend on marketing research to determine what consumers want and what they are willing to pay for. Marketers hope that this process will give them a sustainable competitive advantage. Marketing management is the practical application of this process.

In marketing products, companies pursue a customer orientation or a product orientation. A market-oriented company focuses its activities and products on customer needs. A product-oriented company pursues product innovation, then tries to attract the market to the product. Although many people assume that a market-oriented approach is the most logical avenue, many firms successfully focus on product innovation, such as in research and development focused companies.

Some aspects of marketing, especially promotion, are the subject of criticisms.

A relatively new form of marketing uses the Internal and is called **internet marketing** or more generally e-marketing. It typically tries to perfect the segmentation strategy used in traditional marketing. It targets its audience more precisely, and is sometimes called personalized marketing or **one-to-one marketing**.

Target Market

A **target market** is the market segment which a particular product is marketed to. It is often defined by age, gender and/or socio-economic grouping.

Targeting strategy is the selection of the customers you wish to service. The decisions involved in targeting strategy include:

- how many segments to target
- which segments to target
- how many products to offer
- which products to offer in which segments

There are three steps to targeting:

- market segmentation
- target choice
- product positioning

Targeting strategy decisions are influenced by:

- market maturity
- diversity of buyers needs and preferences
- the company's size
- strength of the competition
- the volume of sales required for profitability

Targeting can be selective (*e.g.* focus strategy, market specialization strategy or niche strategy), or extensive (*e.g.* full coverage, mass marketing, or product specialization).

CONFERENCE

The term **conference** can be used to describe any meeting of people that confer about a certain topic.

- In politics, a conference is usually a multilateral diplomatic negotiation (like the Potsdam Conference).
- In science, a conference is a formalized event where scientists present there research results in speeches, workshops or by other means.
- In evangelical Christianity, a conference is a series of meetings where topics related to Jesus Christ, the Bible, and the church are discussed. Often new books and other media are present for sale in them and original research may be presented.
- In business, a business conference is an event organized by a for-profit or non-profit organization to discuss a pressing issue – like a new product, market trend or government regulation – with a range of speakers. Many are open to the public for a fee.

Sports

- The National Hockey League is divided into a Western and Eastern **Conference.**
- In English association football, the fifth and sixth tiers of the football league are called the Football Conference.
- In the United States, football has two NFL conferences: the National Football Conference (NFC), and the American Football Conference (AFC). The winners of these two conferences go on to play in the annual Super Bowl.
- In American basketball, there are two NBA conferences – the Western Conference and the Eastern Conference. The winners of these conferences go on to play in the NBA Finals for the NBA championship.

2

International Hotel and Restaurant Association (IH&RA)

IH&RA DESCRIPTION

The IH&RA is the only international trade association exclusively devoted to promoting and defending the interests of the hotel and restaurant industry worldwide. It is a non-profit membership organization dedicated to helping members achieve their business objectives and prepare for the future.

- International and National Hotel and/or Restaurant Chains
- National Hotel and/or Restaurant Associations

IH&RA headquarters are in France, 48 Boulevard de Sébastopol, 75003 Paris.

What does Membership of the IH&RA mean?

— Protecting your business interests.
— Building your business network.
— Keeping you informed.

The IH&RA is run on a not- for-profit basis with a team led by a Chief Executive. It is governed by a General Assembly and a Board of Directors.

IH&RA Membership

A world of business benefits

Protection—A passport to the global hospitality industry. We defend members' interests by lobbying international policy-making bodies to oppose regulations that could damage your business.

Networking—A window on the world. We introduce members to the right people, opening doors that help them multiply their business contacts, build profitable partnership and learn from other's experience.

Information—A view of the future. We give members the information they need to do better business, sharing best practice, and keeping you up to date with changes in the industry through e-newsletters, research reports and conferences.

IH&RA Foundation for the Future

Mission of the Foundation for the Future

The IH&RA Foundation for the Future (FFF) is a registered Swiss charity established in 1989. Its purpose is to contribute to the development of education, specifically in the hospitality industry, to contribute to research on this industry and to promote projects in developing countries. Over the past 14 years 200 participants have benefited from an international education which may not otherwise have been available to them.

Summer Education Programme

Due to some very exciting developments, the format for the Foundation for the Future education programme will be changing from 2004. Details of the new programme will be available through IH&RA and through the new website, www.foundationforthefuture.org.

Energy and Indoor Air Quality in Hotels and Restaurants

IH&RA, the International Hotel and Restaurant Association, invited hotels and restaurants around the world to apply today for the IH&RA 2002 "Environmental Award" which recognizes outstanding examples of best environmental practice from both corporate and independent establishments. This award, in its 12th year was sponsored by American Express Establishment Services and focuses on "Energy and Indoor Air Quality in Hotels and Restaurants." Applications were reviewed and judged by industry experts from the United Nations Environment Programme, Green Globe 21, Siemens and Radisson SAS Hotels and Resorts. The winners were announced at IH&RA's 39th Annual Congress, held November 8-11, 2002, in New York City, and selected applications were published as IH&RA best practice case studies.

IH&RA chose the theme of "Energy and Indoor Air Quality in Hotels and Restaurants" recognizing the challenge hotels and restaurants face in improving energy efficiency while ensuring an acceptable indoor environment. This is a real world problem as people spend 80 per cent of their time inside buildings. While energy efficiency is critical to cutting costs and emissions, the indoor environment is the most fundamental element of service quality. Guests want a comfortable environment in order to be productive at meetings and enjoy their leisure time, be it in their rooms, in restaurants or around establishment premises. At the same time, employees need to concentrate to work efficiently and creatively. To guarantee these expectations, a good indoor environment is essential. The challenge is to improve the indoors without compromising on energy efficiency. These two objectives are at the core of environmental management and as such reflect an operator's commitment to corporate social responsibility. With this in mind, IH&RA seeks to honour establishments on the cutting edge of service delivery while making their property a cleaner, healthier and safer place to work and rest.

Applicants were judged on: evidence of long-term commitment to sustainable hotel and/or restaurant management; use and description of technologies and approaches to energy and air quality management and monitoring; results of energy savings and improvements in indoor air quality over time; quality of environment and energy management training provided to employees and chief engineers; the means by which employee and guest complaints on energy and indoor environment are handled and resolved.

IH&RA launched this Environment Award in 1991 with the support of American Express Establishment Services. Over the past years, this Award has become recognized as one of the industry's top honours for excellence in hospitality service and environmental best practice, and sets an industry standard for all hospitality establishments.

The International Hotel and Restaurants Association (IH&RA) is the only international trade association exclusively devoted to protecting, promoting and defending the interests of the hotel and restaurant industry worldwide. It represents a network of international and national hotel and restaurant chains, and national hotel and restaurant associations in more than 100 countries. Through its membership network, IH&RA represents over 300,000 hotels and 8 million restaurants, which employ 60 million people and contribute US$950 billion annually to the global economy.

IH&RA ENVIRONMENTAL AWARD, 2004

The 2004 theme, "Innovation in Environmental Best Practice" aims to embrace the use of new technology as well as original and creative methods employed by hotels and restaurants to protect the environment in their day-to-day operations while promoting long-term sustainable development of travel and tourism.

The IH&RA and founding sponsor American Express created the Environmental Award to recognize environmental leadership in the hospitality industry. American Express is sponsoring the Award for the 13th year, and the 2004 Award is also supported by IH&RA partners Green Globe 21, Shell and Onity. This year's theme, "Innovation in Environmental Best Practice" focuses on the use of new technology, as well as the unique and creative methods that hotels and restaurants use to protect the environment in their day-to-day operations, while promoting long-term sustainable development of travel and tourism.

"IH&RA was one of the first associations in the hospitality industry to launch an annual environmental award, thanks to the support of American Express. Since 1991, our pioneering programme has helped not only to heighten environment awareness but also to identify best practice and highlight the industry's proactive stance on environmental management.

The greeting of the industry is firmly under way, with the growing adoption in properties of environmental management schemes, sound sitting, design principles and relevant staff training. In fact, outstanding examples of environmental good practice are to be found in all comers of the globe. It is these examples of outstanding good practice which will lay the path for a more environmentally sound future.

What is Innovation?

Innovation: "The act of starting something for the first time; introducing something new."

The main difference between an "innovation" and a basic "good' practice" is that "good practice" is something that has been used/applied widely before.

If it is process that is widely used, then it would not be considered "innovative."

In many cases, especially the application of technology, the technology itself may not be new but might be applied in an innovative way.

For example, solar panels have been around for a long time, but their use in the tourism industry has been fairly limited to hot heating. Is your property using solar panels in an "innovative way" outside the "standard use" of water heating? Then this, yes, could be considered innovative. Think of any other examples of "innovation" that your hospitality company is employing to protect and sustain the environment while developing tourism, also ways innovative ways in which your establishment(s) are contributing to the local community.

Innovative people take a product or invention and use it in a clever way that has not previously been widely adopted. It does not have to be technology, but can be any "creative" or "new" idea. Special consideration will also be given to those hotels that use "innovative" ideas that are replicable, *i.e.*, can be used and copied by other properties. This is the idea of "leap-frogging" which is applying a new and innovative concept to other properties so that Environmental Good Practice can continue to evolve, improve and grow in the hospitality industry worldwide.

"Your participation in our Environmental Award will help us inspire the global hospitality industry to create a more environmentally sensitive hotel and restaurant product for our guests, ourselves and our future."

John Bell, President, IH&RA

"As a supporter of the IH&RA Environment Award for more than a decade, we have seen how cultivating environmental and cultural resources can enhance the travel and tourism industry. Past winners are positive proof that we can all do well by doing good."

David Herrick,
President, American Express
Establishment Services Europe

"As a partner of IH&RA, GREEN GLOBE 21 is proud to support this Environmental Award and to be part of the judging panel. We believe that it is vital that the tourism industry shows leadership in building a more sustainable future for the planet. Through the adoption of the GREEN GLOBE 21 worldwide environmental

certification programme, operators in the tourism industry can measurably reduce their environmental impact and demonstrate their credentials to an increasingly discerning traveller."

Cathy Parsons
Global Manager
GREEN GLOBE 21

"The rapidly growing tourism and travel sector does and will increasingly have a major impact on the environment. As a consequence hotels need to look at ways to integrate environmental considerations into day-to-day business decisions," said Moniuqe Barbut, Director of the Division of Technology, Industry & Economics, UNEP, "Innovation and new technologies present a lot of opportunities in this area, and UNEP is once again pleased to be associated with the IH&RA Environmental Award. We strongly support this initiative and applaud those hotels which operate in a sustainable way to protect the environment."

Monique Barbut
Director of the Division of
Technology, Industry & Economics UNEP

3

Global Hotel Industry: Trends and Classifications

NEW TRENDS IN HOTEL INDUSTRY

In cooperation with the International Hotel and Restaurant Association (IH&RA), a WTO Affiliate Member, WTO has responded to a recent initiative of its government Members to convene a world conference on the latest developments in the hotel industry in Saint Petersburg Russia during April 25-28, 2004. This interest by Governments is timely as they need to review and update regulatory measures and incentives to promote investments in the sector in the face of ongoing liberalization and expectations that such investments contribute to sustainable development and poverty alleviation and meet the consumers' demand of competitive, safe and quality services. As a growing trend in the industry is chain affiliation, a special section of the conference will be dedicated to examining measures enabling co-existence and partnership between destination suppliers of tourism services and the mother national and transnational hotel companies and consortia developing and promoting their own brands of hotel services and striving for an effective management of resources. An important issue to be considered relates to the preservation and enhancement of the national idiom of hotel facilities, their effective access to the world's distribution channels and the integration of local labour force. Hotel classification stood at the outset of the conference initiative. Disliked by one part of the industry on the grounds of its legitimate concern over undue Government intervention, but equally preferred by a sizeable consumer representation and practiced in many countries as an orderly measure of both mandatory and voluntary nature, it will stand firmly on the conference agenda. The discussions will be based on a recent joint WTO-IH&RA project, a status report and study on hotel classification.

Finally, the Conference will analyze the critical issue of human resources for the hotel industry which is faced by continuous needs of training new staff and its motivation towards quality service against the sector's seasonality and other challenges, such as safety and security, automation and recognition of qualifications. A set of guidelines and recommendations is expected from this conference on each of the subjects mentioned – investment, chains, classification and training – to which participants from the public and private sector will be invited to contribute. This will be made easy as most of the conference proceedings will be carried out by means of panel discussions. The conference hosts, St. Petersburg and the Russian Federation represented by the Ministry of Economic Development and Trade promise a warm welcome to participants from the world and WTO membership looks forward to a useful and purposeful event.

Joint WTO – IH&RA Conference Calls for Systematic Approach to a New Hotel Classification

The World Conference on New Trends and Measures in the Hotel Industry, jointly organized by the World Tourism Organization (WTO) and the International Hotel and Restaurants Association (IH&RA) suggested a cautious, albeit systematic approach to hotel classification at world level with a view to reconciling the legitimate demands and concerns of consumers and industry with the obligations of the governments.

The Conference held in St. Petersburg, Russia and was attended by 210 participants from 22 countries. The Conference was opened by the WTO Secretary-General Francesco Frangialli, Deputy Minister of Economic Development and Trade of Russian Federation Vladimir Strzhalkovsky and the IH&RA Chief Executive Officer Alain-Philippe Feutr co-chaired by Mr. Henryk Handszuh, WTO Chief of Quality and Ms. Natela Shengeliya, Chief of the Russian Tourism Department.

"Governments need to review and update regulatory measures and incentives to promote investments in the sector in the face of ongoing liberalization and expectations that such investments contribute to sustainable development and poverty alleviation and meet consumers' demand for competitive, safe and quality services, "said the WTO Secretary-General Mr. Francesco Frangialli in his opening address.

The Conference dealt with such important issues for the hotel industry today as the desirability of classification schemes, mechanisms to attract investments, the importance and training of human resources and the role of hotel chains.

Russian representative for classification discussions Ms. Margarita Nemolyaeva said "the current lack of coherence among the variety of existing national hotel classifications is responsible for consumer complaints in her country, adding that there was an urgent need for a solid, objective and universally acceptable referent in this area."

It was observed during the event that a common international understanding on hotel classification could be helpful in multilateral trade negotiations.

The WTO and IH&RA (a WTO Affiliate Member) should devise a methodology and tools for setting up hotel classifications schemes which could be recommended to countries, delegates concluded. This methodology should include:

- provisions for respect of cultural and differences in a systematic manner;
- references to basic norms which could be recognized as minimum standards of universal application irrespective of cultural differences, which are vital to all human beings and consumers and correspond to ethics and the satisfaction of their basic needs;
- mechanisms of consultations and cooperation between the public and private sector;
- consultations with consumers to which effect the provisions of the United Nations Guidelines for Consumer Protection should be used, particularly by devising consumer surveys and soliciting consumer response;
- provisions regarding consumer redress;
- a request for the universal use of common terminology in the hotel industry and respective classifications by adapting and developing standard EN ISO 18513-2000 for this purpose;
- provisions on classification audits and relationship between classification and licenses to operate;

- provisions on additional elements which may be determined through international consultation in order to make this instrument comprehensive and transparent.

"The Conference did not pretend to seek enactment or even to impose an international hotel classification scheme, but a mentioned document could represent a reasonable measure devised by the major stakeholders in addressing the complex nature of tourism and the demands of consumers and industry" said co-chairman Mr. Handszuh. "New hotel classification referents could be used voluntarily in different countries, taking into account the local practices and conditions." According to WTO, public-private partnership is crucial in the development of these endeavours.

The existing approaches to hotel classification issues are rooted in the various cultural and administrative traditions. Some of them, inspired by Roman Law, provide for government intervention and public classification systems aimed at informing and protecting the consumer. It should be noted, though, that such public systems are, as in Spain, increasingly decentralized in favour of regional authorities. On the other hand, models more widely accepted in Anglo-Saxon and Nordic countries provide for either consumer protection through justice, the same as in Germany, or through voluntary certification mechanisms, as in the United Kingdom.

This part of the discussion at the Conference was based on a recent joint WTO-IH&RA project, a status report and study on hotel classification. This study shows that there is a diversity of situations worldwide; that while consumers seek transparency and protection of their rights to truthful information which classifications should carry, the industry requires a fair framework for free competition which classifications should not blur.

WTO and IH&RA therefore concluded that "it would be advisable to devise a methodology providing those countries wishing to set up a national or regional classification scheme with the necessary tools to do so", and that "cultural differences between countries in terms of service and facilities according to destinations, regions and purpose of travel" should be taken into consideration in this exercise.

The picture has become even more complicated due to the expansion of global and national hotel chains. This growing trend in the industry is reflected by the fact that over 20 per cent of a total of 16 million rooms worldwide are now controlled by a dozen leading chains. Major chains often consider that their brands themselves provide appropriate standards, making redundant any classification.

The participants appealed to national and local governments and to the hospitality industry to closely cooperate in advancing the various issues discussed at the Conference in St. Petersburg.

JOINT WTO AND IH&RA STUDY ON HOTEL CLASSIFICATION

Survey rationale. With the dramatic development of domestic and international travel in the past fifty years, the question of how hotel ratings compare across the world is periodically raised by various public and private-sector interests. As a result hotel classification has appeared on the agenda of the World Tourism Organization for a considerable number of years. Most recently, the topic was included in the WTO 2000-2001 Work Programme. The International Hotel and Restaurant Association (IH&RA) proposed that before any new work has undertaken, the first stage of any project should be to draw up a status report on the various schemes existing throughout the world. WTO then appointed IH&RA its designated expert to undertake this status report. In this first stage, IH&RA limited its role to surveying the private sector and specifically to preparing:

- a status report (*i.e.*, inventory) of existing hotel classification schemes
- a comparative analysis of these schemes (qualitative and quantitative elements)

At the same time, WTO surveyed public sector involvement in hotel classification *via* its Member National Tourism Administrations.

Scope and findings of survey. After reviewing previous work by other bodies (IUOTO, ISO, CEN, HOTREC), the present study collates the results of these two surveys and provides a comparative analysis of their findings, 31 countries for the private sector and

89 for the public sector. Overall, of the countries surveyed, 83 have an official hotel classification scheme, while only 23 countries have an official classification scheme covering hotels, apartment hotels, motels and inns. Where the public sector is concerned, 20 countries indicate that classification is used to control or monitor accommodation tariffs and 13 that it is used as the basis for the application of government taxes such as VAT (Value-Added Tax). The private sector report no link between classification and the social obligations imposed on employers. The two bodies most involved in devising and drafting the hotel classification scheme are officials of National Tourism Administrations (NTA) with other government officials (in 49 countries) and the national hotel association, rarely alone and generally when consulted by government authorities (in 48 countries). In addition, 40 countries indicate that the system is based on that of another (usually neighbouring) country. Classification is mandatory for all establishments in 46 countries. In 55 countries it is needed to obtain a license to operate whereas in 32 others, establishments can operate without being classified.

Other forms of classification. Alongside the grading schemes surveyed above, the report reviews other forms of classification. Major Tour Operators often rate hotels according to their own criteria while schemes used in electronic distribution channels (*e.g.*, CRS, GDS) are typically devised for the benefit of the travel professionals (and travel agents in particular). These are often based on guides such as the US Official Hotel Guide originally only available in print and now also electronically. Although the star rating system is the one most in use throughout the world, other symbols are also used (diamonds, crowns etc.), sometimes even in combination. Irrespective of the symbol used, all systems break accommodation down into three or four major bands (usually luxury, superior, mid-market, budget/economy). Major hotel companies prefer to use branding as a means of positioning their product on the market and typically place the customer and his/her profile, needs and desires at the heart of their marketing strategies. Within the hotel industry itself the debate continues as to whether formal classification is necessary or not—as instanced by HORESTA the Danish Hotel Association and the Israel Hotel Association, offering case-studies respectively for and against. Be this as it may, there are currently moves afoot in a number of world regions—Scandinavia, South East Asia,

Middle East and even Europe – for some form of harmonized regional system.

Consumers. While all approaches to classification claim to be for their benefit, consumers or their representative bodies are in fact rarely consulted in the process of establishing a system. The report concludes that systems set up by the private sector are far more responsive to consumer demand, rapidly recognizing new forms of accommodation such as time-share and resorts, whereas standards and criteria laid down by the public sector tend to be infrequently checked and rarely updated to meet changes in consumer taste—or in destination market. More generally, many surveys show that consumer choice is governed first and foremost by considerations of price and destination, rather than on the basis of complex classification systems of which consumers have either little knowledge or little understanding.

Public and Private sector responsibilities. In conclusion, it is important to separate out the respective responsibilities of the public and private sectors in the area of hotel classification. As recent events such as SARS, Mad Cow and Legionnaire's disease have shown, public authorities must obviously ensure minimum standards of safety and hygiene in accommodation establishments. Private sector bodies, being commercially driven, must meet the consumer's demand for better and more transparent information on both products and destinations. This implies the consistent use of recognized and harmonized terminology. Given the interest expressed in the survey, it would seem advisable to provide states wishing to set up a national or regional classification scheme with the necessary tools to do so. It is therefore important to devise the appropriate methodology taking into account cultural differences between states as they relate to services and facilities, markets and purpose of travel. To be sustainable, tourism must be able to consolidate its diversity, not seek uniformity. Failing this, any attempt at regional and even global harmonization of what can only be voluntary systems would, under the guise of clarification, merely end up creating more confusion.

Introduction

Background

Historically, hotel classification systems were developed to ensure safe and reliable lodging and food for travelers at a time when very few such trustworthy establishments existed. With the unprecedented growth of international tourism in the past fifty years, during which hospitality has reach the status of a mature industry, the focus has moved from consumer protection (generally guaranteed by national regulations and legislation) to consumer information. Today, standardization and competitive marketing of hotel services to foreign customers and tourist professionals have emerged as driving forces for instituting a local or national hotel classification systems. With so many people now travelling, both within their own country and often far beyond, the idea has arisen of devising one single scheme which could be applied to hotel accommodation throughout the world for the benefit of both consumers (tourists) and travel professionals (tour operators and travel agents, in particular). Whether this is in fact desirable – and indeed feasible – remains a subject of considerable discussion. As a result, the issue of hotel classification is one that has appeared on the agenda of the World Tourism Organization for a considerable number of years. Most recently, a comparative study of hotel classification systems (the formal determination of hotel ratings or categories) was included in the WTO General Programme of Work for the 2000-2001 biennium, as a specific project (Activity 12: National Tourism Legislations) under Part B (Documentation) of the Section 7. The WTO Quality Support Committee at its 4th meeting (Madrid, 12-13 April 2000) recognized that "in the present changing regulatory framework for tourism, the decentralization of government competence for the sector and the appearance of diverse voluntary quality standards applied to accommodation establishments, hotel classification systems:

(*a*) are challenged by part of industry as unduly interfering with the marketplace and free competition, especially where such systems are established and controlled by government;
(*b*) continue to play the role of consumer guidance as traditional category indicators;
(*c*) however, confuse customers because of the lack of international harmonization and accountability;
(*d*) are requested by a number of developing countries as a regulatory measure, especially for small business, and in

order to achieve compatibility with tourist-sending countries."

In consideration of the above, the Committee requested the Secretariat to carry out a comparative study of existing hotel classification schemes world-wide with a view to:

(*a*) identifying the common characteristics prevailing in such classifications;
(*b*) establishing minimum international classification criteria as reference values and guidelines which could be used by interested parties in rating hotels and similar accommodation establishments;
(*c*) defining recommended procedures and rules for classification;
(*d*) preparing the WTO position on classification outlining the various types classification available (voluntary, corporate, industry-controlled, government-controlled, etc.) and the prevention of its use as a barrier to free competition and trade in hotel services."

Also, the same Committee strongly recommended that this activity be closely coordinated with representatives of the operational sector, to begin with WTO's Affiliate Member, the International Hotel and Restaurant Association (IH&RA). The recommendation of this Committee was subsequently endorsed by the WTO Executive Council at its 63rd and 64th session (Madrid, 28-30 November 2000). Based on this recommendation, the Secretary-General of WTO formally consulted the International Hotel and Restaurant Association (IH&RA). After an exchange of letters and various meetings between representatives of both organizations, IH&RA proposed that before any new work was undertaken, the first stage of any project should be to review the various schemes existing throughout the world tapping the experience and expertise of the national hotel associations across the globe. WTO then appointed IH&RA its designated expert on this aspect of the project. IH&RA officially advised the Secretary-General early in January 2001 that it was prepared to cooperate with WTO initially in two areas, *viz.*:

- to prepare a status report on existing hotel classification schemes
- to carry out a comparative analysis and interpretation of such schemes and their functions.

It was understood that in the light of the conclusions of the study, which could give rise to recommendations, both organizations would examine the possibility of undertaking a follow-up to this activity as already outlined in the recommendations of the WTO Quality Support Committee.

1. Objectives

This joint WTO/IH&RA study is expected to produce the following results considered to be of interest to governments, industry professionals and consumers:

(*a*) to achieve transparency regarding existing hotel classification schemes and policies, on the basis of comprehensive research and international comparisons; and,

(*b*) to bring into focus the implications of the present situation in order to guide governments and industry in any further action they may wish to undertake in this area.

2. Previous work

IUOTO–Hotel Trade Charter. In 1952, a Hotel Trade Charter was drawn up by the International Union of Official Travel Organizations (IUOTO) – the predecessor to the World Tourism Organization. This marked the beginning of expressions of interest in the issue of hotel classification, taken up at IUOTO as of 1969. In 1971 it was decided that any overall system, to be successful, should be evolved at the regional level, in close consultation with hotel industry professionals.

World Tourism Organization (*WTO*). When the World Tourism Organization was created in 1975 it formally took over the functions previously covered by IUOTO. As a result, between 1976 and 1982, all WTO Regional Commissions came to adopt standardized hotel classification systems on a regional basis, using the model established by IUOTO. In 1985, the WTO General Assembly adopted a resolution to include the issue of hotel classification in its Work Programme for the period 1986-1987 as part of its standard-setting activity. Two surveys of Member States were carried out in 1985-1987. They form the basis of the Report on "*Interregional Harmonization of Hotel Classification Criteria on the Basis of the Classification Standards adopted by the Regional Commissions*" [*PG(VI)/B.5.2*] presented to the Executive Council in Fez, Morocco, in November 1988. The surveys showed that out of the 74 respondents to the questionnaire, 54 (*i.e.* 73 per cent) had national hotel standards consistent – either fully or partially – with WTO-recommended classification standards. In the remaining 20 Member States, national standards were either not consistent with WTO standards – or there was no classification system in place.

European Union–HOTREC. In the spring of 1982 the then European Economic Community (EEC) proposed a common EEC grading of Hotels. This gave rise to discussions between the Confederation of Hotels, Restaurants and Cafes in the European Community (HOTREC) and the Commission Services on whether or not grading was the most satisfactory way of providing the consumer with relevant information on which to base his/her choice of accommodation. HOTREC favoured providing more efficient consumer information and proposed a standardized EEC hotel information system based on graphical symbols without grading. These discussions ultimately led to the adoption of Council Recommendation of 31 December 1986 on *Standardized Information in Existing Hotels* (*86/665/EEC*) stating that Member States should encourage the use by their national tourist bodies or other competent bodies, in collaboration with bodies representing hoteliers, of the set of standard graphical symbols designed to cover hotel facilities. The Recommendation also invited the Commission "to make an analysis, in cooperation with Member States, of their tourist bodies and/or representatives of their hotel industries, of existing hotel-grading systems and to examine the practical usefulness and the desirability of producing a Community-wide grading system for hotels." In response to this invitation, HOTREC produced its study in 1988 on "*Proposed Uniform Hotel Information System for Hotels in Member States of the European Economic Community*" (*Doc.88.31*). This document reviewed and compared existing grading systems within the EEC, analyzed the problems inherent in grading as well as those specific to the EEC and reviewed consumer information needs and booking patterns. In view of the practical difficulty of setting up a worthwhile and workable European hotel grading system, it concluded that consumer information needs would be far better met by a standardized information system.

Signs, Symbols and Terminology–WTO, CEN & ISO. The question of graphical symbols and standardized terminology was then taken up by a number of different bodies. The World Tourism Organization reported in 1989 on *The Standardization of Tourist Signs and Symbols* (*PG(VI)B.5.1* in relation to tourist attractions, services and facilities, without however any particular reference to hotel facilities. Work was also undertaken on public information symbols in the early 1990s by the Comité Européen de Normalization (CEN – the European Standardization Committee bringing together the national standards bodies of Europe) in conjunction with the International Organization for Standardization (ISO). Some of these symbols specifically covered hotel and restaurant services. By the late 1990s, European efforts were focused on the harmonization of description criteria for tourist services. In 1996, CEN set up a Working Group within its Technical Committee (TC 329) in charge of Tourist Services to study the advisability of setting up an international standard on hotel classification. This was in response to a request formally made to ISO for an international standard by AIT/FIA, the international trade association representing automobile clubs (Alliance Internationale du Tourisme and International Automobile Federation). Members of the CEN TC had reservations regarding a standard but agreed on the need to clarify terminology. Immediately both HOTREC and IH&RA officially made known their strongly opposition to the idea of an international standard for the classification of hotels on the grounds that "creating a single grading system that transcends national boundaries would be an impossible and undesirable task." At the same time, both organizations supported the idea of improving consumer information. Then in 1997, ISO set up a Working Group specifically on "Accommodation Facilities." While agreeing to let CEN continue to lead the work on the harmonization of "terminology and description criteria," it was proposed to extend the group's area of investigation to cover the quality of accommodation services. This led to a formal proposal to use ISO 9000 as the basis for an international hotel classification standard. This was once again vigorously opposed by IH&RA and HOTREC on the grounds that ISO 9000 only assures that predetermined standards are consistently provided but gives no indication of the level of that standard. In addition, ISO 9000 does not address consumer expectations on service delivery. A series of meetings of the ISO WG followed in 1997-1998, where IH&RA consistently voiced its opposition to the proposals under discussion and where no consensus could be reached between participants. Noting this irreconcilable division the ISO Technical Management Board decided to disband the WG and refer the work on a terminology standard back to CEN in February 1999. The CEN work in this area was completed with the publication in January 2001 of the European Standard on Tourism Services – Hotels and other types of tourism accommodation – Terminology (prEN ISO 18513).

Latest developments at the EU level. In May 2003 the European Parliament Committee on Regional Policy, Transport and Tourism (RETT) requested the EU Directorate-General Research to carry out a study on hotel classification in the European Union. The stated purpose was to review existing classification schemes in Member States.

3. *Methodology*

The Study was mainly based on desk research. Background documents include:

- National laws and regulations on hotel classification. (These are available at the WTO Documentation Centre.)
- The results of studies and reports prepared by other sources. (Reference is made to the HOTREC surveys on Classification of Lodging Establishments in Countries Represented within HOTREC of 1988, 1996, 2001.)
- The results of periodic surveys on classification of lodging establishments conducted by IH&RA among its member National Hotel and Restaurant Associations. (This survey was conducted in 1995, 1997, and 2000.)

Twin survey methodology. After a series of consultations and internal meetings, including a debate at the IH&RA National Association Chief Executives Council (NACE) in Amsterdam in April 2001, IH&RA and WTO agreed that the most efficient way of covering the hotel classification issue would be to devise two parallel questionnaires, one intended for the National Tourism Administrations (NTAs) *i.e.*, the public sector, the other for National Hotel Associations, *i.e.*, the private sector. These two sectors may both be involved either separately or jointly in establishing and running a country's hotel classification scheme, so it was essential to be able to track the form this involvement took as well as the overlap, where it occurred.

In April 2002, these two questionnaires were devised by WTO with input from IH&RA. WTO then circulated the public sector questionnaire to all its Members while IH&RA circulated the private sector questionnaire to its National Association members as well as to non-Member associations. Hasteners were sent out in the following months and additional information sought from respondents where this was considered necessary or particularly interesting, especially regarding new or evolving schemes. At the same time the WTO undertook the same process at its end. Given the difficulty in obtaining replies from some key Member States or Associations, compilation was deferred in order to achieve as broad a coverage as possible. This was undertaken by IH&RA in 2002-2003, with preliminary results of both questionnaires consolidated by late 2002 and a first draft report submitted to WTO in April 2003. Late replies continued to be received after this date up to January 2004 have been incorporated into the final analysis. The following chapter gives the consolidated replies to the IH&RA questionnaire followed by those of the WTO questionnaire and finally a comparative analysis of findings of both surveys. Given below is the explanatory note to the IH&RA questionnaire sent to National Hotel Associations, as well as the slightly different note accompanying the WTO questionnaire sent to National Tourism Administrations.

Explanatory Note to IH&RA Questionnaire

Purpose: The findings of this survey will contribute to the "joint IH&RA and WTO study on hotel classification" which follows on the recommendation of the WTO Quality Support Committee, the WTO work programme for 2002-2003 and the *Memorandum of Understanding* between the International Hotel and Restaurant Association (IH&RA) and the WTO Secretariat. (WTO and IH&RA have agreed to undertake jointly a study on hotel classification to include a status report on existing hotel classification schemes and a comparative analysis and interpretation of such schemes and their functions.)

Object: The scope of the survey is limited to hotels and similar establishments (Such establishments provide services entered as number 63110.0 in the Central Product Classification (CPS) and coincide with "tourism characteristic activities" in the Tourism Satellite Account: Recommended Methodological Framework) [*e.g.*, apartment hotels, motels, inns, etc.(These terms are subject to debate and regional interpretation. At the European level, standardized terminology has been adopted to this effect by CEN (European Committee for Standardization)], irrespective of their location (urban, rural, coastal, etc.). Other types of accommodation facilities, irrespective of their denotation and regional interpretation (*e.g.*, holiday centres, holiday homes, youth hostels, holiday camps, camping and caravanning sites, time-share, *etc.*), are excluded from the survey.

Definitions: For the purpose of the survey, the term "classification of accommodation establishments" denotes a system, duly published, in which accommodation establishments of the same type (*e.g.*, hotels, motels, inns, *etc.*) have been conventionally broken down into classes, categories or grades according to their common physical and service characteristics and established at government, industry or other private levels.

Scope of replies: In view of their national situation and the availability of information, NACE respondents may provide information on classification (governmental, non-governmental or both, if both systems co-exist or are complementary).

Document: The respondent's efforts to provide simple and unequivocal answers, whether affirmative (yes, underline), non-affirmative (no) or factual (specify) is much appreciated. As a principle, you are not requested to attach additional supporting documents, unless you feel that such existing documents (if possible, in English or French) need to be sent to IH&RA to further clarify your replies.

It would greatly assist us if you could use the opportunity of the survey to attach to the completed questionnaires the latest relevant regulatory instruments and/or indicate their country website from which such instruments could be viewed and/or downloaded. This will facilitate clearer investigation of classification criteria.

Explanatory Note to WTO Questionnaire

Purpose, Object and Definition were identical to those given for the IH&RA questionnaire.

Scope of replies: In view of their national situation and the availability of information, NTA respondents may provide information on government classification (covered by Part A of the survey) or non-governmental classification (Part B), or both systems (should such systems co-exist or are complementary), as well as on announced classification (Part C).

Documents: The respondents' efforts to provide simple and unequivocal answers, whether affirmative (yes, underline), non-affirmative (no) or factual (specify) will be appreciated. As a principle, they are not requested to attach additional supporting documents, unless the respondents feel that such existing documents (if possible, in English, French, Russian or Spanish) need to be sent to the WTO Secretariat to further clarify their replies.

With respect to national legislation and regulations governing accommodation classification, which are normally requested and received by the WTO Documentation Centre on a regular basis, respondents are kindly requested to check on this situation and, when appropriate, use the opportunity of the survey to attach to their completed questionnaires the latest relevant regulatory instruments and/or indicate their country website from which such instruments could be viewed and/or downloaded. This will allow the researchers to better investigate the classification criteria.

Status Report on Classification

Compilation of Replies from the Private Sector to IH&RA.

Questionnaire on the classification of accommodation establishments (hotels and similar establishments), completed by national hotel associations (NACE).

The questionnaire was circulated to 68 national associations in 61 countries. The following is the analysis of the 32 replies received.

Participating National Associations

Country/ Territory	*Association*	*Respondent*
Austria	Austrian Professional Hotel Association	Gregor Herzog Chief Executive Officer
Canada	Hotel Association of Canada	Anthony P. Pollard President
Caribbean	Caribbean Hotel Association	John Bell Director General & CEO
Chile	Asociación Gremial de Empresarios Hoteleros de Chile	Gustavo Abel Ernst Manager
Colombia	Colombian Hotel Association	Manuel Bermudez General Manager
Czech Republic	Czech National Federation of Hotels and Restaurants	Dr. Vladimir Stentina General Secretary
Denmark	Danish Hotel, Restaurant and Tourism Association	Torben Kaas Head of the Classification Dept.
Egypt	Egyptian Hotel Association	Baghat Badawy Director of Marketing, Promotion & Training
Estonia	Estonian Hotel and Restaurant Association	Donald Visnapuu Managing Director
Finland	Finnish Hotel and Restaurant Association	Pekka Ropponen Consultative Manager
France	Union des Métiers et des Industries de l'Hôtellerie	
Georgia	National Hotel Association of Georgia	George Mtvaradze General Manager
Germany	Hotelverband Deutschland Germal Hotel and Restaurant Association	Markus Luthe Deputy Chief Executive
Greece	Hellenic Chamber of Hotels	Agni Christidou Manager
Hungary	Hotel Association of Hungary	Gabor Lombosi General Secretary
Iceland	Icelandic Travel Industry Association	Erna Hauksdottir Director
Iraq	Hotel and Restaurant Association in Iraq	Dleir Ismail Chairman
Israel	Israel Hotel Association	Abraham Rosental Director General

(*Contd.*)

(*Contd.*)

Country/ Territory	*Association*	*Respondent*
Jordan	Jordan Hotel Association	**Fakhri Twal** Director
Kuwait	Kuwait Hotel Owners Association	**Mohamed A. Najia** General Secretary
Lebanon	Syndicate of Hoteliers of Lebanon	**Melhem Hage**
Malaysia	Malaysia Association of Hotels	**Sophia Maxwell** Administration Manager
Netherlands	Koninkljik Horeca Nederland	**Hans van der Kooij** Sector Manager Hotels
Norway	Norwegian Hospitality Association	**Bjorn Arnesen** Senior Manager
Romania	Romanian Hotel Industry Federation	**Mihai Rajnita** Chief Executive Officer
Slovak Republic	Slovak Association of Hotels and Restaurants	**Zora Dundekova**
Sultanate of Oman	Ministry of Commerce and Industry Directorate General for Tourism	**Dr. Heba A. Aziz** Advisor-Research and Development **Ali Al Sudairi** Statistical Analyst
Sweden	Swedish Hotel and Restaurant Association	**Rikard Bergsten** Head of Classification Dept.
Switzerland	Swiss Hotel Association	**Annette Siegwart** Classification
Turkey	Turob-Turkish Hotel Association	**Kasim Zoto** Board Member
United Arab Emirates	Dubai Government Department of Tourism and Commerce Marketing	**Majid Sager Abdulla Al Merri** Executive, Hotel Classification
United Kingdom	British Hospitality Association	**Martin Couchman** Deputy Chief Executive
United States of America*	American Hotel and Lodging Association	**Tia Gordon** Director of Communication
Total		**32 Countries**

* There is no official hotel classification system, hence no replies to the questionnaire

1. Is an official classification system in place in your country?

2. If yes, at what level?

Country/Territory	Yes	No	Level
Austria	×		National; responsibility of the Austrian Professional Hotel Association
Canada	×		Provincial; each province has different regulation
Caribbean			Varies from country to country
Chile	×		National; Tourism Board
Colombia		×	
Czech Republic	×		National; under tourism law in cooperation with Czech National Federation of Hotels and Restaurants
Denmark	×		National; cooperation between hotel association and Tourist Board/Ministry for Trade and Industry
Egypt	×		Government
Estonia	×		Government
Finland		×	
France	×		National
Georgia	×		Government
Germany	×		National; voluntary system operated by DEHOGA
Greece	×		National
Hungary	×		Government
Iceland	×		National; it is open to every hotel and guesthouse, but voluntary
Iraq	×		Government
Israel		×	
Jordan	×		
Kuwait	×		Government; in coordination with Kuwait Hotel Owners Association
Lebanon	×		Government
Malaysia	×		Government, Ministry of Culture Arts and Tourism of Malaysia
Netherlands	×		International, with Belgium and Luxemburg
Norway		×	
Romania	×		Government; Ministry of Tourism
Slovak Republic	×		Government
Sultanate of Oman	×		Government; Ministry of Commerce and Industry/Directorate General of Tourism
Sweden	×		National, voluntary system operated by SHR for the first year (2004)
Switzerland	×		National; the classification system of the Swiss Hotel Association is under private law
Turkey	×		Government
United Arab Emirates	×		Government
United Kingdom	×		Regional; 4 systems: England, Scotland, Wales and Northern Ireland
United States of America*		×	

3. Application to facilities.

(*a*) Current classification in force applies to:

Country/Territory	*Hotels*	*Apartments hotels*	*Motels*	*Inns*	*Others*
Austria	×	×	×	×	B+B's, 'campagnards'
Canada	×	×	×	×	
Chile	×	×	×	×	
Czech Republic	×		×		
Denmark	×				
Egypt	×				Floating hotels
Estonia	×				
France	×				Tourism residences
Georgia	×	×	×	×	All kinds of hotels with 10 and more rooms
Germany	×	×	×	×	
Greece	×	×	×		
Hungary	×		×	×	Health and spa hotels
Iceland	×	×	×	×	
Iraq	×	×	×	×	Restaurants
Jordan	×	×	×	×	
Kuwait	×				
Lebanon					
Malaysia	×	×	×	×	
Netherlands	×	×	×	×	
Romania	×	×	×	×	
Slovak Republic	×	×	×	×	
Sultanate of Oman	×	×	×	×	Guesthouses
Sweden	×				
Switzerland	×	×	×	×	
Turkey	×	×	×		Historic buildings
United Arab Emirates	×	×			Guesthouses
United Kingdom	×		×	×	

Country/Territory	*All or specific types*	*Last date*	*Graphical symbol*
Austria			
Canada			
Chile	Optional	August 1987	Stars
Czech Republic		1998	Stars
Denmark			Stars
Egypt			
Estonia		2001	Stars
France		1986	Stars
Georgia			

(*Contd.*)

(*Contd.*)

Country/Territory	*All or specific types*	*Last date*	*Graphical symbol*
Germany	All	1999	Stars
Greece	All types of hotels	1987 (2002)	Letters (stars)
Hungary	All	24 June 1998	Stars
Iceland			
Iraq			
Jordan			
Kuwait		1994	
Lebanon			
Malaysia	All		Stars for hotels, apartment hotels and motels, Orchid for Inns
Netherlands	All	1 January 1999	Stars
Romania	Specific types	1999	Stars
Slovak Republic	Specific types	October 2001	Stars
Sultanate of Oman	All		Stars
Sweden	Specific types		Stars
Switzerland	Members of SHA	2000	Stars for hotels, motels special symbol for apartment hotels, inns
Turkey	All	06 July 2000	Stars
United Arab Emirates			
United Kingdom	All	1997	Stars

(*b*) Additional comments:

Country/Territory	*Comments*
Czech Republic	Basic classification is in force all types of facilities classification of CNFHR as ticked above.
Germany	Private guest houses and Bed & Breakfast accommodation (non-commercial) are classified according to a different system run by the German Tourist Association (DTV).
Greece	In March a new classification system has been legislated, but it has not been applied yet. The relevant decree provides that all the hotels must be classified according to the new system by the end of September 2003.
United Kingdom	Some group hotels are permitted entry into the scheme guidebooks without having a star rating.

4. Basis for establishing classification.

1. State Constitution
2. Tourism law
3. NTA competence
4. Agreement between government bodies concerned
5. Recommendation in a government-adopted tourism development plan
6. Prerogative/declared objective of a national hotel association
7. Decision (ad hoc) of a national hotel association
8. Agreement between independent hotels
9. Government recommendation
10. Recommendation in a tourism development plan implemented by industry

Country/Territory	*Basis for establishing classification*										*Types of establishments concerned*
	1	*2*	*3*	*4*	*5*	*6*	*7*	*8*	*9*	*10*	
Austria						×	×				
Canada	×			×					×		Varies in provinces
Chile		×							×		All
Czech Republic		×				×					All
Denmark	Agreement between national hotel association and government bodies										
Egypt		×									
Estonia		×									
France				×							
Georgia		×									
Germany							×				
Greece		×	×								All hotels
Hungary			×		×						All
Iceland				×					×	×	
Iraq		×			×	×	×	×		×	
Jordan		×								×	
Kuwait				×					×		
Lebanon						×	×	×	×	×	
Malaysia	×	×		×					×		
Netherlands		×		×							
Romania		×	×	×	×						All accommodation and F&B
Slovak Republic	×		×						×		All hotels
Sultanate of Oman		×							×		
Sweden					×		×				
Switzerland						×					
Turkey	×	×	×	×	×	×	×			×	All hotels
United Arab Emirates	×	×			×				×		
United Kingdom			×						×		

5. Rationale and use of classification.

Classification is justified by:

Country/Territory	*Consumer concerns*	*Marketing (industry's wish to better communicate its offer)*	*Need to have a tool to monitor sector development*
Austria	×	×	×
Canada	×	×	
Chile	×	×	
Czech Republic	×		
Denmark	×	×	×
Egypt			
Estonia	×	×	
France	×	× (hotel chains)	
Georgia	×		×
Germany	×	×	
Greece	×	×	×
Hungary	×	×	
Iceland	×	×	
Iraq	×	×	
Jordan	×	×	×
Kuwait		×	×
Lebanon	×	×	×
Malaysia	×	×	×
Netherlands	×	×	
Romania	×	×	×
Slovak Republic		×	×
Sultanate of Oman			
Sweden	×	×	
Switzerland	×	×	×
Turkey	×	×	×
United Arab Emirates	×	×	×
United Kingdom	×	×	

Country/ Territory	*Is it used to promote quality?*	*Is it used to promote investments?*	*Does it seek compatibility with existing classification systems in other countries?*	*Other rationale and use*
Austria	Yes	Yes	Yes	
Canada	Yes	Yes	Yes, to a certain degree (Mobil and CAA/AAA)	
Chile	Yes	No	Yes	
Czech Republic	Yes	No	Yes, Austria	
Denmark	Yes	No	No	Raise the quality of the hotel sector

(Contd.)

(Contd.)

Country/ Territory	*Is it used to promote quality?*	*Is it used to promote investments?*	*Does it seek compatibility with existing classification systems in other countries?*	*Other rationale and use*
Egypt	Yes		Yes	Control and monitor accommodation tariffs within established classes
Estonia	Yes		Yes	
France	No	No	No	
Georgia	Yes	No	Yes	
Germany	Yes	Yes	No	
Greece	Yes	Yes	Yes	Control and monitor accommodation tariffs within established classes
Hungary	Yes		Yes, Germany, Austria, Switzerland	
Iceland	Yes		Yes	
Iraq	Yes	Yes	No	Differentiate government taxes; monitor acorn, tariffs within establishments
Jordan	Yes	Yes	Yes	
Kuwait	Yes			
Lebanon			Yes	Differentiate government taxes; control and monitor accommodation tariffs within established classes
Malaysia	Yes	No	Yes	
Netherlands	Yes	Yes	Yes	
Romania	Yes	Yes	Yes	
Slovak Republic	Yes	Yes	Yes	Differentiate government taxes
Sultanate of Oman	Yes		Yes	Control accommodation tariffs within established classes
Sweden				
Switzerland	Yes	Yes	Yes	
Turkey	Yes	Yes	Yes	
United Arab Emirates	Yes	Yes	No	Differentiate government taxes
United Kingdom	Yes		No	

6. Classification authority/body deciding each classification. (Classification authorities such as National Tourism Ministry/ Hotel Association, etc. The following (hotels, apartment hotels etc.) may each be classified by a different authority)

Country/ Territory	*Hotels*	*Apartment hotels*	*Motels*	*Inns*	*Others*	*Classification authority*
Austria	×	×	×	×		Austrian Professional Hotel Association
Canada	×	×	×	×	×	
Chile	×	×	×	×	×	National Tourism Board
Czech Republic	×		×			Single body in cooperation with CNFHR
Denmark	×					Classification Board (3 rep. from Danish Tourist Board and 3 rep. from the national hotel association)
Egypt	×				×	Ministry of Tourism
Estonia	×					Ministry of Economy
France	×					DGCCRF
Georgia	×	×	×	×	×	Single body for all types of establishments
Germany	×	×	×	×		DEHOGA in cooperation with regional tourism associations
Greece	×	×	×			Tourism Directorates of the 13 regional authorities; in the new system the competent body will be the Greek National Tourism Organization
Hungary	×		×	×	×	Local authority/ municipality
Iceland	×	×	×	×		Icelandic Tourist Board
Iraq	×	×	×	×		Tourism Board
Jordan						
Kuwait	×					Government authority in coordination with hotel association
Lebanon						

(*Contd.*)

(*Contd.*)

Country/ Territory	*Hotels*	*Apartment hotels*	*Motels*	*Inns*	*Others*	*Classification authority*
Malaysia	×	×	×	×		Ministry of Culture, Arts and Tourism of Malaysia
Netherlands	×	×	×			One single authority which inspects the star-system; this is obligatory to be able to use the name 'hotels'
Romania	×	×	×	×		Ministry of Tourism with Industry Representatives
Slovak Republic	×					Each establishment
Sultanate of Oman	×	×				Directorate General of Tourism
Sweden	×					Swedish Hotel and Restaurant Association
Switzerland	×	×	×	×		5 regional and 1 national commission, all bodies of the SHA
Turkey						
United Arab Emirates	×	×			×	Department of Tourism and Commerce Marketing
United Kingdom	×		×	×		England: AA/RAC Scotland, Wales and Northern Ireland: national org.s

7. Bodies involved in devising and drafting classification. Was the classification system in question prepared by:

(*a*) NTA/NOT and other government officials
(*b*) An expert designated/recommended by WTO/OMT
(*c*) In consultation with an international hotel and/or restaurant association
(*d*) In consultation with national hotel association
(*e*) A private national/international consultant
(*f*) Collaboration between hotel industry and NTA/Government/NOT experts
(*g*) On the basis of another country's classification system
(*h*) By revising the previous system
(*i*) In consultation with Consumers' Association

Country/ Territory	*Bodies involves*									*Others*
	1	*2*	*3*	*4*	*5*	*6*	*7*	*8*	*9*	
Austria				×	×	×		×		Extensive market research project on tourist expectations and needs is the basis for the current system. The research project was government funded and carried out by the Vienna University of Economics.
Canada				×	×	×	×	×		
Chile	×			×		×				
Czech Republic						×				
Denmark				×		×				
Egypt	×			×			×	×		
Estonia	×			×		×	×			
France			×							
Georgia		×								
Germany				×		×				Consumers' Association demanded a national classification scheme. Market introduction in 1996, relaunched in 1999.
Greece	×			×				×		There has been research into the classification systems existing in Europe.
Hungary	×			×			×			
Iceland	×			×						
Iraq			×	×						
Jordan	×					×				
Kuwait				×						
Lebanon							×	×		
Malaysia	×			×		×	×			
Netherlands	×									
Romania	×			×		×	×	×		
Slovak Republic	×			×		×		×	×	
Sultanate of Oman					×		×			Directorate General of Tourism in consultation with other ministries concerned
Sweden				×			×			Based on HORESTA (Denmark's) system
Switzerland			×	×		×		×	×	
Turkey				×		×		×		
United Arab Emirates					×		×			
United Kingdom	×			×		×		×		

8. Applicability of Classification

(*a*)

Country/ Territory	*Is classification mandatory?*	*Can establishments operate without being classified?*	*Can classification be mandatory in certain areas, e.g., as a condition for membership of a hotel association?*	*Is it necessary to obtain license/ permission/ registration to operate?*
Austria	No	Yes	No	Yes
Canada	Varies from province to province			
Chile	No	Yes	No	No
Czech Republic	Yes	No	No	No
Denmark	Yes, hotels	Yes	Yes	No
Egypt	Yes	Yes, but will not be classified as a tourist establishment	Yes	Yes
Estonia	No	Yes	No	Yes
France	No	Yes	No	No
Georgia	Yes	No	No	Yes
Germany	No	Yes	No	No
Greece	Yes	No		Yes
Hungary	Yes	No	No	Yes
Iceland	No	Yes	No	No
Iraq				
Jordan	Yes	No	No	Yes
Kuwait		Yes		
Lebanon	Yes	No		No
Malaysia	Yes	No according to the ne Tourism Act 2002 which was implemented for mandatory classification, before yes	No	Yes
Netherlands	Yes	Yes	No	Yes
Romania	Yes	No	No	No
Slovak Republic	Yes	No	No	No
Sultanate of Oman		No		Yes
Sweden	No	Yes	No	
Switzerland	Yes, for SHA members	Yes, non-members of SHA	No	Yes
Turkey	Yes	No	Yes	Yes
United Arab Emirates	Yes	No	No	Yes
United Kingdom	No, except in Northern Ireland	Yes, except in Northern Ireland	Yes, e.g., in order to obtain advertisement space in Tourist Board publications	No

(b)

Country/Territory	*Of establishments (by type of establishments) %*	*Of room capacity (by type of establishments) %*	*Can all establishments apply to be classified?*
Austria	70	75	Yes
Canada	90	95	Yes
Chile	20	35	Yes
Czech Republic	100	100	Yes, space of rooms according to law act 173/98 Sb
Denmark	70	90	No, only national hotel association's members
Egypt			Yes
Estonia	25 of hotels	50 of hotel rooms	Only certified hotels can be classified
France			No
Georgia	65	50	Yes
Germany	15	30	Yes, more than 8 beds
Greece	100	100	Yes
Hungary	100	100	Yes
Iceland	Most of the largest hotels in the country and most of the hotels in Reykjavik are classified but there are very many small guesthouses and few are classified.		Yes
Iraq			
Jordan			Yes
Kuwait	80	80	Yes
Lebanon			No
Malaysia			Yes, if they have appropriate infra-structure as a tourist accommodation premise and valid business license
Netherlands	100	100	Yes
Romania	963 hotels, motels, inns and similar	~ 120.000 rooms, of which 45% seasonal	Yes, all minimum criteria recommended by WTO are applied
Slovak Republic	100	100	Yes
Sultanate of Oman	30		Yes
Sweden	35% of the members	40% of the members	No, establishments have to be members of SHR
Switzerland	45	80	No, established have to be members of the SHA
Turkey	55	75	No
United Arab Emirates	100	100	Yes
United Kingdom	30-40	60	Yes

9. Verification of compliance with classification system

(*a*) Is verification performed by:

Country/Territory	*Central government inspectors*	*Local government inspectors*	*Hotel industry (second party) inspectors*	*Independent (third party inspectors)*	*Other parties*
Austria			×	×	
Canada				×	
Chile					
Czech Republic			×		
Denmark			×		
Egypt	×	×			
Estonia					Classification Commission (Ministry of Economy)
France					
Georgia	×	×			
Germany			×		NTA and RTA
Greece	×	×		×	
Hungary	×	×			Consumer protection organizations, municipality
Iceland	×				
Iraq					
Jordan			×		JHA inspectors
Kuwait		×			
Lebanon	×			×	
Malaysia	×	×	×	×	Third party inspectors are Authorities for fire department and health
Netherlands	×				
Romania	×	×	×		
Slovak Republic	×		×		
Sultanate of Oman	×				
Sweden			×		
Switzerland			×		
Turkey	×		×		
United Arab Emirates		×			
United Kingdom				×	

(*b*) Mode of verification:

Country/Territory	*Announced visits at fixed date*	*Mystery checks*	*Other methods*
Austria	×		Frequent questionnaires to be answered by the hoteliers
Canada	Yes, except for 5*	Yes, except for 5*	
Chile	×		One time visit upon application
Czech Republic	×	100	
Denmark	×	×	
Egypt	×		
Estonia	×		
France		×	
Georgia		×	
Germany	×		
Greece	×		Non-announced visits of the competent public authorities
Hungary	×		
Iceland	×		
Iraq			
Jordan		×	
Kuwait	×		
Lebanon	×		
Malaysia	×	×	
Netherlands	×		
Romania	×	×	
Slovak Republic			
Sultanate of Oman			DGT inspectors random surprise visits
Sweden	×		
Switzerland	×		
Turkey	×	×	
United Arab Emirates	×	×	
United Kingdom		×	

(c-d) Cost of verification borne by:

Country/Territory	*The verifying authority*	*The hotel company concerned*	*Periodically of verification*
Austria	×		
Canada		×	Every year
Chile	×		Once upon registration
Czech Republic		×	Every two year
Denmark		×	Every year
Egypt	×		
Estonia	× (State)		Every two year
France			Occasionally
Georgia		×	Every year
Germany		×	Every three year
Greece	×	×	Can occur at any time
Hungary	×		Occasionally
Iceland		×	Every year
Iraq			
Jordan	×		Every year
Kuwait		×	Every three year
Lebanon			
Malaysia	×		Every two year
Netherlands	×		Every two year
Romania	×		Every three year
Slovak Republic		×	Occasionally
Sultanate of Oman	×		Every year and when necessary
Sweden		×	Every year
Switzerland	×		Every five year
Turkey	×		Occasionally
United Arab Emirates	×	×	Every year or when asked by the establishment for classification
United Kingdom		×	Every year

10. How frequently is the classification system updated?

11. Who finances the system?

12. What are the main criteria referred to for classification?

Country/ Territory	*How frequently is classification system updated?*	*Who finances the system?*	*What are the main criteria referred to for classification?*
Austria	Every year	Membership establishments of the Austrian Professional Hotel Association	Hard- and software
Canada	Every year	The hotels	Numerous
Chile	Quarterly, regarding registered and classified establishments	National Tourism Administration	Availability of services, e.g., restaurant facilities, meeting rooms, recreational, parking
Czech Republic	Every two year	Respective facilities	Law act 137/98 Sb and classification of CNFHR
Denmark	Every three year	The classified hotels	All services and facilities that can be measured
Estonia	Every five year	Government	
France		Hotel concerned	Number of rooms, surfaces, service
Georgia	Every year	Hotel company	Georgian National Standard; 12 December 1996
Germany	After 4-5 years the criteria are checked and updated to market needs	Hotels (classification fees)	237 objective criteria, mainly hardware; minimum criteria by category and assessment points to be reached
Greece	Every five years hotels have to update certain supporting documents	Government and hoteliers	Compulsory technical specifications and functional standards which can be compulsory or optional
Hungary	Every five years	Government	The level of comfort provided
Iceland	Every year	The participant hotels	Objective
Iraq			
Jordan		Jordan Hotel Association	The JHA hotel classification system
Kuwait	When it is needed	Kuwait Hotel Owners Association	
Lebanon		Government	Location, building, indoor units, personnel

(*Contd.*)

(*Contd.*)

Country/ Territory	*How frequently is classification system updated?*	*Who finances the system?*	*What are the main criteria referred to for classification?*
Malaysia	Every 3 year	Ministry of Culture, Arts & Tourism Malaysia	Qualitative & aesthetic requirements of Common areas (lobby, reception, bar, restaurant, banquet halls, recreation), Services (F&B, Frong desk), Safety Standards & hygiene, Staff and rooms
Netherlands	Every 3 year	All enterprises in the hotel, restaurant and catering industry	Hardware, very the little attention to service-related aspects
Romania	Almost every 3 year	Ministry of Tourism and taxes paid by operators	Minimum recommended by WTO
Slovak Republic	Irregularity	Government	Qualified personnel, quality and number of services
Sultanate of Oman	Every year and when necessary	Directorate-General for Tourism	Location, outlets, building, indoor units
Sweden	Just initiated so only minor adjustments regularly	Initial one time cost covered by Swedish Tourist Delegation (Government). On-going costs covered by the hotels through a yearly fee based on number of rooms.	Hotel standard and service functions
Switzerland	Information: every year standards of class: every five year	Swiss Hotel Association	Quality of infra-structure and services
Turkey	Every year	Government	Standard of rooms and other social activities of the hotel
United Arab Emirates	Every year or when changes are announced at a hotel	Government	Services, health standards, infrastructure
United Kingdom	Every year	Fees paid by participating hotels	England: facility based Scotland, Wales: quality based

13. Is there any link between the classification scheme and:
    Social obligations of the employer (i.e., rating as a criterion to determine social charges);
    Other burdens on the employer (i.e., rating as a criterion to determine other charges/taxes imposed on the employer).
14. Are you satisfied with the existing system in your country?
15. Plans to introduce new classification or revise current classification?

Country/Territory	*Obligations relating to employer*	*Are you satisfied with the existing system in your country?*	*Plans to introduce new classification or revise current classification?*
Austria	None	Yes, they have just modernized the system	
Canada		Yes, but there is always room for improvement	There is an ongoing revision
Chile	Not considered	No, the actual system does not evaluate quality of service; infrastructure nor minimum requirements; it should be also mandatory and incentivated as a marketing tool; classification and verification should be periodical	Yes, the local hotel association and national tourism administration are working on a plan to review the current classification system to include above mentioned aspects
Czech Republic	None	Not in all respects	With two or three years
Denmark	The hotels must comply with all relevant laws (tax, working conditions, license, etc.)	Yes, it is easily understood as all criteria are measurable; grading meets the expectations of the customers, and the independent classification board ensures the credibility of the scheme	They are currently revising the classification as they do at least every three years
Estonia	None	Yes, in general, only periodically of verification should be every five years	Government system includes a lot of bureaucracy, so it is more effective to be managed by NTA, may be in cooperation with NOT

(*Contd.*)

(*Contd.*)

Country/Territory	*Obligations relating to employer*	*Are you satisfied with the existing system in your country?*	*Plans to introduce new classification or revise current classification?*
Finland		Yes, as far as there is no official hotel classification system in Finland	
France	None	Yes	
Georgia	Needs to be improved	Lack of information in both parties	Plan for new classification based on international experience and laws
Germany	None	Yes, it is their own marketing system with the possibility of changing aspects immediately	Existing system will be revised regularly in 2003
Greece		The old system had to be modernized; the new one has not yet come into force, so cannot be evaluated	
Hungary	To provide minimal services plus additional services	Yes	There is a need to renew it every five years
Iceland	None	Yes, quite satisfied, but many hotels find it too expensive, would like to add subjective criteria in the future	No, not yet; we have only had this system, which is the Danish one, for a few years
Iraq			
Jordan	Out of 16 per cent social security fees, the owner pays 11, 6 per cent		
Kuwait	None	Might need update	Revise current classification
Lebanon	CNSS transportation, education	Yes, it has just been revised and the new one is quite modern	

(*Contd.*)

(*Contd.*)

Country/Territory	*Obligations relating to employer*	*Are you satisfied with the existing system in your country?*	*Plans to introduce new classification or revise current classification?*
Malaysia	No	Exist plans for the system to be managed by the national hotel association but not for certain yet	Yes, to differentiate criteria for service apartments
Netherlands	Officially no, but there are examples of real estate taxes being based on the star rating of the hotel concerned	The are in the process of evaluating the system; they have conducted a survey among their members and 44 per cent want to maintain the present system, 28 per cent prefer a voluntary system and 18 per cent want no classification at all	
Norway			They are working on hotel classification and now they have conducted a survey among the consumers and tour operators
Romania		Could be better, but state regulations, control and certification is still necessary till privatization is ready and operators will be more checked by market consumers than by official bodies	Within one month, but the only change refers to F&B sector
Slovak Republic		Yes	Not in near future
Sultanate of Oman	None	Yes, the system is currently satisfactory; there is a tourism law which will amend and improve further the classification	The tourism law will add and revise certain points
Sweden	No	Yes, and there is an intention to build a Nordic System with Sweden and Denmark as a base	Studying to classify apartment hotels and conference facilities

(*Contd.*)

(Contd.)

Country/Territory	Obligations relating to employer	Are you satisfied with the existing system in your country?	Plans to introduce new classification or revise current classification?
Switzerland	None	Yes	The current classification will be revised during the next three years and enter in force in 2005
Turkey	None	No, the changes in the industry are very fast and the classification system is not very effective actually	Involve more the hotel association instead of central Government
United Arab Emirates	Hotel must respect local traditions, social values and Muslim religion; facilities must be given to employees	Yes, but intend to develop and improve the system in 2003	Always trying to keep up with the development of the industry
United Kingdom	None	No, three schemes is too many	The governments in England, Scotland and Wales are moving towards accepting the need for a combined system

1. Additional comments

Country/ Territory	*Additional comments*
	Each province has different rules, regulations, laws; classification is not mandatory in many provinces.
Canada	According to the Canadian Constitution, property and civil regulation is a provincial matter, so there are four different classification systems in Canada.
	Many countries such as Barbados, St. Lucia, Bahamas and Jamaica had plans to establish a system, but none of them had implemented it. 'Les departments d'outre mer Francais' are part of France and therefore subject to French legislation. Cancun, Cozumel and the Riviera Maya are subject to Mexico's star system.
Caribbean	CHA's official position has always been to oppose the setting up of national classification programmes, on the grounds that with different criteria, they would totally confuse an already turbulent marketplace. It is conceivable that a case could be made for a Caribbean regional programme, but it would require an awesome amount of preliminary discussion and could meet difficulties in implementation. More to the point would be a common approach to hotel licensing, with proper criteria in place for space requirements, fire safety and health standards, etc.
Colombia	Due to the last government tourism reform law in 1996, there is not an official hotel or similar establishment classification in Colombia at this moment.
Czech Republic	The system is basically established on the law/act 137/98 Sb./Czech National Federation of Hotels and Restaurants (CNFHR) built it up to the quality of services and equipment.
France	Besides of government classification, 'Hotelcert' has a private additional rating system.
Hungary	International chains (e.g., ACCOR Group) do not like the valid categorization system.
Netherlands	In The Netherlands the name 'hotel' is protected by law. Accommodations need to have at least one star to be able to call themselves hotel.
	The scheme is updated whenever one of the participants (i.e., Belgium, Luxembourg and Holland) asks modification.
	The national automobile association ANWB operates its own system. This system is a voluntary system, paid for by the individual hotels. Around 60 per cent of all establishments with at least one star in the official classification participate. If one is willing to pay the fee, it will be 'ANWB preferred supplier' and will receive a label on or near the front entrance.
Romania	Operators should submit a written request (a complete file). For new developments, a pre-project visa must be obtained from Ministry of Tourism. Generally speaking, all criteria are applying of those minimum recommended by WTO. Compliance with

(*Contd.*)

(Contd.)

Country/ Territory	*Additional comments*
	minimum requirements of norms and consequently with health, sanitary-veterinary, work safety, fire safety bodies certificates. It applies to: buildings, room size, safety and security criteria, staff certificates proving graduation of hospitality schools (front desk, restaurant waiters, cooks, chefs) and a certificate for hotel director/General Manager, issued by Ministry of Tourism/. Restaurants are part of the classification scheme, rated by stars by Ministry of Tourism. The only and very recent private classification guide appeared on the market—House—and it created rumours among Ministry of Tourism officials. The Romanian Hotel Industry Federation's position is that as long as it is a free market, government can rate hotels much more objectively than inspectors, who can be 'Convinced'.
Switzerland	The classification system of the Swiss Hotel Association is the only classification system in Switzerland. It was adopted by SHA in 1979 and has been revised every 5 years.
United Kingdom	The classification system is not very clear, some hotel groups award themselves star ratings.

2. *Compilation of Replies from Public Sector to WTO*

Questionnaire on the classification of accommodation establishments (hotels and similar establishments). Completed by responsible officers of National Tourism Administrations (NTAs) in collaboration with their national hotel association(s).

145 questionnaires were sent out. The following is the analysis of the 89 replies received.

Participating Countries

Country/ Territory	*Respondent*	*Address*
Algeria	*Salid Rebach* Vice-Director	Ministry of Tourism R. N. 36 El-Balir, Alger
Andorra	*Monica Bonell Tuset* Tourism Technician	Ministry of Presidency and Tourism, Department of Tourism Carrer Prat de la Creu 62-64, Andorra la Vella
Argentina	*German Luis Perez* Executive Coordinator	Secretariat of Tourism Suipacha 1111, piso 20 (1368), Buenos Aires
Armenia	*Aram Torosyan* Senior Expert	Ministry of Trade and Economic Development, Tourism Development Department 5 Mher Mkrtchian str., 375010, Yerevan

(Contd.)

(*Contd.*)

Country/ Territory	*Respondent*	*Address*
Azerbaijan	*Bakhtiyar Gylyndzhov* Senior Official	
Belgium	*Mouling Alfons* General Assistant	Flemish Tourism Grasmarkt 61, 1000, Brussel
Benin	*Paul C. Akoha* Director of Tourism & Hotellerie	Ministry of Culture, Industry and Tourism
Bolivia	*Tec. Monica V. Vargas O.* Responsible for Tourism Services	Ministry of Foreign Trade and Investment Av. Mariscal Santa Cruz, Edificio Palacio de las Comunicaciones, Piso 16, Laz Paz
Bosnia and Herzegovina	*Dunja Pejic* Senior Advisor	Ministry of Trade and Tourism Vuka Karadzica 4, 78000 Banjaluka
Botswana	*Kenneth Bentinck* For/Director	Department of Tourism Private Bag 0047, Gaborone
Brazil	*Nelson Faria Lins d'Albuquerque Junior* Chief of Tourism Product Quality Department	Ministry of Sports and Tourism, Brazilian Institute of Tourism SCN—Quadra 2, Bloco G, Sala 204, 70712-907 Brasilia/DF
Burundi	*Nsabimana* Grading Service of Tourism Establishments	BP 902, Bujumbura
Cambodia*	*Om Sornsun* Under Secretary of State	Ministry of Tourism
Chad	*Akia Abouna* Minister of Tourism Development	Ministry of Tourism Development
Chile	*Humberto Rivas Ortega* Chief of Planification Department	Av. Providencia 1550, Santiago
China	*Zhou Zhang* Deputy Director of Hotel Division	China National Tourism Administration 9A, Jianguomennei Ave., 100749 Beijing
Costa Rica	*Lic. Martin Quesada Rivera* Chief of Tourism Services and Enterprises Department	
Croatia	*Zdenko Micic* Deputy Minister	Ministry of Tourism Ul. Grada Vukovara, 78, Zagreb
Cuba	*Maria Elena Lopez Reyes* Director of Quality Department	Ministry of Tourism Calle 19 No. 710 esq. Paseo Vedado, La Habana
Cyprus	*Kyriakos Kyriakou* Tourist Officer	Cyprus Tourism Organization P. O. Box 24535, 1390 Nicosia

(*Contd.*)

(*Contd.*)

Country/ Territory	*Respondent*	*Address*
Czech Republic	*Petr Houska* Deputy Director	Old Town Square 6, 110 15 Prague 1
Ecuador	*Monica Jaramillo Luque* Chief of National Tourism Resources	Ministry of Tourism
Eritrea	*Tseggai Mogos* D/G/T Service	Ministry of Tourism
Ethiopia	*Matewos G/Mariam* Head of Standardization & Licensing Department	Tourism Commission P.O. Box 2183, Addis Ababa
France	*Michel Veneau* Assistant Chief of Tourism Industries & Professions Department	Direction of Tourism 2, rue Linois, 75015 Paris
Gambia	*Jimmo Jawneh* For: Director General	Gambia Tourism Authority Kololi, P. O. Box 4085, Bakau, K.M.C.
Georgia	*Maya Margvelashvili* Deputy Chairman	State Department of Tourism and Resorts of Georgia 80, Chavchavadze Str., 380062, Tbilisi
Germany	*Markus Luthe,* Deputy Chief Executive	DEHOGA and IHA 10873 Berlin, Germany
Ghana	*Adeline Boateng* Quality Assurance Manager	Ghana Tourist Board P. O. Box 3106, Accra
Greece	*Evangelia Papadopoulou* International Relations Department	Ministry of Development, General Secretariat of Tourism 2, Amerikis street, 10564 Athens
Guatemala	*Hugo Armando Ruiz Garcia* Chief of Registration and Supervision of Tourism Enterprises Department	Guatemala Tourist Commission 7a. Ave. 1-17, Guatemala, C.A.
Guinea Equatorial	*Gabino-Muemba Molonguaivina* General Director of Tourism	Ministry of Information, Tourism and Culture, General Secretariat of Tourism Malabo
Haiti	*Marie-Jo Bredy Planification* Director Georges Belin Investments Director Jn-Claude Rolles Consultant	
Hungary	*Gabor Lombosi* Secretary-General	Hotel Association of Hungary P. O. Box 233, H-1444, Budapest
India*	*J. Dash* Joint Director-General	Tourism India C-1 Hutments Dalhousie Road, 110011 New Delhi

(*Contd.*)

(*Contd.*)

Country/ Territory	*Respondent*	*Address*
Indonesia	*I Gede Ardika* Minister of Culture and Tourism	Ministry of Culture and Tourism of the Republic of Indonesia Jl. Medan Merdeka Barat 17-19, 10110 Jakarta
Iran	*Fereidoun Nateghi Elahi* Technical Advisor to the Deputy Minister and Chairman of Iran Touring and Tourism ITTO	Ministry of Culture & Islamic Guidance, Iran Touring & Tourism Organization Hajj and Pilgrimage Bldg., Azadi Ave., P. O. Box 14155-1555, Tehran
Italy	*Mauro Di Pietro*	Ministry of Productive Activities General Tourism Board Via della Ferratella, 51, 00184 Rome
Ivory Coast	Director of Tourism	B.P.V. 184
Jamaica	*Carrole A.M. Guntley-Brady* Director-General	Ministry of Tourism and Sport Jamaica Tourism Center 3rd Floor, 64 Knutsford Boulevard, Kingston 5
Jordan	*Nader Dahabi* Minister of Transport	Ministry of Tourism & Antiquities P. O. Box 224, Amman 11118
Kazakhstan	*Shaikenova Rashida* Executive Director	Kazakhstan Association of Hotels and Restaurants 98 Zheltoksan str., office 509, 480091
Kenya	*Clement Mwatsama* Director of Tourism	Ministry of Tourism and Information P.O. Box 54666, Nairobi
Lebanon	*Mohammed Zantout* Inspector at Minister of Tourism	Ministry of Tourism Rue de la Banque Centrale, Beyrouth
Macau	*Maria Isabel da Costa Alves* Head of Licensing Division	Macau Government Tourist Office Largo do Senado, 9 Edf. Ritz
Madagascar	*Rasolofoniaina Haga* Director of Tourist Development Department	Ministry of Tourism Rue Fernand Kassanga, B.P. 610 Tsimbazaza, Antananarivo 101
Madeira	*Bruno Camacho Pereira* Regional Director	Regional Secretariat of Tourism and Culture, Regional Tourism Board Avenida Anniaga, 18, 9004-519 Fonchal
Malawi	*Isabel T. Chakhumbira* Senior Tourism Officer	Ministry of Tourism P. O. Box 402, Blantyre
Malaysia	*Dato' Tengku Alaudin Tengku Abdul Majid* Secretary General	Ministry of Culture, Arts and Tourism 36 Floor, Menara Dato' Onn, Putra World Trade Centre, 45, Jalan Tun Ismail, 50694 Kuala Lumpur
Maldives*	*Ahmed Solih* Assistant Director, Trade Standards	Ministry of Tourism info@visitmaldives.com

(*Contd.*)

(*Contd.*)

Country/ Territory	*Respondent*	*Address*
Mali	*Alion. I. Mâiga*	BP 191 Omatho, Bamuko
Malta	*Albert Callus*	Ministry of Tourism
	WTO Deputy Permanent Representative	Auberge d'Italy, Merchants Street, Valletta CMR 01
Mauritius	*C. I. Mijoo*	Ministry of Tourism
	For Permanent Secretary	Level 12, Air Mauritius Centre, John Kenedy Street, Port Louis
Mexico	*Eduardo Barroso Alarcon*	Secretariat of Tourism
	Secretary of Tourism Operation Department	Presidente Masarik 172, 7 piso, Colonia chapultepec Morales, Delegacion Migue Hidalgo C.P. 11587 Mexico, D.F.
Moldova	*Kalmyk Serdzhiu*	National Tourism Agency
	Consultant	Office 901-A, 180, Stefan cel Mare Blvd, MD-2004 Chisinau
Monaco*	*Dario dell'Antonia*	Direction du Tourisme et des Congrés,
	Délégué Genéral au Tourisme	2a boulevard des Moulins, MC 98030 Monaco CEDEX
Mongolia	*L. Enkhnasan*	Ministry of Infrastructure, Government Building-2, United Nations Street 5/2 Ulaanbaatar-210646
Montenegro	*Predrag Nenezic*	Ministry of Tourism
	Minister of Tourism	Trg Vektre b.b., 81000 Pongorica
Morocco	*M. El Ouardighi Abderrahmade*	Ministry of Tourism, Board of Tourist Activities and Enterprises
	Chief of Tourism Establishments Department	22, Avenue d'Alger Hassane Rabat
Mozambique	*António José Filipe Saia*	PO Box 614, Maputo, Fax 307677
	National Director	
Netherlands	*A.K. Vis*	Bedrijfschap Horeca en Catering Bar.
	Project Manager Benelux-Hotel Classification	De Coubertinln. 6, 2719 EL Zoetermeer, Postbus 121, 2700 AC Zoetermeer
Niger	*Madougai Ousmane*	Ministry of Tourism and Arts
	Regulation Service	B. P.. 480/12130, Niamey
Nigeria	Embassy of Nigeria Madrid	Embassy of Nigeria Madrid
Pakistan	*Khalid Hussain Warraich*	Department of Tourist Services
	Deputy Controller	B6 Markaz F-7, Islamabad
Paraguay	*Aurelio Rojas*	Operations Department
	Chief of Operations Department	Palma 468—Asuncion

(*Contd.*)

(*Contd.*)

Country/ Territory	*Respondent*	*Address*
Peru	*Miguel Antonio Zamora S.* National Director of Tourism	Ministry of Industry, Tourism, Integration & International Commercial Negotiation, Department of Tourism Calle Uno Oeste, 50 Urb. Corpac, San Isidro, Lima 27
Philippines	*Atty. Ma. Victoria V. Jasmin* Director of the Office Tourism Standards	Department of Tourism, Office of Tourism Standards RM. 204, 2nd Floor DOT Bldg., T, M. Kalaw St. Ermita, 1000 Manila
Poland	*Mrs. Malgorzata Milka-Bryska* Director of Department of Tourism	Ministry of Economy, Department of Tourism Pl. Tizech Krzyzy 3/5, 00-507 Warsaw
Portugal	*Jose Sancho Silva* General Director	General Tourism Board Av. Antonio Augusto de Aguiar, 86, 1069-021 Lisboa
Puerto Rico	*Jose M. Tirado* Economic Research Specialist	Puerto Rico Tourism Company, Department of Business Intelligence, Division of Research & Development P. O. Box 902390, Old San Juan Station, San Juan
Russia	*N. Shenguelia* Chief of Tourism Department	Ministry of Economic Development and Trade
San Marino	*Gloria Licini, Dominique Morolli*	Officer of Tourism Promotion and Programming Sector Contrada Omagnano, 20, San Marino
Sao Tome et Principe		Hotel and Tourism Board Caixa Postal 40, St. Tome
Seychelles	*Sinha Levkovic* Assistant Director of Inspectors Quality Assurance Unit	Inspectors Quality Assurance Unit P. O. Box 92, Victoria, Mahe
Sierra Leone	*Joseph O. Mansaray* Planning & Development Manager	National Tourist Board of Sierra Leone Room 100, Cape Sierra Hotel, P. O. Box 1435, Freetown
Slovak Republic	*Eliska Romanova* Senior Officer	Ministry of Economy, Department of International Cooperation in Tourism Mierova 19, 827 15 Bratislava
Slovenia	*Ana Bozicnk* Senior Counselor	Ministry of Economy Trubarjeva 11, 2000 Maribor
South Africa	*Dr. Joseph Raputsoe*	Department of Environment and Tourism Private Bag x447, 0001 Pretoria

(*Contd.*)

(Contd.)

Country/ Territory	Respondent	Address
Spain	*António Nieto Magro* Sudirector General de Cooperacióny Coordinatión Turistica	José Lázaro Galdiano 6 28036 Madrid
Sri Lanka	*Director/Trade Standards (Hotels and Guest-Houses)*	Sri Lanka Tourist Board, No. 80, Galle Road, Colombo 03
Switzerland	*Andrea Kammer* Hotel Classification Service	Swiss Society of Hoteliers Monbijoustrasse 130, CH-3001 Bern
Tanzania	*Salama A. Kibogoyo* Principal Tourism Officer	Ministry of Natural Resources P. O. Box 9352, Dar-Es-Salaam
Togo	*Anate S. Bagnah* Director of Tourism Professions	Ministry of Tourism B.P. 1289, Lome
Tunisia		Ministère du Tourisme et de l'Artisanat, Office National du Tourisme
Turkey	*Turkay Can* Manager	The Union of Turkish Municipalities Guesthouse Selanik Cad. 57, Kizilay/Ankara
Ukraine	*Ludmila A. Mechterskih* Chief of Accommodation Establishment Classification Sector	Accommodation Establishment Classification Sector 36, Yaroslaviv Val. 01034 Kyiv,
Vietnam	*Vu Quoe Tri* Deputy Director of Hotel Department	Vietnam National Administration of Tourism 80-Quan Su Street, Hanoi
Yugoslavia	*Aleksandar Susa* Advisor	National Tourism Organisation of Serbia Dobrinsjka 11, 11000 Belgrade, Serbia, FR
Zambia	*Micheal Lengalenga* Principal Standards Inspector	Ministry of Tourism Environment and Natural Resources P. O. Box 30575, Lusaka

Cambodia*	Letter of 17 July 2002, advising that they are preparing the replies.
Germany*	There is no government classification, hence no replies to questions in part A.
India*	Survey returned void.
Maldives*	E-mail of 10 July 2002. They do not have a Hotel Classification System in the Maldives
Monaco*	They only sent the legislation and have not replied to the survey.
Nigeria	Verbal note of 12 June 2002: "the questionnaire has been transmitted to the appropriate Nigerian Authorities for their necessary action."
Tunisia	Sent the classification system of hotels "Normes 2000" but did not reply to the survey.

Part A: Government Classification

1. Application to Facilities

(*a*) Current classification in force applies to:

Country/ Territory	*Hotels*	*Apartment Hotels*	*Motels*	*Inns*	*Others*
Algeria	×	×	×	×	Holiday villages, pensions, chalets
Andorra	×	×		×	Pensions, chalets and bungalows
Argentina	×	×	×	×	
Armenia	×	×	×	×	
Azerbaijan	×		×	×	
Belgium–Flemish	×	×	×	×	
Benin	×		×	×	
Bolivia	×	×		×	Complimentary hospitality, resort
Bosnia and Herzegovina	×	×	×		
Brazil	×				
Burundi	×		×	×	
Chile	×	×	×	×	
China	×				
Costa Rica	×	×			
Croatia	×	×	×		Holiday villages, tourist apartments, guesthouses, pensions
Cuba	×	×	×		Tourist villages
Cyprus	×	×	×		Tourist villages, traditional houses, guesthouses, tourist apartments and furnished apartments which are regarded as perishing classes of accommodation
Czech Republic	×		×	×	
Ecuador	×		×	×	Floating hotels, pensions
Equatorial Guinea	×	×		×	
Ethiopia	×	×			Pensions, guesthouses
France	×	×			
Ghana	×	×	×	×	Resorts
Greece	×	×			
Guatemala	×	×	×	×	
Hungary	×				Bed and breakfast, apartment house, tourist hotel
Indonesia	×	×	×	×	
Iran					
Italy	×	×	×	×	

(Contd.)

(*Contd.*)

Country/ Territory	*Hotels*	*Apartment Hotels*	*Motels*	*Inns*	*Others*
Ivory Coast	×		×	×	
Jordan	×	×	×		Hotel suites, hostels
Kazakhstan	×				
Kenya	×	×	×	×	
Lebanon	×	×	×	×	Chalets
Macau	×	×			
Madagascar	×		×		Ecolodges
Madeira	×	×		×	Rural tourism
Malawi	×		×	×	Lodges
Malaysia	×		×	×	
Mali	×	×	×	×	
Malta	×	×			Self-catering
Monaco	×				
Moldova	×	×	×		Villas, bungalows, pensions, holiday villages, tourist ships
Mongolia	×				Traditional ger camp (ger-traditional house)
Montenegro	×	×	×		Resort hotel complexes
Morocco	×	×	×	×	Holiday villages, pensions, restaurants
Mozambique	×	×	×	×	
Netherlands	×	×	×	×	
Nigeria	×				
Pakistan	×	×	×	×	Guesthouses
Paraguay					
Peru	×	×		×	Ecolodges, pensions, resorts
Philippines	×	×		×	Pensions, homestays
Poland	×		×		Pensions, guesthouses, bivouac grounds
Portugal	×		×	×	Apartment hotels, pensions, holiday villages, guesthouses
Puerto Rico	×	×		×	Puerto Rico Inn
Sao Tome et Principe	×	×	×	×	
San Marino	×	×	×		
Seychelles	×				
Slovak Republic	×		×		Boarding houses
Slovenia	×	×	×	×	Camps, marines, apartments
South Africa	×		×	×	
Spain	×	×	×	×	
Sri Lanka	×				Guesthouses
Tanzania	×	×	×		Lodges, villas, cottages, restaurants

(*Contd.*)

(*Contd.*)

Country/ Territory	*Hotels*	*Apartment Hotels*	*Motels*	*Inns*	*Others*
Togo	×		×	×	
Tunisia	×				
Turkey	×		×		Holiday villages
Ukraine	×		×		
Vietnam	×				
Yugoslavia	×	×	×	×	Pensions
Zambia	×		×	×	Lodges

Country/Territory	*All or specific types*	*Last date*	*Graphical symbol*
Algeria	all	1999	stars
Andorra			
Argentina			Stars
Armenia			
Azerbaijan			
Belgium–Flemish	All	1984	Stars
Benin			
Bolivia	All		Stars
Bosnia and Herzegovina			
Brazil	All	All	Stars
Burundi	Specific types	1978	Stars
Chile		1992	
China		1988	Stars
Costa Rica		26 February 1997	Stars
Croatia	All	10 May 2002	Stars
Cuba	All	2002	Stars
Cyprus	All	1969	Stars, letters
Czech Republic	All hotels	2002	Stars
Ecuador			
Ethiopia	Specific types		
France	All	14 February 1986	
Ghana	All	1979	Stars
Greece			
Guatemala			
Hungary	All	24 June 1998	Stars
Italy	All	1983	Stars
Ivory Coast			
Jordan	All hotels, apartment hotels & motels	Hotels 1 January 1994	Stars, ABC

(*Contd.*)

(*Contd.*)

Country/Territory	*All or specific types*	*Last date*	*Graphical symbol*
Kazakhstan			
Lebanon	All	2000	Stars
Macau			
Madagascar	All	19 April 2001	Stars
Madeira			
Malawi			
Malaysia	All	1995/2001	
Mali			
Malta			Stars; 'standard', 'comfort', 'superior' (self-catering)
Moldova	All	2002	Stars
Montenegro	All		Stars
Monaco	Hotels		Stars 1-4L
Mongolia	All hotels all tourist ger camps	1998 2000	Stars 1.2 grade
Morocco	All	25 November 1986	Stars
Netherlands	All	1999	Stars
Nigeria	All	1978	Stars
Pakistan	All	1977	
Paraguay			
Peru	All	13 July 2001	Stars
Philippines	All		None
Poland	All	13 June 2001	Stars
Portugal	All	1997	Stars
Puerto Rico	Specific, hotels		N/A
Sao Tome et Principe			
San Marino		18 March 1993	
Seychelles			
Slovak Republic	All	1 November 2001	Stars
Slovenia	All	23 May 1997	Stars
South Africa			
Spain			
Sri Lanka	Hotels		Stars
Tanzania			
Togo	All	1989	Stars
Turkey	All		Stars
Tunisia		2000	Stars
Ukraine			
Vietnam	All	27 April 2001	Stars
Yugoslavia	All		Stars
Zambia			

(*b*) Additional comments, if any:

Country/Territory	*Comments*
Jordan	Established at Central government level, Ministry of Tourism and Antiquities
Mongolia	Both standards expected to be revised by end 2002. The draft of motel, guest house standards is in process.
Spain	Classifications made bv Regional Governments
Tunisia	The system "Normes 2000" includes 3, a start system which is compulsory plus a Quality Label and Specialization, which are both voluntary.

2. *Basis for Central/Local Government Authority an Role in Establishing Classification*

1. State constitution
2. Tourism law
3. NTA competence
4. Agreement between government bodies concerned
5. Recommendation in a government-adopted tourism development plan

Country/ Territory	*Bodies involved*					*Others*
	1	*2*	*3*	*4*	*5*	
Algeria		×	×			
Andorra		×		×	×	Agreement between each group's representatives and Hotel Union of Andorra and Chamber of Commerce of Andorra representatives.
Argentina		×	×			
Armenia		×				
Azerbaijan			×	×		
Belgium–Flemish		×				
Benin			×			
Bolivia			×			
Bosnia and Herzegovina		×				
Brazil		×	×		×	
Burundi		×				
Chile		×				
China					×	
Costa Rica		×				
Croatia		×				
Cuba		×	×			
Cyprus		×	×			

(*Contd.*)

(*Contd.*)

Country/ Territory	*Bodies involved*					*Others*
	1	*2*	*3*	*4*	*5*	
Czech Republic		×			×	
Ecuador		×				
Ethiopia						
France		×				
Ghana		×			×	
Greece		×	×			
Guatemala		×				
Guinea Equatorial		×				
Hungary				×		
Indonesia	×	×	×	×	×	
Italy		×				
Ivory Coast		×	×			
Jordan		×	×			
Kazakhstan		×			×	
Kenya		×			×	
Lebanon		×	×		×	
Macau		×	×	×	×	
Madagascar		×				
Madeira	×	×	×	×	×	
Malawi		×			×	
Malaysia		×				
Mali		×	×		×	
Malta		×				
Moldova				×		
Mongolia		×	×		×	Government guideline
Montenegro		×			×	
Morocco		×				
Mozambique			×		×	
Netherlands						Treaty with Belgium and Luxemburg
Nigeria			×			
Pakistan		×				
Paraguay						
Peru	×	×	×	×		
Philippines		×				
Poland		×	×			
Portugal		×	×			
Puerto Rico		×			×	
Sao Tome et Principe	×	×	×			
San Marino		×	×		×	
Seychelles					×	
Slovak Republic			×			
Slovenia		×		×		Catering law
South Africa		×			×	
Spain		×				

(*Contd.*)

(*Contd.*)

Country/ Territory	*Bodies involved*					*Others*
	1	*2*	*3*	*4*	*5*	
Sri Lanka		×				
Tanzania		×			×	
Togo		×			×	
Turkey		×				
Ukraine		×		×	×	
Vietnam		×	×			
Yugoslavia		×			×	
Zambia	×	×	×			

3. *Rationale and Use of Government Classification*

Country/Territory	*Is classification justified by consumer concerns?*	*Does it seek compatibility with the existence of classification systems in other countries?*	*Is it used to control accommodation tariffs within established classes?*	*Is it used as the basis for applying different taxes (e.g., VAT)?*
Algeria	Yes	Yes	No	No
Andorra	Yes	Yes	No	No
Argentina	Yes	Yes	Yes	No
Armenia	Yes	Yes	No	No
Azerbaijan	Yes	Yes	Yes	Yes
Belgium – Flemish	Yes	No	No	No
Benin	No	Yes	Yes	No
Bolivia	Yes	Yes	No	No
Bosnia and Herzegovina	Yes	No	No	No
Brazil	Yes	Yes	No	No
Burundi	Yes	Yes		
Chile	Yes		No	No
China	Yes	Yes	No	No
Costa Rica	Yes	Yes	No	No
Croatia	No	Yes	No	No
Cuba	Yes	Yes	Yes	No
Cyprus	Yes	No	No	No
Czech Republic		Yes	No	No
Ecuador	No	Yes	No	Yes
Ethiopia	No	Yes	No	No
France	Yes	No	No	Yes
Ghana	Yes	Yes	No	No
Greece	Yes		Yes	
Guatemala		Yes	Yes	Yes
Hungary	Yes	Yes	No	No
Indonesia	Yes	Yes	No	No

(*Contd.*)

(*Contd.*)

Country/Territory	*Is classification justified by consumer concerns?*	*Does it seek compatibility with the existence of classification systems in other countries?*	*Is it used to control accommodation tariffs within established classes?*	*Is it used as the basis for applying different taxes (e.g., VAT)?*
Italy	Yes	Yes	?	?
Ivory Coast	yes	Yes		
Jordan	Yes	Yes	No	Yes
Kazakhstan	Yes	Yes	Yes	No
Kenya	Yes	Yes	No	No
Lebanon	Yes	Yes	Yes	Yes
Macau	Yes	Yes	No	No
Madagascar	Yes	Yes	No	Yes
Madeira	Yes	No	No	Yes
Malawi	Yes	Yes	Yes	No
Malaysia	Yes	Yes	No	No
Mali	Yes	Yes	Yes	No
Malta	Yes	Yes	Yes	
Moldova	Yes	Yes	No	No
Mongolia*	No	No	No	No
Montenegro	yes	Yes	No	Yes
Morocco	Yes	Yes	Yes	Yes
Mozambique	No	No	Yes	
Netherlands	Yes	Yes	No	No
Nigeria	Yes	Yes	Yes	Yes
Pakistan	Yes	Yes	Yes	No
Paraguay				
Peru	Yes	Yes	No	No
Philippines	No	Yes	No	No
Poland	Yes	Yes	No	No
Portugal	Yes	Yes	No	No
Puerto Rico	No	Yes	No	Yes
Sao Tome et Principe	Yes	Yes	Yes	Yes
San Marino	No	Yes	Yes	No
Seychelles	Yes	Yes	No	Yes
Slovak Republic	Yes	Yes	Yes	No
Slovenia	No	Yes	No	No
South Africa	Yes	Yes	No	No
Spain	Yes	Yes	No	No
Sri Lanka	Yes	Yes	No	No
Tanzania	No	Yes	Yes	No
Togo	Yes	Yes	Yes	No
Turkey	Yes	Yes	No	No
Ukraine	Yes	Yes	No	Yes
Vietnam	Yes	Yes	No	No
Yugoslavia	Yes	Yes	No	No
Zambia	Yes	Yes	No	No

(*Contd.*)

(*Contd.*)

Country/Territory	*Is classification justified by consumer concerns?*	*Does it seek compatibility with the existence of classification systems in other countries?*	*Is it used to control accommodation tariffs within established classes?*	*Is it used as the basis for applying different taxes (e.g., VAT)?*
Moldova	Yes	Yes	No	No
Mongolia*	No	No	No	No
Montenegro	yes	Yes	No	Yes
Morocco	Yes	Yes	Yes	Yes
Mozambique	No	No	Yes	
Netherlands	Yes	Yes	No	No
Nigeria	Yes	Yes	Yes	Yes
Pakistan	Yes	Yes	Yes	No
Paraguay				
Peru	Yes	Yes	No	No
Philippines	No	Yes	No	No
Poland	Yes	Yes	No	No
Portugal	Yes	Yes	No	No
Puerto Rico	No	Yes	No	Yes
Sao Tome et Principe	Yes	Yes	Yes	Yes
San Marino	No	Yes	Yes	No
Seychelles	Yes	Yes	No	Yes
Slovak Republic	Yes	Yes	Yes	No
Slovenia	No	Yes	No	No
South Africa	Yes	Yes	No	No
Spain	Yes	Yes	No	No
Sri Lanka	Yes	Yes	No	No
Tanzania	No	Yes	Yes	No
Togo	Yes	Yes	Yes	No
Turkey	Yes	Yes	No	No
Ukraine	Yes	Yes	No	Yes
Vietnam	Yes	Yes	No	No
Yugoslavia	Yes	Yes	No	No
Zambia	Yes	Yes	No	No

(*a*) Other rationale and use:

Mongolia: It is used to update hotel and ger camp service quality.

4. Classification Authority/Body Deciding Each Classification

Country/ Territory	*Hotels*	*Apartment hotels*	*Motels*	*Inns*	*Others*	*Classification authority*
Algeria	×	×	×	×	×	National Tourism Administration
Andorra	×	×		×		Tourism Department
Argentina	×	×	×	×		Local Government
Armenia	×	×	×		×	
Azerbaijan	×		×	×		Central Executive Body
Belgium–Flemish	×	×	×	×		Toerisme Vlaanderen
Benin	×	×	×	×		National Tourism Administration
Bolivia	×	×	×	×		National Tourism Administration, motels: local Government
Bosnia and Herzegovina						
Brazil	×					Embratur, National Consulting and Regional Committees
Burundi	×		×	×		Ministry of Environment and Tourism
Chile	×	×	×			National Tourism Service
China	×					National Technology and Supervision Administration
Costa Rica	×	×			×	Tourism Institute of Costa Rica
Croatia	×	×	×		×	Ministry of Tourism
Cuba	×	×	×		×	Ministry of Tourism
Cyprus	×	×	×		×	Hotels Committee and Board of Directors of Cyprus Tourism Organisation
Czech Republic	×		×	×		National Hotel and Restaurant Association
Ecuador						
Ethiopia	×	×	×		×	
France	×	×				Local prefecture
Ghana	×	×	×	×	×	National Tourism Administration
Greece	×	×	×		×	National Tourism Administration
Guatemala						
Hungary	×				×	National Tourism Administration

(*Contd.*)

(Contd.)

Country/ Territory	*Hotels*	*Apartment hotels*	*Motels*	*Inns*	*Others*	*Classification authority*
Italy	×	×	×	×		Provincial Government
Ivory Coast	×		×	×		Classifying Committee
Jordan	×	×	×	×	×	Ministry of Tourism, Jordan Hotel Association
Kazakhstan						
Kenya	×	×	×	×		Hotels and Restaurants Authority, Ministry of Tourism and Information
Lebanon	×	×	×	×	×	Ministry of Tourism
Macau	×	×				Macau Government Tourist Office
Madagascar	×		×		×	Ministry of Tourism
Madeira	×	×		×	×	Tourism Chamber, Regional Tourism Board, Regional Secretariat of Social Subjects, Civil Protection
Malawi	×		×	×	×	Government conjunction with the Tourism and Hotel Boards
Malaysia	×		×	×		Panel set up under the Ministry of Culture, Arts & Tourism, consisting of ministry officials and members from non-governmental organizations (hotel association, tour operator association and other relevant government agencies)
Mali	×	×	×	×		National Classification Committee
Malta	×	×			×	Malta Tourism Authority
Moldova	×	×	×		×	National Tourism Agency
Monaco	×					Ministre de l'Etat et Commission Hôelière
Mongolia	×				×	Hotel and ger camp classification committee
Montenegro	×	×	×			Ministry of Tourism
Morocco	×	×	×	×	×	National Tourism Administration
Netherlands	×	×	×	×	×	Bedrijfschap Horeca and Catering

(Contd.)

(Contd.)

Country/ Territory	*Hotels*	*Apartment hotels*	*Motels*	*Inns*	*Others*	*Classification authority*
Nigeria	×					National Tourism Administration
Pakistan	×	×	×	×	×	Department of Tourist Services
Paraguay						
Peru	×	×		×	×	National Tourism Board
Philippines	×	×	×		×	Department of Tourism
Poland	×		×		×	16 representatives of the government at regional level
Portugal	×		×	×	×	Central Administration, General Board of Tourism
Puerto Rico						
Sao Tome et Principe	×	×	×	×		National Tourism Office
San Marino	×	×	×			Committee of Hotel Classification
Seychelles	×					Ministry of Tourism and Transport
Slovak Republic	×		×		×	Ministry of Economy
Slovenia	×	×	×	×	×	Classification Council
South Africa	×		×	×		
Spain	×	×	×	×	×	Regional government authority
Sri Lanka	×					
Tanzania	×	×	×		×	National Hotel Board
Togo	×		×	×		National Committee of Licensing and Classification
Turkey	×		×			A commission consisting of two inspectors from NOT and a representative from NTA
Ukraine	×		×			State Standardization Entity Gosstandart, National Tourism Administration of Ukraine
Vietnam	×					Vietnam National Association of Tourism
Yugoslavia	×	×	×	×	×	Commission of Ministry of Trade, Tourism and Service
Zambia	×		×	×		Hotel Board of Zambia

5. Methods and Bodies Involved in Devising and Drafting Classification

Was the classification system in question prepared by:

1. An expert NTA/NOT official(s)
2. A team of NTA/NOT and other government officials
3. A private national consultant
4. A private international consultant
5. An expert designated/recommended by WTO/OMT
6. On the basis of another country's classification system
7. By revising the previous system
8. In consultation with National Hotel Association(s)
9. In consultation with Consumer's Association

Country/ Territory	*Bodies involves*									*Others*
	1	*2*	*3*	*4*	*5*	*6*	*7*	*8*	*9*	
Algeria	×	×					×	×		
Andorra				×		×		×		
Argentina	×	×				×				
Armenia	×									
Azerbaijan	×	×				×				
Belgium – Flemish	×	×	×			×	×	×		
Benin	×	×				×				
Bolivia	×	×		×		×	×	×		
Bosnia and Herzegovina		×					×			
Brazil	×						×	×		
Burundi	×					×				
Chile	×					×	×	×		
China	×	×				×	×			
Costa Rica	×			×		×	×	×		
Croatia				×						Ministry of Tourism prepared the regulation consulting national hotel association and foreign consultant
Cuba		×					×	×		
Cyprus		×		×			×	×		
Czech Republic	×		×				×	×		
Ecuador						×		×		
Ethiopia	×	×			×		×			
France	×	×					×	×	×	
Ghana	×				×		×			Classification is in line with Hotel Classification Standards for Africa

(*Contd.*)

(*Contd.*)

Country/ Territory	*Bodies involves*									*Others*
	1	*2*	*3*	*4*	*5*	*6*	*7*	*8*	*9*	
Greece		×					×	×		
Guatemala						×		×		
Hungary						×	×	×		
Indonesia	×	×	×			×	×	×	×	
Ivory Coast		×					×	×		
Jordan		×					×	×		
Kazakhstan						×	×			
Kenya	×	×				×	×	×	×	
Lebanon		×	×			×	×	×		
Macau	×	×				×	×			
Madagascar	×					×	×	×		
Madeira	×	×					×	×		
Malawi		×					×			Study tours were undertaken in Zimbabwe and Zambia system before amending the classification
Malaysia		×						×	×	
Mali	×	×					×	×	×	
Malta		×		×		×	×	×	×	
Moldova	×		×		×	×				
Mongolia	×	×	×	×		×*	×*	×		Ministry of Infrastructure; Mongolian Tourism Board; Ministry of Health and Welfare; Ministry of Nature; other government controlling authorities; Mongolian Tourism Association; Mongolian Hotel Association, Standards Authority
Montenegro	×	×		×		×*	×			*USA, Germany, UK, Switzerland, Spain, Crotia, Austria and international hotel companies; tour operator organizations
Morocco		×		×			×	×		
Mozambique		×				×	×	×		
Netherlands		×	×				×	×		
Nigeria	×	×					×	×		
Pakistan										Rules have been frames by the Federal Government of Pakistan
Paraguay										
Peru	×						×	×		
Philippines		×				×		×		
Poland		×	×			×	×	×	×	

(*Contd.*)

(*Contd.*)

Country/ Territory	*Bodies involves*									*Others*
	1	*2*	*3*	*4*	*5*	*6*	*7*	*8*	*9*	
Poland		×	×			×	×	×	×	
Portugal	×	×					×	×	×	Elaborated by the State Secretariat of Tourism in collaboration with the General Board of Tourism
Puerto Rico				×						
Sao Tome et Principe					×	×				
San Marino		×	×			×				
Seychelles		×				×		×		
Slovak Republic	×	×	×			×	×	×	×	
Slovenia	×	×		×		×	×	×		Chamber of Economy
South Africa	×						×	×	×	
Spain		×					×	×	×	
Sri Lanka		×					×	×		
Tanzania	×	×	×			×	×	×		
Togo		×				×	×	×		
Turkey		×				×	×	×		
Ukraine						×	×	×	×	
Vietnam	×					×	×			
Yugoslavia		×	×			×	×	×		
Zambia	×			×			×	×		

Notes: Mongolia 6* Based on Russian standard
7* Existing standards expected to be revised by end 2002

6. *Applicability of Classification*

Country/Territory	*Is it mandatory for all establishments?*	*Is it necessary to obtain license/ permission/ registration to operate?*	*Can establishments operate without being classified?*
Algeria	Yes	Yes	No
Andorra	Yes	Yes	
Argentina	Yes	Yes	No
Armenia			Yes
Azerbaijan	Yes	Yes	No
Belgium – Flemish	Yes	Yes	No
Benin	Yes	Yes	No
Bolivia	Yes	Yes	No
Bosnia and Herzegovina	Yes	Yes	No
Brazil	No	Yes	Yes
Burundi	No	Yes	Yes

(*Contd.*)

(Contd.)

Country/Territory	*Is it mandatory for all establishments?*	*Is it necessary to obtain license/ permission/ registration to operate?*	*Can establishments operate without being classified?*
Chile	No		Yes
China	No	No	Yes
Costa Rica	No	Yes	Yes
Croatia	Yes	Yes	No
Cuba	Yes	Yes	Yes
Cyprus	Yes	Yes	No
Czech Republic	Yes	No	No
Ecuador	Yes	Yes	No
Ethiopia	Yes	Yes	
France	No	Yes	Yes
Ghana	Yes	Yes	Yes
Greece	Yes	Yes	No
Guatemala	Yes	Yes	Yes
Hungary	Yes	Yes	No
Indonesia	Yes	Yes	No
Italy	Yes		No
Ivory Coast	yes	Yes	No
Jordan	Yes	Yes	No
Kazakhstan	No	No	Yes
Kenya	Yes	No	Yes
Lebanon	Yes	Yes	
Macau	Yes	Yes	No
Madagascar	Yes	Yes	Yes
Madeira	Yes	Yes	No
Malawi	No	Yes	Yes
Malaysia	Yes	Yes	
Mali	No	Yes	Yes
Malta	Yes	Yes	No
Moldova	Yes	Yes	No
Mongolia	Yes	Yes	Yes
Montenegro	yes	Yes	No
Morocco	No	Yes	Yes
Mozambique	Yes	Yes	No
Netherlands	Yes	No	Yes
Nigeria	No	Yes	Yes
Pakistan	Yes	Yes	Yes
Paraguay			
Peru	No	Yes	Yes
Philippines	No	Yes	Yes
Poland	No	No	Yes
Portugal	Yes	Yes	No
Puerto Rico	No	Yes	Yes
Sao Tome et Principe	Yes	Yes	No

(Contd.)

(*Contd.*)

Country/Territory	*Is it mandatory for all establishments?*	*Is it necessary to obtain license/ permission/ registration to operate?*	*Can establishments operate without being classified?*
San Marino	Yes	Yes	No
Seychelles	No	No	Yes
Slovak Republic	Yes	Yes	No
Slovenia	Yes	Yes	No
South Africa	No	Yes	Yes
Spain	Yes	Yes	No
Sri Lanka	No	Yes	Yes
Tanzania	Yes	Yes	No
Togo	Yes	Yes	No
Turkey	Yes	Yes	Yes
Ukraine	No	No	Yes
Vietnam	Yes	Yes	No
Yugoslavia	Yes	Yes	Yes
Zambia	Yes	Yes	Yes

7. *Verification of Compliance with Classification System*

(*a*) Is verification performed by:

Country/ Territory	*Central government inspectors*	*Local government inspectors*	*Hotel industry (second party) inspectors*	*Independent (third party) inspectors*	*Other parties*
Algeria	×	×			
Andorra	×		×	×	
Argentina		×			
Armenia		×			
Azerbaijan	×	×			
Belgium – Flemish	×				
Benin	×				
Bolivia	×				
Bosnia and Herzegovina	×				
Brazil	×	×	×	×	
Burundi	×				
Chile					
China	×	×	×	×	
Costa Rica	×				
Croatia	×				
Cuba	×		×	×	

(*Contd.*)

(Contd.)

Country/ Territory	*Central government inspectors*	*Local government inspectors*	*Hotel industry (second party) inspectors*	*Independent (third party) inspectors*	*Other parties*
Cyprus					Cyprus Tourism Organization
Czech Republic	×		×		
Ecuador	×		×		
Ethiopia	×				
France		×			
Ghana	×				
Greece	×	×			
Guatemala	×				
Hungary	×	×			
Indonesia	×	×	×	×	
Italy		×			
Ivory Coast	×				
Jordan	×	×	×		
Kenya	×		×	×	Hotel and Restaurant Association Board
Lebanon	×				
Macau		×			
Madagascar	×	×	×		
Madeira		×			
Malawi	×				A grading/classification committee, appointed by the Board will be responsible
Malaysia	×	×	×	×	
Mali	×				
Malta	×				
Moldova	×	×			
Mongolia	×	×			
Montenegro	×	×			
Morocco	×	×	×		
Mozambique	×	×			
Netherlands			×	×	
Nigeria	×	×			
Pakistan	×				
Paraguay					
Peru	×	×			
Philippines	×				

(Contd.)

(Contd.)

Country/ Territory	*Central government inspectors*	*Local government inspectors*	*Hotel industry (second party) inspectors*	*Independent (third party) inspectors*	*Other parties*
Poland	×			×	
Portugal	×	×			
Puerto Rico	×				Many hotel chains have their own inspection personnel
Sao Tome et Principe					
San Marino	×				
Seychelles		×			
Slovak Republic		×			
Slovenia	×	×			
South Africa			×		
Spain		×			
Sri Lanka	×				
Tanzania	×				
Togo	×				
Turkey	×		×		
Ukraine	×		×		
Vietnam	×	×			
Yugoslavia	×				
Zambia	×		×		

(*b*) Mode of verification:

Country/Territory	*Announced visits at fixed date*	*Mystery checks*	*Other methods*
Algeria	×		
Andorra		×	
Argentina			Local government's decision
Armenia	×		
Azerbaijan	×		
Belgium–Flemish	×	×	
Benin	×		
Bolivia			Unannounced visits by identified inspectors
Bosnia and Herzegovina		×	
Brazil	×		
Burundi		×	

(Contd.)

(*Contd.*)

Country/Territory	*Announced visits at fixed date*	*Mystery checks*	*Other methods*
Chile	×		
China	×		
Costa Rica			Unannounced visits by identified inspectors
Croatia	×		
Cuba	×		Unannounced visits
Cyprus			Announced and unannounced visits by inspectors at regular time intervals
Czech Republic		×	Accommodation establishments must fill in the classification questionnaire
Ecuador			Unannounced visits by identified inspectors
Ethiopia	×	×	
France	×	×	
Ghana	×	×	
Greece		×	
Guatemala		×	
Indonesia	×	×	
Italy	×		
Ivory Coast	×	×	
Jordan			
Kenya		×	
Lebanon		×	Unannounced visits
Macau		×	
Madagascar		×	
Madeira	×	×	
Malawi	×		A questionnaire will be distributed to operators and after being completed, it will be sent to the grading committee for verification and inspectors will inspect the establishment
Malaysia			Based on public complaints, public requests and requests from hotels
Mali	×		
Malta			Unannounced visits by identified inspectors
Moldova		×	
Mongolia	×		Between June and August
Montenegro	×		
Morocco	×		
Mozambique	×		
Netherlands	×	×	
Nigeria		×	
Pakistan	×		

(*Contd.*)

(*Contd.*)

Country/Territory	*Announced visits at fixed date*	*Mystery checks*	*Other methods*
Paraguay			
Peru			Unannounced visits by identified inspectors
Philippines		×	
Poland	×		
Portugal	×	×	
Puerto Rico	×	×	Comment cards
Sao Tome et Principe			
San Marino	×		
Seychelles	×	×	
Slovak Republic		×	
Slovenia		×	Proposed self-estimation level is verified by classification commission with pre-announced visits before establishments acquire fixed classification symbol
South Africa	×		
Spain		×	
Sri Lanka	×	×	
Tanzania			
Togo		×	
Turkey	×		
Ukraine	×		
Vietnam	×		
Yugoslavia	×		
Zambia		×	

(*c-d*) Cost of verification borne by:

Country/Territory	*The verifying authority*	*The hotel company concerned*	*Periodicity of verification*
Algeria	×		Depends on NTA's decision
Andorra	×		Every year
Argentina	×		Every year
Armenia			Every two years
Azerbaijan			Every year
Belgium–Flemish	×		Every three years
Benin			
Bolivia	×		Every year or when necessary
Bosnia and Herzegovina		×	Every three years
Brazil		×	Every year

(*Contd.*)

(Contd.)

Country/Territory	*The verifying authority*	*The hotel company concerned*	*Periodicity of verification*
Burundi			Every year
Chile	×		Not established, only in case of changes detected
China			Every year
Costa Rica	×		Every year
Croatia		×	Every two years
Cuba	×		Every three years
Cyprus	×		Every two years, routine inspections every two months
Czech Republic		×	Every two years
Ecuador			Every year
Ethiopia	×		Every year
France			Occasionally
Ghana	×	×	Every year
Greece	×		Every year
Guatemala	×		Every month
Indonesia	×	×	Every three years
Italy	×		When characteristics change
Ivory Coast	×		Every year
Jordan	×		Irregularly, at least once a year
Kenya	×		Every two years
Lebanon	×		Not a particular date
Macau			Once or twice a year
Madagascar	×	×	
Madeira	×	×	When necessary
Malawi	×		Every two years
Malaysia	×		Every three years
Mali	×		Every year
Malta	×		When necessary
Moldova	×		Every year
Mongolia			Depends on hotel company request
Montenegro		×	Every three years
Morocco	×		Every two years
Mozambique		×	
Netherlands	×		Every two years
Nigeria	×		Every three years
Pakistan	×		Every year

(Contd.)

(*Contd.*)

Country/Territory	*The verifying authority*	*The hotel company concerned*	*Periodicity of verification*
Paraguay			
Peru	×		Every year
Philippines	×		Every year
Poland		×	Every two year
Portugal	×	×	Every year
Puerto Rico	×	×	Twice a year
Sao Tome et Principe			
San Marino	×		Every five years
Seychelles	×	×	Every year
Slovak Republic	×		Every year
Slovenia		×	Every three year
South Africa		×	Every year
Spain	×		
Sri Lanka			Every year
Tanzania	×	×	Every two years
Togo	×		Every year
Turkey	×		When necessary
Ukraine		×	Every year
Vietnam	×	×	Every two years
Yugoslavia		×	Every five years
Zambia	×		Every year

8. Plans to Introduce New Classification or Revise Current Classification

Country/ Territory	*Comments*
Algeria	Classification is at central administration level and local level.
Andorra	
Argentina	The National Tourism and Sport Secretariat has set up a co-operation agreement to develop the 'Tourism Quality System' with representative private-sector entities. Its objectives include stimulating national legislation for tourism establishments and facilitating national and/or international technical assistance from countries which implemented similar systems in terms of categorization criteria and quality systems.
Azerbaijan	A new classification preparation is underway and few changes are being introduced in the existing normative legislative base
Benin	Project in process
Bolivia	There is a compulsory development of the 'National Recategorisation Programme' every five years, obliged by the tourism establishment's regulation.
Brazil	The revision and actualization of classification criteria is defined by National Technical Consultancy

(*Contd.*)

(*Contd.*)

Country/ Territory	*Comments*
Burundi	Current classification is under revision
Chile	The presentation of a study is in process, which helps to elaborate the technical basis and standards for a new classification system, according to the actual market expectations.
China	It is being revised.
Costa Rica	Classification is used to define the level of quality and competition within regional markets. They are interested in reforming the actual hotel classification system, implementing ISO 9001-2000 norms for detailed grading of guest-related service's quality as well as quality documentation developed by the enterprise.
Cuba	The Cuban Norm, which includes classification requirements was revised in 2001. Revisions are planned every five years or when necessary.
Cyprus	Under consideration. Municipality taxes are levied according to classification.
Czech Republic	In the end of 2002
Ecuador	Technical regulation has been elaborated under the assistance of a national consultant and taking other countries' (e.g. Spain, USA, etc.) classfication and categorization system as a reference. This regulation is adequate to the actual situation in Ecuador.
Ethiopia	Government level of classification is much preferred to promote quality service in the tourist facilities industry. Although, classification is a new phenomena, intensive explanation of the use of classification and related ideas must be detailed. There is a plan to revise current classification on the basis of WTO criteria (standards for Africa) introducing new names like 'five star delux' in the classification system.
Ghana	Classification is in the line with 'Hotel Classification Standards for Africa. Revise current criteria.
Greece	Introduction of new classification on the basis of star system.
Guatemala	There is a need for a non-governmental support of classification procedure to make it competitive at international level.
Jordan	A new revision of the current classification will be introduced within the next 5 years.
Kenya	East African Regional Classification Document is being prepared as an improvement of the current Kenyan criteria.
Lebanon	The new classification system is very recent and in process of application.
Malawi	Has already drafted or amended classification system to conform international standards.
Malta	New classification system was introduced recently.
Moldova	The classification in question is a new one and will be implemented till the end of 2002.

(*Contd.*)

(*Contd.*)

Country/ Territory	*Comments*
Mongolia	Revise current classification.
Montenegro	Establishment of new classification in harmony with international procedures is in progress.
Peru	
Philippines	Department of Tourism is planning to adopt the star classification for hotels.
Poland	Is revising its provisions connected with hotel facilities classification.
Puerto Rico	Next year a new classification system will be introduced with new standards of classification and evaluation for all properties.
Sao Tome et Principe	
San Marino	Revise in project.
Slovenia	Ongoing project of renewing classification system for all types of establishments.
Ukraine	A new classification preparation is underway and few changes are being introduced in the existing normative legislative base.

III. Comparative Analysis

Sources of Information

WTO surveyed the public sector, specifically the role of governments in hotel classification in the various countries. The survey has been completed by National Tourism Administrations (NTAs) in collaboration with their national hotel association(s).

IH&RA surveyed the private sector specifically to prepare:

- a status report (*i.e.*, inventory) of existing hotel classification schemes.
- A comparative analysis of these schemes (price, qualitative and quantitative elements).

The survey was completed by National Hotel and Restaurant Associations.

The findings of the two reports were collected from a total of:

32 countries, surveyed by the private sector
89 countries, surveyed by the public sector
13 countries replied to both IH&RA and WTO questionnaire

Official Classification Systems in the Various Countries Covering Hotels, Apartment Hotels, Motels and Inns

Number of countries having an official hotel classification system in their country

Public Sector: .... 70 countries
Private Sector: .... 26 countries
Total (by crossing) .... 83 countries

Number of countries having a classification system applying to Apartment hotels

Public Sector: .... 43 countries
Private Sector: .... 17 countries
Total (by crossing) .... 51 countries

Number of countries having a classification system applying to Motels

Public Sector: .... 49 countries
Private Sector: .... 19 countries
Total (by crossing) .... 56 countries

Number of countries having a classification system applying to Inns

Public Sector: .... 38 countries
Private Sector: .... 15 countries
Total (by crossing) .... 46 countries

Number of countries having a official classification system for all four categories

Public Sector: .... 16 countries
Private Sector: .... 13 countries
Total (by crossing) .... 24 countries

Number of countries having an official classification system for three categories

Public Sector: .... 25 countries
Private Sector: .... 4 countries
Total (by crossing) .... 25 countries

Number of countries having an official classification system for two categories

Public Sector: .... 8 countries
Private Sector: .... 2 countries
Total (by crossing).. 9 countries

Number of countries having an official classification system for one categories

Public Sector: .... 6 countries
Private Sector: .... 6 countries
Total (by crossing).. 11 countries

N.B. In this case the category is always hotels

Note: Where a classification system exists the graphical symbol most widely used is the star. Systems are mostly set up by the government, a region or the Tourism Board of the country and the establishments are only consulted. Afterwards they are adopted into the Tourism Law, the State Constitution or regional constitutions.

20 countries state that there is a relation between Classification and Room Rates

13 countries state that there is a relation between Classification and Taxation

According to the private sector a majority of countries report no link between classification and the social obligations of the employers

Which bodies are involved in devising and drafting classification or by whom have the classification system in question been prepared

An expert NTA/NOT official(s)

Public Sector: .... 33 countries
Private Sector: .... 5 countries
Total (by crossing).. 36 countries

A team of NTA/NOT and other government officials

Public Sector: .... 43 countries
Private Sector: .... 14 countries
Total (by crossing).. 49 countries

A private national consultant

Public Sector: .... 12 countries
Private Sector: .... 6 countries

Total (by crossing) .... 14 countries

A private international consultant

Public Sector: .... 12 countries

Private Sector: .... 7 countries

Total (by crossing) .... 16 countries

An expert designated/recommended by WTO/OMT

Public Sector: .... 4 countries

Private Sector: .... 5 countries

Total (by crossing) .... 7 countries

On the basis of another country's classification system

Public Sector: .... 36 countries

Private Sector: .... 8 countries

Total (by crossing) .... 41 countries

By revising the previous system

Public Sector: .... 48 countries

Private Sector: .... 5 countries

Total (by crossing) .... 49 countries

In consultation with National Hotel Association(s)

Public Sector: .... 47 countries

Private Sector: .... 4 countries

Total (by crossing) .... 48 countries

In consultation with Consumer Association

Public Sector: .... 13 countries

Private Sector: .... 9 countries

Total (by crossing) .... 17 countries

Applicability of Classification in the Countries

In 46 countries it is mandatory for all establishments to have a classification to operate.

In 55 countries it is necessary to obtain a license/permission/registration to operate.

In 32 countries establishments can operate without being classified.

N.B. According to the private sector only two countries oblige establishments to become members of a national association to obtain a license to operate.

Methods of Verification

In general verification of establishments is undertaken between every one to five years and in some countries more irregularly.

Plans to Revise Existing System or Introduce New One

Cf question 15 (private sector) and question 8 (public sector)

Questions appearing only in the private sector questionnaire

Q. 11. *Who finances the system?*

11 countries: individual establishments

3 countries: national hotel associations

9 countries: government

1 country: shared between national association and government

Q. 12. *What are the main criteria?*

As this was an open question, replies vary considerably listing a range of objective (quantitative) and subjective (qualitative) criteria.

Q. 14. *Satisfaction with existing system.*

Of the respondents who replied to this question:

16 countries are satisfied with the existing system in their country

4 countries are not satisfied with the existing system in their country

5 countries would like improvements to the existing system

Current Trends in Hotel Classification

New Information Technologies

Electronic distribution in the form of Central Reservation Systems (CRS) was initially developed in the 1960's by the major airlines as a way of managing their inventory and controlling the rising number of flights and fares. Originally only used by airline reservation staff, in the1970's CRS were gradually made available to travel agents to facilitate the reservation process and give access to inventory data. As the systems developed, user demand and high capital costs prompted the owners of these systems to expand their product offering from solely airline seat to include hotel accommodation, car hire, cruises and almost every other travel product. This gave rise to today's one-stop-travel-shops, *i.e.*, the Global Distributions Systems (GDS). Four main companies dominate the sector – Amadeus, Galileo, Worldspan and Sabre – with a number of smaller GDSs active regionally. Most GDSs subsequently developed their own CRS with data structures more closely adapted to their particular product (*e.g.*, hotels), linking them electronically to the GDS to gain access to the powerful travel agent market and paying a transaction fee to the GDS owners fòr each booking processed. The limited space available on the display screens in CRSs and GDSs strongly influenced the choice of criteria and abbreviations in which a hotel could be described for selling purposes. From the perspective of the travel agent, these systems using a text-based interface are far from ideal as hotel sales and marketing tools, as they can provide only very sparse information.

Since the emergence in 1994 of the Web as an additional and competing electronic distribution channel there has been a rising number of consumer-oriented websites offering a much wider range of information, as well as booking facilities, some of them effectively bypassing both the travel agent and the GDS to create a direct link to the consumer. Once again, the question of categorizing hotels for the benefit of consumers or travel professionals (specifically the travel agent) has come to the fore.

This prompted one of the major third-party marketing and reservation providers, Utell, a Pegasus Solutions Company, to introduce its own hotel classification system.

> Phoenix (June 4, 2001) – Utell today introduced Utell selections, an innovative approach that categorizes its portfolio of 6,400 hotels to assist travel agents in finding the perfect hotel for clients. Utell selections classifies Utell properties into well-defined categories, and is based where possible on the American global industry publication Official Hotel Guide (OHG).
>
> Utell selections provides global consistency in segmenting hotels, since some ranking systems, such as the "star system," vary from country to country. *Utell selections enables* hotels to match customers' expectations with the experience, and uses a universally accepted travel publication, OHG, as the foundation for classification.
>
> Utell selections segments hotels into three core categories and four niche categories. All hotels are classified in one of the

core categories: luxury, superior and value. Hotels can be further identified as one of four niche categories – style, resort, apartment or airport, dependent upon the defined category criteria.

The three core categories are defined as:

- **Luxury** selection. Properties in leisure and business locations that provide the ultimate hotel experience for guests who demand the highest standards. Corresponds to the OHG system as Superior Deluxe, Deluxe, and Moderate Deluxe.
- **Superior** selection. Hotels and resorts that offer excellent quality rooms and facilities for both business and leisure. Classified by OHG as Superior First Class, First Class, and Limited Service First Class.
- **Value** selection. Hotels that create a comfortable atmosphere providing excellent value for money. Includes the OHG Moderate First Class, Superior Tourist Class, Tourist Class and Moderate Tourist Class.

The four niche categories are defined as:

- **Style** selection. Boutique and historic hotels each with distinctive decor and design characteristics.
- **Resort** selection. Includes properties that have recreational activities in the hotel or adjacent to the hotel.
- **Apartment** selection. Caters to travelers who need extended stays and amenities that include a kitchenette.
- **Airport** selection. Must be within seven miles of an airport and many offer transportation to and from the airport.

Based on extensive research carried out over nine months with travel agents and hotels, Utell realized the need to better segment its growing number of independent and chain hotels into a consistent classification system. Hotels wanted to be promoted in easy-to-understand groups in a manner similar to how their customers view them, instinctively. "The 'star system,' for instance, is not consistent around the world – a five-star hotel in Spain and a five-star hotel in Indonesia are not comparable, leading to inconsistency in service levels and expectations," said Michael Prager, Operations Managing Director, Utell.

The Utell selections classification system will be introduced on June 4, 2001, and is profiled on all of Utell's distribution channels, including international voice representation, Utell's proprietary Web site http://www.utell.com/ and the four major global distribution systems (GDSs). Utell's voice reservation agents who handle calls from over 40 countries have also been trained to describe hotels and help customers identify the hotel that best meets their needs based on *Utell selections*.

It is obvious from this example that the prime motivation is to simplify the travel agent's task in matching supply and demand in order to "help increase reservations and revenue." This classification system is based on an American trade publication which itself does not refer to the star system, which is only one of the various systems in use in the USA where neither the American Hotel and Lodging Association (AH&LA) nor the federal government is involved in hotel classification. This is generally left to automobile or petrochemical-related interests.

Hotel Industry – The Role of Branding

The major international hotel chains focus far more on defining and positioning their brands than on hotel classification per se (*e.g.*, star or other ratings) as granted by national hotel associations or other bodies. According to the country, properties managed by these chains will be classified according to the local or national scheme operating in the country in which the properties are located if this is mandatory or considered beneficial.

However, rather than focusing exclusively on the quantitative and qualitative criteria displayed by individual properties, for brands, the customer is the key focus. Brands are generally defined in terms of price tier (*e.g.*, Luxury, Upper scale, Mid-market, **Economy/Budget) with specific target customers in view – individual business travellers, individual leisure travellers,** Meetings, Incentive, Conference and Event (MICE) travel, group leisure travel etc. Branding also takes into account the location and the type of market in which the property is located – urban, suburban, airport, leisure destinations, gateway cities and major metropolitan areas.

An interesting example of this is given by Marriott International's brand reference chart. Each brand is defined in terms of price position, types of markets, brand essence, brand positioning, target customers and customer value proposition (also listing hotel benefits and features). Marriott Hotels, for instance are targeted principally at Upper-Upscale Frequent Business Travellers. A detailed customer profile is then used as the basis for defining and positioning the brand in relation to the company's other brands, and in relation to competition. The following gives some (but not all) of the features listed – and illustrates how customer-centric this approach is. (Note that Hotel benefits and Features, i.e. qualitative and quantitative criteria, are used specifically to support the Customer Value Proposition.)

Marriott International – Marriott Hotels Brand
Upper-Upscale Frequent Business Travellers

Target Customer

- "Grounded Achievers": travellers focused on productivity and accomplishment, looking for predictable/consistent hotel experiences and genuine caring service

Price Tier

- Quality

Brand Positioning

- "For grounded achievers who value dependable familiarity"

Brand Essence

- "Confidence for people going places"

Customer Value Proposition

- "Helps you achieve your business objectives"
- "Helps you Relax and recharge for the next day" etc

Hotel Benefits and Features

- Well-lit desks with large workspace, task lighting, ergonomic seating and easy access to electrical and data ports
- One in-hotel contact for all needs
- Express check-out
- Complimentary in-room coffee/tea

Focusing on the customer's lifestyle and needs, the idea is to enhance the customer's overall experience and gratify his sense of identity.

Travel Industry – Tour Operators

The hotel classification systems devised and run by national hotel associations and/or government authorities are not necessarily used by travel professionals, particularly when they are dealing with clients from outside the market where the accommodation is provided. It is well known that the major Tour Operators assess prospective hotels according to their own criteria and then provide their own description in their promotional material.

Reproduced below are very general descriptions given by some of the major tour operators in the UK as to what their classifications mean. In this case, *First Choice* is the most specific.

First Choice

- Basic, comfortable, budget ranged
- Standard popular accommodation. These hotels normally feature a selection of public areas including a restaurant
- Large, modern or well-established accommodation with a wide range of facilities
- High standards of comfort and service

The company points out that "Accommodation of similar ratings, but in different countries, cannot always be meaningfully compared."

Thomson Holidays

> Thomson T ratings are based on our annual appraisals and customers' views taken from the end-of-season Customer Satisfaction Questionnaires. Hotels and apartment? are rated from "2T" for no-frills, good value accommodation to "5T" for more comfort and a wider range of facilities. To a very few of our best hotels, we award a Blue Ribbon classification. These are internationally renowned luxury hotels which offer an exceptional standard of comfort. There may be some differences between accommodation that shares the same T rating category. This is where our T-plus rating can be a useful extra guide.

Airtours

The "A" ratings are awarded by specially trained Airtours staff, based on such criteria as the public area furnishings, food and drink outlets, room and leisure facilities and service. They range from AA for simple accommodation to AAAAA offering the highest quality and level of service.

Thomas Cook

The universal ratings system is based on the views (at the time of publication) of senior managers both in the UK and overseas.

As can be seen, none of these are particularly objective, but this information at least provides some insight into how the tour operators go about rating accommodation.

Travel Industry – Hotel Guides

The Official Hotel Guide (OHG)–USA: This Guide is widely recognized by travel agents as a comprehensive and reliable source of information on hotels around the world.

The Official Hotel Guide (OHG) provides comprehensive, in depth profiles of 29,000 hotels and resorts worldwide. For over 38 years, travel professionals have relied on its unique classification system and unbiased profiles to help them successfully match their clients to the right hotel. Its rich content has made it the hotel directory that travel professionals pay hundreds of dollars to subscribe to year after year.

NorthStar, parent company of OHG, has now incorporated OHG into its Hotel and Travel Index which it claims is the industry's leading print and online hotel information source for travel professionals with 79,000 hotels online.

Views of Main Stakeholders

(a) National Tourism Administrations (NTAs) and the World Tourism Organization (WTO)

Since 1988 WTO ceased to be engaged in harmonizing hotel classification standards region-wise and worldwide, partly due to the lack of coordinated and clear approach in favour of hotel classification by its Government Members and partly in response to the negative view on government intervention in this area by its Affiliate (private sector) Members representing the hotel industry. On an individual basis, however, both governments and private consultants have never ceased to approach the Organization and its Secretariat to ask for "WTO hotel classification", fielding sectoral support missions and technical cooperation to establish classification in respective countries and regions (at the time of preparing this report, a WTO-sponsored mission is taking place in Maldives), or at least for recommending WTO-trusted experts to do this job. The Secretariat has also taken note of such projects taking place without WTO having been consulted as an intermediary. As a result, WTO has never "freed itself" from hotel classification and over the years has sent dozens of missions and consultants to interested countries and regions to do hotel and related classification, but without defining common "WTO standards" for such missions and consultants.

It has been seen through this experience that, certainly, States are sovereign and that it is legitimate for their governments represented by NTAs to seek classification and that they need international referents and support in this effort. Their objectives appear to be similar to those sought by the private sector, first of all to ensure fair competition in the hotel industry, also to provide for "transparency at first sight" for the consumer. Trade related aspects of classification have also become important for the national hotel industry, especially in developing countries where private and government investors have made important investments and great sacrifices to upgrade their hotel facilities and now expect to be fairly remunerated for this effort while observing that differences in their favour with the attributes of the same category establishments in the tourism sending countries appear to be widening. Reference to unequivocal internationally-recognized standards can therefore help them defend their economic interests when it comes to negotiating contracts with wholesale tour operators.

From the WTO perspective, the lack of common understanding of hotel classification standards has also led to confusing quality aspects of the supply of hotel services (largely responding to the general question of HOW they are supplied) with physical and quantitative aspects of hotel establishments (required to respond to the question of WHAT) which normally intervene in classifications, while both aspects are important for competition. This converging approach can be seen, for example, in CEN

(European Committee for Standardization) standard EN ISO 18513-2000 followed by ISO, while WTO experience, also expressed in the WTO definition of quality in tourism as well as national experience, such as Spanish ICTE, shows that attribution of a hotel establishment to a given category level does not imply an automatic attainment of quality criteria, although the higher the category, the higher the quality potential of the establishment.

These considerations suggest that an international agreement on the meaning and guidance on hotel classification could satisfy the various demands and constitute a service to Governments, the private sector, consumers and the international community at large.

(b) Hotel Industry–National Hotel Association Involvement in Classification

Within the hotel industry, views can diverge diametrically on the need (or not) for a national classification scheme. Two classic examples are provided by the national hotel associations of Israel and Denmark, the former having abandoned classification, while the latter has adopted it after operating without classification for a number of years.

The Hotel Industry in Israel -12 years without Classification or Grading

(Information provided by Abraham Rosental, Director-General, Israel Hotel Association-IHA)

In April 1992, the system of grading hotels according to stars was cancelled and no other official system has taken its place.

Today, twelve years later, IHA can evaluate if the decision to cancel the grading system proved itself correct or not, if the "great damage to tourism to Israel", which many in the tourism industry predicted, came true, or if perhaps the goals of cancellation were realized.

In order to determine what happened since then, it is necessary to take into consideration the situation of hotels before the government cancelled the regulations for grading hotels, the situation today and expectations for the future.

Background

(i) *Government involvement*: The rationale behind the government grading system was to give official information on the standard of hotels in the country and to control the criteria for grading according to the star system. But in reality, from the 300 or so hotels in Israel, some 60 of them did not have star grading at all. They were published under the classification as "not yet graded", "not recommended", holiday villages, camping grounds, apartment hotels, and so on. The official information concerning their level did not exist at all.

The rest of the hotels were grouped into 6 grades mainly in the 3-4 and 5 star categories. Therefore, most if the hotels were concentrated in total; into three standards of grading. For instance, there were about 80 hotels in the 4 star category and it was obvious to all that there were great differences among them and it was not possible to ascertain much about a specific hotel in a similar large group.

The grading of part of the hotels did not reflect the reality. There were hotels which, having received their high grade, lowered their standards during the years and it was difficult, if not downright impossible to change their grade. Additional difficulties in grading were discovered also in comparisons between city hotels and holiday hotels, new hotels and old hotels, small and large hotels and between regular hotels and apartment hotels and suite hotels.

The grading of a hotel created certain expectations from the client. A great part of the complaints received about hotels were in the style of "this is not the service of a hotel graded X stars.... Who gave the hotel the stars..." etc....

(*ii*) *Travel agent reaction*: The situation was worsened by travel agents who published tour packages to Israel in the old and known manner of "overnight in a 4 star hotel in Jerusalem...". These travel agents did not promise a specific hotel, or certain level of services – they only promised to give the client a hotel of a certain grade and nothing more.

(*iii*) *Hotel reaction*: When there are many hotels with the same grade, it is clear that there is a very good 4 star hotel whose rates are expensive and there is a bad 4 star hotel whose rates are cheap. In fact, there have been many cases in which travel agents ordered the cheaper hotels for their clients ... however, they stood by their promise to supply a 4 star hotel, but the once who suffered where the clients themselves who thought that this was the level of hotels in Israel.

A situation was created whereby hotels used to sell their grading and not their diverse and various services. The grade influenced the rates and it was acceptable, of course, that a higher graded hotel would receive a higher rate. As a result of this, there was a fear that lower graded hotels would not make any special effort – because in any case they would not get anything for their efforts, while hotels of higher grades also will not try improve themselves since their grades are solid and go on forever.

Healthy Competition

With the cancellation of the grading, the new name of the game is competition. Each hotel must establish itself from the aspect of the product, the service, publicity and marketing.

The Name of the Game is the Name

That is to say, that which determines now is the name of the hotel – what does it supply, what services does it give and what is its real level. In short, does it have a good name or a bad name in the market?

Indeed, with the cancellation of grading, we have witnessed a wave of renovations by hotels. Hotels began to publicize themselves more and in particular to publicize their services and their amenities which they offer their clients.

They started to be concerned about their good name and understood that this would bring clients. This healthy competition became a regular method of operation.

Moreover, wholesalers abroad began to sell hotels and not grades. Israeli agents "were forced" to become better acquainted with hotels in the country and to know what they were selling – no longer to be satisfied with knowledge of the grade of the hotel alone.

Hotels entered into intensive competition, the power of the market did its work and stabilized the hotels in the country according to actual levels.

Hotels aspire to improve themselves diligently in order to put themselves in better standing in the hotel market.

The Hotel Industry is no longer frozen and conservative.

Other Forms of Classification

In addition, readers must remember that there exists a worldwide hotel guide called OHG, which is kept by most travel agents in the world. This voluminous guide grades hotels in the world and is considered the most trustworthy among travel agents.

The large tourism wholesalers in the world (TUI, Thompson, Neckerman, etc.) grade the hotels that they sell by themselves. A potential client in Germany who takes a "TUI: prospect in his hands, for instance, knows with certainty which level hotel he can expect.

We are in the era of the internet and the huge store of information available to the user. For most hotels in Israel, there are today, independent sites with a lot of information, pictures and details describing the hotels' services and amenities.

There are more than 42,000 hotel rooms in Israel, 26,000 of them about 60 per cent belong to internationally known chains. IHA are sure that a potential tourist well appreciates the difference between a "Crowne Plaza" hotel room and a "Days Inn" hotel room and he doesn't need the grading information.

Hotel Classification in Denmark

(Information provided by HORESTA Denmark, the Danish Hotel Association)

1. Background

Prior to 1997, there was no hotel classification system in Denmark. The Danish Tourist Board had produced an official accommodation guide for the country but it had not rated the hotels listed in it. The guide included only basic information. Reading through this information, the consumer had sufficient information to guide his/her choice of hotel. There was no monitoring or assessment of facilities listed in the guide.

2. Hotel Industry Reaction

The hotel industry in Denmark was historically opposed to the introduction of an official scheme. The Danish Hotel Association – HORESTA Denmark – had a definite policy opposing "official, compulsory classification systems." The Association felt that such systems left the way open to government intervention and gave government the opportunity to impose tariff levels and to control pricing.

The industry was aware that users such as tour operators and consumers expressed a need for classification systems. However, such systems were dependent on the criteria requirements behind the grades and on the types of control and monitoring involved.

3. Travel Industry Reaction

As there was no classification system in Denmark, tour operators in general had their "own" system. All the grading was done by the individual operators themselves.

4. Danish Tourist Board Reaction

Originally, the Danish Tourist Board did not plan to introduce a classification system because:

- Such a system was not considered necessary.
- The Board could not afford to implement a system.
- The Danish Hotel Association was opposed to official classification system and would fiercely oppose any attempt to introduce such a scheme in the country.
- The travel industry was at that time implementing its own schemes which it felt were ore reliable and trustworthy.

The country's accommodation sector had very high standards in both facilities and service and it was common opinion that there was no need to introduce a classification system at that time.

5. Current Situation

HORESTA introduced the new Hotel Classification System in Denmark on 14 May 1996 and approved the classification of member hotels by the star scheme. This scheme is reserved for HORESTA members. All Danish hotels associated with

HORESTA which have at least 8 rooms are classified on a scale ranging from 0-5 stars. The classification scheme is based upon objective criteria, *i.e.*, the presence or absence or a wide range of facilities and service. The number of stars is therefore not indicative of subjective features such as atmosphere, quality of food and service, location or view.

The Danish Tourist Board welcomed this new classification scheme, firstly, because such a scheme had long been called for by both customers and tour operators; secondly, because experience from abroad showed that a star classification scheme was a tool for improving hotel standards. This was a quality improvement that was crucial if Danish hotels were to hold their own in the increasingly competitive international tourist market.

6. Why a Star-rating?

Everywhere in the world guests are accustomed to inquire about hotels in terms of the number of stars. Even though the criteria vary from one country to the another, a national classification nevertheless offers customers greater opportunity of finding a hotel which conforms to the standard desired, thereby avoiding the wrong choice of hotel – something which is disagreeable for both parties. The most important objective for HORESTA was to satisfy their customers' wishes as well as they can.

Moreover, experience from other countries showed that in many instances classification was a useful aid for a hotel manager is interested in improving his/her product. With the criteria and inspection report in hand it is easier to make improvements precisely where guests will gain most from them.

8. Role of the Classification Board

- Lays down the criteria according to which the classification will be undertaken
- Ensures that these criteria are consistently adapted to developments taking place in the world
- Has the initiative of discussing alterations to criteria and taking decisions about such alterations

9. What Does the Classification Scheme Cost?

HORESTA contributes financially to the establishment of the scheme. Running the classification scheme will subsequently be paid for by the hotels, according to the following criteria:

- Hotels with less than 20 rooms/apartments
- Hotels with at least 20 rooms/apartments
- Annual price rate
- Annual extra charge per room/apartments

These charges, to be paid by quarterly instalments, were instituted as of March 1997.

10. Five Categories

A prerequisite for classification is that the hotel is deemed to have reached an overall satisfactory standard of cleanliness and maintenance.

The HORESTA classification scheme is not based on an assessment of the hotels, but is a recording of actual conditions.

If "Hotel Garni" is displayed on the sign or listed here on www.danishhotels.dk, it means that the hotel restaurant usually only serves breakfast. A small selection of the more than 100 criteria is shown below:

- All rooms have at least a hand-basin with hot and cold running water. There is at least one bathroom and toilet per 10 rooms.
- Telephone box, or suitable sound-proofing for a communal telephone. At least 20 per cent of the rooms have private bath/shower and toilet.
- All rooms have private bath/shower and toilet, as well as telephone, TV, radio and writing desk.
- Comfortable chairs in the rooms. TV with international channels and film channel or in-house video service. Modem connection in at least 10 per cent of the rooms. Round-the-clock reception, à la carte restaurant and bar. Mini-bar in all rooms, or round-the-clock room service with refreshments.
- Luxurious interior decor. Rooms with safebox and some form of air-conditioning – with suites available. Modem connection in all rooms. Room service until 11 pm for

meals. Indoor swimming pool, or fitness centre with professional staff. Large selection of toilet articles, etc.

Hotels fulfilling a number of specified requirements concerning meeting facilities can apply for the designation 'Hotel and Conference Centre'. As far as holiday centres are concerned, a special set of criteria was drawn up in close collaboration with the 'Association of Holiday Centres in Denmark.' These describe both the facilities available and the activities on offer.

11. What the Classification Does Not Say...

The aim of the classification scheme is to provide guests with an immediate overview of the hotel's general and objectively recorded standard as regards facilities and services. It is not designed to provide a qualitative or subjective evaluation.

Certain types of information are not covered by the classification, which is why sensible marketing on the part of the hotel ought to contain such information. This can be indicated with the aid of symbols, text, photographs or a combination of all three.

Regional Classification Schemes

1. Towards a Nordic Classification Scheme? Sweden Opts for the Danish Model

In March 2003, after lengthy consultations with representatives of hotel chains, cities/destinations, distributors and various consumer organizations, the Swedish Hotel and Restaurant Association (SHR) took the decision to classify Swedish hotels that are members of the Association. For the time being, this is on a voluntary basis. In principle, SHR has adopted the Danish scheme, with certain adjustments to suit Swedish conditions and the requirements of certain key players on the Swedish market. It will also use the Danish website as a model, specifically in terms of data flow.

The classification process started in Stockholm and the Gothenburg area and is gradually being extended to cover Member hotels throughout the country. It is anticipated that by late 2004 all SHR members, some 1000 hotels, will be graded. To do this, SHR has recruited a staff of four people to run the scheme and carry out the inspections.

Costs will be covered by the hotels on a no profit/no loss basis. The government is covering the introductory cost in order get the scheme launched, thus enabling SHR to reduce the level of financial risk involved. So far, the system is being rolled out successfully, with key players backing the project. However, some hoteliers still have strong reservations about classification. SHR believes the timing is right and that the website model will offer a distinct competitive advantage to members.

Both Norway and Finland are closely following developments in Sweden. Ultimately, the vision is to establish a Nordic classification system common to all the players in the region.

(Information provided by the Swedish Hotel & Restaurant Association)

2. *Adapting the Swiss Hotel Association (SHA) System to Other Countries?*

In 1979 SHA introduced a hotel classification system which was the fist and only private one of its kind in the world. It is based on self-assessment by the hotelier which is subsequently reviewed by one of SHA's five regional committees.

Following comprehensive overhauls in 1985, 1989 and 1994, the SHA hotel classification scheme underwent its fourth review in 2000. The new standards give hoteliers the option of applying for a maximum of three specialization categories (*e.g.* Family, Historic, Golf, Congress Health Hotel) as well as an optional Seal of Quality qualification, in recognition of the fact that the quality of individual hotels has steadily increased over the years. Reviews are undertaken every five years to allow for periodic reclassification well received by SHA members, despite the substantial investment involved.

The SHA system is used in Switzerland by the Canton Ticino Tourist Office (for classifying hotels which are not SHA members) and has been adopted at the international level by Germany, Austria, various North Italian provinces. South Tyrol and Trinidad and Tobago. HOTREC is studying the system as a discussion basis for further projects at the European level.

3. The Association of South East Asian Nations (ASEAN)

Starting in 1976, the ten States Member of the ASEAN (Brunei Darussalam, Cambodia, Indonesia, Lao People's Democratic Republic, Malaysia, Myanmar, Philippines, Singapore, Thailand and Vietnam) have developed comprehensive programmes and plans of actions on cooperation in tourism. Among the different activities included under these programmes and plans in favour of ASEAN cooperation in tourism, the establishment of a common hotel classification scheme is under consideration.

4. The Economic Community of West African States (ECOWAS)

ECOWAS, which groups fifteen countries (Benin, Burkina Faso, Cabo Verde, Côte d'lvoire, Gambia, Ghana, Guinea, Guinea-Bissau, Liberia, Mali, Niger, Nigeria, Senegal, Sierra Leone, and Togo) has established a programme of cooperation in the tourism sector which focuses on three areas, namely: Promotion and marketing of tourism products; Facilitation and Harmonization of regulations applicable to tourism activities and the hotel industry.

With regard to hotel classification, at its 45th session (Lome, Togo, 5 December 1999), the Council of ECOWAS Ministers adopted regulations on proposed standards for classification of hotels, motels and guest inns in the sub-region, taking into account those drafted and proposed by WTO for the African region in 1984. ECOWAS has however introduced in its proposed standards new elements, such as minimum ceiling standards, billing and payments rules, insurance requirements and services entrances.

A workshop on the implementation of this harmonized hotel classification system was jointly organized by ECOWAS and WTO in Dakar, Senegal, in July 2001. Participants in this workshop have recommended to ECOWAS Member States to establish their respective national classification committees, in order to take responsibility for classification of hotels and the setting up of inspection teams in each state, based on the standards as approved in 1999 by the Council of Ministers.

Participants also agreed that the ECOWAS Secretariat should take responsibility for sourcing of the funds necessary to meet the classification training and human resource development requirements for the implementation of the aforementioned regulations between 2002 and 2003.

Review of Graphical Symbols – Stars, Diamonds and Other Crown Jewels

A variety of graphical symbols are used in the hotel and lodging industry throughout the world. In the USA, both the American Automobile Association (AAA) and the petrochemical company Mobil provide information on hotel and lodging facilities, rated according to their own system.

1. Mobil "Star" Ratings

- A Mobil One-Star Lodging Establishment is a limited service Hotel/Motel/Inn that is considered a clean, comfortable and reliable establishment.
- A Mobil Two-Star Lodging Establishment is a Hotel/Resort/Inn that is considered a clean, comfortable and reliable establishment, but also has expanded amenities, such as a full-service Restaurant on the property.
- A Mobil Three-Star Lodging Establishment is a Hotel/Resort/Inn which is well-appointed, with a full-service Restaurant and expanded amenities, such as, but not limited to: fitness centre, golf course, tennis courts, 24-hour room service, and optional turndown service.
- A Mobil Four-Star Lodging Establishment is a Hotel/Resort/Inn which provides a luxury experience with expanded amenities in a distinctive environment. Services may include, but are not limited to: automatic turndown service, 24 hour room service, and valet parking.
- A Mobil Five-Star Lodging Establishment provides consistently superlative service in an exceptionally distinctive luxury environment with expanded services. Attention to detail is evident throughout the Hotel/Resort/Inn from the bed linens to staff uniforms.

Lodging Criteria and Expectations

The following criteria are suggested—criteria of what a guest can generally expect at each star level. They are not individually mandated nor are they limited to those items listed below. These are merely a representative sampling of the hundreds of points covered during our inspection process.

Additionally, at each level the lodging establishment is required to meet or exceed the requirements of the previous star rating. For example, a Two-Star hotel meets the criteria expectations of a Two-Star hotel as well as the One-Star hotel. A Three-Star hotel meets the criteria expectations of a Three-Star hotel, a Two-Star hotel and One-Star hotel, and so forth.

2. *American Automobile Association (AAA) "Diamond" ratings*

(*a*) *One Diamond*: These establishments typically appeal to the budget-minded traveller. They provide essential, no-frills accommodations. They meet the basic requirements pertaining to comfort, cleanliness and hospitality.

(*b*) *Two Diamond*: These establishments appeal to the traveller seeking more than the basic accommodations. There are modest enhancements to the overall physical attributes, design elements and amenities of the facility typically at a moderate price.

(*c*) *Three Diamond*: These establishments appeal to the traveller with comprehensive needs. Properties are multifaceted with a distinguished style, including marked upgrades in the quality of physical attributes, amenities and level of comfort provided.

(*d*) *Four Diamond*: These establishments are upscale in all areas. Accommodations are progressively more refined and stylish. The physical attributes reflect an obvious enhanced level of quality throughout. The fundamental hallmarks at this level include an extensive array of amenities combined with a high degree of hospitality, service and attention to detail.

(*e*) *Five Diamond*: These establishments reflect the characteristics of the ultimate in luxury and sophistication. Accommodations are first class. The physical attributes are extraordinary in every manner. The fundamental hallmarks at this level are to meticulously serve and exceed all guest expectations while maintaining an impeccable standard of excellence. Many personalized services and amenities enhance an unmatched level of comfort.

Both AAA and Mobil award ratings on a scale of 1 to 5 (5 being the highest rating–signifying the absolute ultimate in service, luxury, atmosphere and price). Both organizations conduct annual on-site physical inspections and both provide inspections, evaluations and rating free of charge to hotels.

AAA overhauls its ratings standards about every five years and invites industry representatives to comment on them before issuing the final version; while Mobil does not disclose detailed criteria to hotels or provide them with any feedback. AAA is currently implementing a major revision of standards for its 2005 awards to be announced in the autumn of 2004. This revision was delayed by the events of 11 September 2001.

3. Mexico favours "Stars and Diamonds"

Cancun, Mexico – 2 September 1999 – During the XXV Tianguis in Acapuico, Mexico's Secretary of Tourism, presented the new Mexican hotel rating classification, called "Stars and Diamonds".

This system is the result of several years of extensive research, and has integrated criteria from various sources like AAA, Mobil, Michelin, Small Luxury Hotels, Relais et Chateaux, The Leading Hotels of the World and Spain's ITQ2000, among others.

"Stars and Diamonds" has been sponsored by the Mexican Hotel Association, as well as the Mexican Chain Hotels Association and approved by the Ministry of Tourism.

This classification is voluntary and will be based on a certification by an independent board. It will consider, on the one side, the quality of a hotel (basically the room), which will be rated with stars, and on the other side, the quality of its services and staff, to be rated in diamonds. This certification will be renewed every year after a site inspection.

4. United Kingdom Seeks to Harmonise Three Systems

Information provided by the British Hospitality Association – BHA

There are new, harmonized, quality standards for hotels under a unified system agreed between the two major motoring organizations – the Automobile Association (AA) and the Royal Automobile Club (RAC), and the English Tourist Board (Scotland and Wales will have slight variances with these standards). Quality standards will be signified with the award of 'Stars'. The minimum number of stars is one and the maximum is five.

There is no legal compulsion for hotels to seek quality recognition, although they are subject to local controls and licensing. Requirements for the granting of stars, crowns etc. can be found inside the cover of the AA and RAC Hotel Guides. These guides can generally be found in the Information Section of local libraries.

Hotel Classification (Stars)

(*a*) *One Star Hotels*: Hotels in this classification are likely to be small and independently owned, with a family atmosphere. Services may be provided by the owner and family on an informal basis. There may be a limited range of facilities and meals may be fairly simple. Lunch, for example, may not be served. Some bedrooms may not have en suite bath/shower rooms. Maintenance, cleanliness and comfort should, however, always be of an acceptable standard.

(*b*) *Two Star Hotels*: In this classification hotels will typically be small to medium sized and offer more extensive facilities than at the one star level. Some business hotels come into the two star classification and guests can expect comfortable, well equipped, overnight accommodation, usually with an en-suite bath/shower room. Reception and other staff will aim for a more professional presentation that at the one star level, and offer a wider range of straightforward services, including food and drink.

(*c*) *Three Star Hotels*: At this level, hotels are usually of a size to support higher staffing levels, and a significantly greater quality and range of facilities than at the lower star classifications. Reception and the other public rooms will be more spacious and the restaurant will normally also cater for non-residents. All bedrooms will have fully en suite bath and shower rooms and offer a good standard of comfort and equipment, such as a hair dryer, direct dial telephone, toiletries in the bathroom. Some room service can be expected, and some provision for business travellers.

(*d*) *Four Star Hotels*: Expectations at this level include a degree of luxury as well as quality in the furnishings, decor and equipment, in every area of the hotel. Bedrooms will also usually offer more space than at the lower star levels, and well designed, co-ordinated furnishings and decor. The en-suite bathrooms will have both bath and fixed shower. There will be a high enough ratio of staff to guests to provide services like porterage, 24-hour room service, laundry and dry-cleaning. The restaurant will demonstrate a serious approach to its cuisine.

(*e*) *Five Star Hotels*: Here you should find spacious and luxurious accommodation throughout the hotel, matching the best international standards. Interior design should impress with its quality and attention to detail, comfort and elegance. Furnishings should be immaculate. Services should be formal, well supervised and flawless in attention to guests' needs, without being intrusive. The restaurant will demonstrate a high level of technical skill, producing dishes to the highest international standards. Staff will be knowledgeable, helpful, well versed in all aspects of customer care, combining efficiency with courtesy.

Guest House Classification (Diamonds)

The Diamond awards assess guest accommodation at five levels of quality, from one Diamond at the simplest, to 5 Diamonds at the luxury end of the spectrum.

Terminology

1. WTO Thesaurus on Tourism and Leisure Activities

Due to the considerable growth worldwide in the volume of information on tourism activity and at the same time the sizeable increase in automated documentation systems regarding this sector, the World Tourism Organization (WTO) set itself the task of creating a structured multilingual tool to facilitate indexing and bibliographical search into tourism and allied fields: The Thesaurus on Tourism and Leisure Activities.

This linguistic instrument was developed between 1996 and 1999 – by the means of an effective partnership between the WTO Secretariat – and the Secretariat of State for Tourism of France through its Tourism Directorate.

The Thesaurus – which was initially established as a specific documentation language to help search for information relating to tourism activities – can be also used as a guide to tourism terminology as well as for the standardization and normalization of a common indexation and retrieval language, at the international level. Its basic framework is made up of semantic fields, which include terms, definitions and relations linking the terms to each other.

The 8,185 terms thus selected are distributed over 20 fields representing tourism activity. Field 08 concerns *Accommodation* and its main related aspects, *i.e.* Accommodation Capacity; Holiday Accommodation; Youth Accommodation; Rural Accommodation; Hotel Trade and Other Means of Accommodation.

The first edition (French-English-Spanish) of the Thesaurus was published in 2001 and the Italian version in 2003. The Croatian and Portuguese versions of the Thesaurus was published in 2004. The objective set for this linguistic tool during 2004-2005, is to provide updated on line editions and also expand it to other languages.

2. WTO Tourism Legislation Database (LEXTOUR)

As from mid-November 2003, the WTO Documentation Centre launched the Tourism Legislation Database – LEXTOUR. This database has been designed to act as a referral system facilitating via the WTO Website (www.world-tourism.org), direct access through links to external websites, databases and information servers on tourism legislative data produced and distributed by authoritative sources, such as national parliaments, central government bodies (including national tourism administrations – NTAs), professional associations, universities, etc.

Presently, some three hundred information systems have been identified in more than 130 countries.

A number of webservers recorded in LEXTOUR (especially those administrated by NTAs) provide references to and/or full text of legislative and regulatory instruments governing tourism accommodation and, in particular, hotels and similar establishments.

CEN - ISO

After many years of work, investigation and broad industry consultation both at the European and international levels the CEN work in this area was completed with the publication in January 2001 of the European and International Standard on *Tourism Services – Hotels and other types of tourism accommodation – Terminology (prEN ISO 18513).*

This was released as an official ISO publication in 2003, described by ISO in the following terms:

> This is a dictionary of core terms for the tourist industry, meaning that when one person uses a term, the others anywhere in the world know exactly what is being described and what they can expect.
>
> ISO 18513 can serve as a reference for the explanations given in travel brochures or in automatic booking systems; in business-to-business communications; in definitions given in tourist statistics; or consumer advisory services, to avoid misunderstandings when tourist offers are provided; and for interpretation in legal conflicts.

Conclusions

Synthesis of findings

It is obvious from this study, based on a survey of both the public and private sectors, that not only is the situation complex – but that the solutions are just as complicated.

1. Classification by Other Entities

First and foremost, it should be noted that the study does not attempt to do more than refer briefly to classification standards or criteria used by consumer bodies or travel professionals *e.g.*:

- Consumer guides (Michelin, RAC, AA etc.)
- Global Distribution Systems (GDS) (Amadeus, Galileo, Sabre etc.)
- Computer Reservation Systems (CRS) and brokers
- GSM codification used by computers and telephone technology in cars
- Major voluntary chains and consortia
- Major hotel chains
- Major hotel franchisors
- Tour Operators
- ISO (International Organization for Standardization)

It would also be useful to take a look at furnished rentals, *i.e.*, neither hotels nor resorts, which form a large share of the holiday rental market. These are often subject to the same rules and regulations as regular private rentals, rather than those applying to tourist accommodation.

In addition to all these classification standards or criteria, others are laid down by governments, professional bodies or private enterprises.

2. Consumer-driven?

One point is obvious – all these approaches claim to be for the benefit of the consumer. Yet consumers are very rarely consulted even though many organizations claim to be acting on their behalf. Here one fundamental difference can be noted between the public and private sectors. When such standards and criteria are laid down by governments, they tend to remain in force for years at a time, are infrequently checked and rarely updated to meet changes in fashion and consumer taste or take account of changes in destinations and markets.

In this respect, the private sector is much quicker at responding to demand, as instanced by such developments as timeshare, resorts, villas providing traditional hotel services etc. Similarly, the criteria set out in private-sector consumer guides are much more responsive to consumer and market demand. Many surveys show that consumer choice is governed first and foremost by price and destination, rather than by classification systems that are so complex that the consumer is either unaware of them or unable to decipher them.

In fact, where the public sector is concerned, government interest in having a classification system is often prompted by the need to organize the domestic market, obtain statistics and assess competition from neighbouring countries/destinations.

3. Summing up

In the light of recent events such as 9/11, SARS, Mad Cow disease and Legionnaire's disease, ensuring minimum standards for safety and hygiene should obviously fall to governments. As most of the other aspects of classification are basically commercial, or market-driven, this could be a first consideration guiding the classification debate.

The two notions, destination, whether country or region, and purpose of travel (business, leisure, etc.) are fundamental. As noted in the report, Europe is currently considering the feasibility of an EU classification system; similar investigations are underway within ASEAN (Association of South East Asian Nations); in the Nordic countries and in the Middle East; while Central African states have expressed interest in some such system.

4. Key Considerations

1. *Private sector requirement*: consumer information—There is strong consumer demand for better and more transparent information on both the products and destinations on offer. This implies the consistent use of a given and recognized terminology. It also raises the problem of the language(s) in which the information is made available. On the positive side, the diversity of information available can also be considered an advantage.
2. *Public sector responsibility*: Hygiene and safety—Government concern should focus more on ensuring hygiene and personal safety than on the commercial aspects of classification.
3. *Methodology*—It would be advisable to devise a methodology providing those states wishing to set up a national or regional classification scheme with the necessary tools to do so. The point here is to provide a systematic way of taking into account the cultural differences between states in terms of service and facilities according to destinations, regions and purpose of travel. To be sustainable, tourism must be able to consolidate its diversity, not seek uniformity.

Without these intermediary stages, any international classification system would run the risk of being irrelevant and therefore inefficient, especially as it could necessarily only be voluntary. In the long run, this would end up merely creating more confusion.

4

Global Hospitality Enterprise Management

GOLDEN BLUE HOSPITALITY

Golden Blue Hospitality Enterprises SA

A Leading Business-To-Business Hospitality Organization founded by Hospitality Industry Executives and commenced its activity a few years ago.

While actively involved in expanding its network, presence and customer base, it has also introduced Internationally accepted Hospitality Concepts in a well developed and pioneering way to various Local and Regional Markets.

Golden Blue's mission is to be a catalyst of Innovative and Positive Change targetting sustainable operational success, growth and profitability.

Pixel Point 2000 POS

Pixel Point R 2000 T SQL for Windows 95/98/ME or Windows NT/2000 is a fully integrated 32-bit Point of Sale and BackOffice software solution for table service and quick service restaurants. Its unmatched reliability, remarkable flexibility and unprecedented ease-of-use set a new benchmark in POS software for today's hospitality environments. Whether you are running a fine dining restaurant, a quick service chain or even a high volume bar, Pixel Point POS software can be configured to meet your needs.

Pixel Point 2000 Out of the Box

(*i*) Table Management
(*ii*) Membership
(*iii*) Client Loyalty
(*iv*) Time and Attendance

(*v*) Delivery
(*vi*) Recipe Management
(*vii*) International Ready
(*viii*) Menu Management
(*ix*) Extensive Reporting
(*x*) Table or Quick Service

Add-on Modules that Expand Your POS

CreditCheck TM
Credit Management: Transform your POS into a powerful credit processor.

StockBoy TM
Perpetual Inventory Management: Take real-time perpetual inventory.

StaffTime TM
Labour Scheduling: Create a more controlled and secure labour management environment.

TalkTime TM & WebTime TM
Remote Schedule Retrieval: Automate scheduling through phone or Internet access.

SalesCall TM
Remote Sales Retrieval: Retrieve sales information by touch - tone phone.

PMS Connect TM
Property management driver: Communicate and post payments to front desk folios.

PixelLinks TM
Third party applications links: Link with third party accounting, liquor control, inventory control and payroll solutions.

BarLinks TM
Beverage Dispensing System Link: Drive and poll third party beverage dispensing systems.

F&B and Materials Management

Including Food & Beverage Management

The most Advanced Software Application of its kind developed by Hospitality and Specialized Technology Industry professionals with years of worldwide or local expertise in their respective fields. It covers in the most comprehensive way all Hospitality Operational Aspects of Purchasing, Inventory, Stores Management, Cost Control, Recipe & Buffet Engineering and Corporate Procurement or Consolidation while providing an extensive variety of reporting flexibility. Its dynamic "data interchange" with the leading POS and Accounting Systems and also its fast and effortless adaptability to any Language or Legal requirement in addition to its scalability constitute the ideal solution for any Hospitality Organization like Hotels & Resorts (Independent or Chain), Casinos, Theme Parks, Cruise Ships, Restaurants of any kind, Bars etc.

Introduction

E-Revenue Management previously called Yield Management, is an advanced technology "New Generation Solution" that allows for the generation of the highest profit expected from an activity.

This is a result of the calculation of the best suitable price to offer (taking into consideration the offer and demand) in order to reach the maximum profit from the sale of a perishable product or service.

On the basis of collected information from the PMS data regarding demand, booking pickup, special events and budgets, the Revenue Management Solution will help to make the Right Decisions for the Optimization of your Total Revenues.

This objective is obtained with innovative business process design and is greatly enhanced with a combination of advanced information technology and sophisticated mathematical algorithmic models.

The principle is simple: *"Sell the right product, to the right customer, at the right time, for the right price and for the right duration"* with the objective of optimizing product price and availability in order to reach the maximum profit.

The Technological Platform ASP

ASP mode =Application Service Provider – WEB based.

It means that there is no need to purchase a RMS software package and Hardware. You simply use the Internet and rent the RMS Solution, without any operational constraint linked to maintenance, service and software updates. This kind of application should tempt single average size properties that sometimes are hesitant to invest, even in a new advanced PMS (Property Management System) for instance. It will delight hotel chains or groups as well as they will benefit from the economy of scale and important operational cost savings.

(a) System's Features
The system offers/allows

- The application of special Management Strategies, relative to product price and availability.
- The management of e-Distribution Channels (GDS, IDS, Hotel websites).
- Immediate and clear decisions/recommendations.

- Very early repayment of the involved investment (needed for its application) from he additional revenue and profits that its application will generate.

(b) And Substantially Contributes

- To the decrease of exploitation costs.
- To Market Share increase.
- To Revenue increase by 4-8 per cent, thus
- Resulting in Profit increases of 20-40 per cent.

E-Pricing and E-Revenue (Yield) Management

In the modern time highly competitive new environment, created - amongst other reasons - by the rapid development of e-Pricing and e-Distribution possibilities offered by the GDS (Global Distribution Systems), IDS (Internet Distribution Systems) and Hotel websites, you cannot avoid the imperative need for an automated e-Revenue Management Solution.

Since, in the struggle to preserve your market share, you operate using E-Pricing and E-Distribution possibilities, you inevitably need an e-Revenue Management Solution, which is indispensable as a TACTICAL SUPPORT TOOL, to supporting the optimization of your hotel's earnings!

E-Pricing and E-Distribution need to be supported by an automated E-Revenue Management Solution (a Decision Support System) that taking into consideration the market's particularities, together with the historical data trends from the PMS, substantially supports the RIGHT decision regarding the calculation of the RIGHT price in each case (time, market segment, duration etc) to achieve the maximum occupancy from the existing demand at the highest possible price per case.

Therefore, the current HOT issue for the Hotelier it is not whether he needs an E-Revenue Management Solution, since this is currently an IMPOSED need, but which Solution to select that will fit better to the size and the financial capacity of his company!

The Selection of the E-Revenue Management

Looking for the Best Solution, it will be useful and wise, to select the one that has the most ACCURATE FORECASTING, as well as the built in possibility of direct access to the COMPETITOR'S RATE ANALYSIS, thus indirectly revealing their Pricing Strategy!!!! These possibilities are available ONLY today within the EzRMS ™ Solution.

It is an Affordable Solution, offered at The Best Price Globally, therefore.......

It's not reasonable not to have EzRMS™ in your Hotel!!!

The EzRMS ™ Price list, Client List and Testimonials, together with other useful information can be found at the Global Site of EzRMS.

For further information or a live demo:

Please contact Mr. Stelios G. Stylianou

Manager - Revenue Management Solution

E-mail: s.stylianou@goldenblue.com

SKYPE name: Sgstelios

What is Revenue Management (Revenue Optimization)?

Revenue Management, previously called Yield Management is an advanced technology "New Generation Solution" that allows the generation of the highest profit expected from a given activity.

This is a result of the calculation of the best price to offer, in order to optimize the contribution coming from the sale of a product or of a service, on the basis of real time graphics and forecasts of the behaviour of the customers in a micro segmented market and demand.

In other words, Revenue Management is the result of the calculation of the best suitable price to offer (taking into consideration the offer and demand), in order to reach the maximum profit from the sale of a perishable product or service.

This objective is obtained with innovative business process design and greatly enhanced with a combination of advanced information technology and sophisticated mathematical algorithmic models.

The principle is simple: *"Sell the right product, to the right customer, at the right time, for the right price and for the right duration"* with the objective of optimising product price and availability in order to reach the maximum profit.

On the basis of information collected from the PMS, data on demand, booking pickup, special events and budgets, the Revenue Management Solution will help to make the Right Decisions for the Optimization of Revenues.

Revenue Management is an Indispensable Tactical Weapon that ensures the profitability (if not the viability) of any business operating in the highly competitive environment, created by the development of electronic distribution, in the form of the GDS (Global Distribution Systems).

Watching what occurred to the American Airline Companies in the 1980's we will realize that the companies that did not invest or waited too long to invest in these tools have disappeared (People Express, Pan Am etc). Those who implemented the most effective Revenue Management systems (especially American Airlines and Delta Airlines) were in fact the companies who adapted best to this new competitive environment.

American Airlines calculated that the systematic use of Yield Management enabled the company to generate $1.4 billion dollars in additional revenue between 1989 and 1991.

ASP the Technological Revolution

What is ASP? (=Application Service Provider -WEB based)

RMS/ASP mode is a contractual service for distributing, implementing, managing and renting computer applications hosted in an external centralized location.

It means that there is no need to purchase an RMS software package and Hardware. You simply use the Internet and rent the RMS Solution, without any operational constraint linked to maintenance, service and software updates.

Substantial Savings of Exploitation Costs

RMS ASP does not require heavy investment either in Hardware or in Software. Various studies underline that using the ASP technology involves a significant decrease of exploitation costs.

This kind of application should tempt single average size properties that sometimes are hesitant to invest, even in a new advanced PMS (Property Management System) for instance. It will delight hotel chains or groups as well as they will benefit from the economy of scale, important operational cost savings.

Other ASP Advantages

The use of ASP mode applications not only means cost savings, but also:

- Flexibility and modernity
- Low cost investment
- Reduced damages and repair expenses
- Automatic, free and current updating of software

- Service accessibility via an Internet connection
- Assistance and trouble-shooting support through the Internet
- Automatic backup of all your data.

Finally, when these benefits come from a system that generates Optimization of Revenues and Profits, then it is a must-have System, That Should Not Be Missing from any modern Hospitality Unit.

EzRMS™ Advantages over the competition

EzRMS™ is the World's Leading provider of ASP based Revenue Management Solutions, having competitive advantage over its competitors worldwide, for the following indisputable reasons:

- It is the only RM provider worldwide that has foreseen, designed and executed from the very beginning the first Hospitality Revenue Management Solution on the technological platform of ASP, since 1999.
- EzRMS™ is operating RM Solutions in ASP mode for more than six years, whilst the competitors have ASP systems for only six months. Therefore, it is logical that EzRMS™ is years ahead in terms of both functionality and the stability of the solution.
- Although competitors now announce the availability of ASP RM products, their Customer list mainly consists of Hotels that Do Not Operate On Asp Mode!
- It is the Easiest solution for the user in the global market!
- It is the Only solution that has an Accurate Forecast, reaching the 95 per cent level of accuracy within a 3 to 6 months period (from commencement of data capture)!
- It is the Only Solution that has fully integrated the possibility of direct access to the competitors rate analysis and there of revealing the Competitor Pricing Strategy!!!!! (Ez-COMPETE™)
- The EasyRMS pricing policy is the Most Competitive of the Market!
- EzRMS™ provides the option of Centralized Revenue Management for many Hotels of the same Group (Multi Property) which is very useful for Hotel Groups or Chains.
- For Resort Hotels that operate mostly on Allotment based contracts, EzRMS™ offers among others: 28 Day Length of Stay Optimization and the Market Mix and Contract

Evaluation, evaluating whether business from one Tour Operator is in fact important to take or not.

Conclusion

Summarizing, the EzRMS™ Revenue Management Solution:

- Involves a significant decrease of exploitation costs.
- Generates the maximum of revenues, thus substantially increases the bottom line profits.
- ALL EzRMS™ customers have RM Solutions that operate ONLY in ASP mode.
- It is indisputably the BEST RM Solution in ASP mode, Globally.
- Is a Low Cost Solution, offered at The Best Price Globally, having a Surprisingly early pay-back period of the involved investment.

Therefore, It is Not Reasonable Not To Have the EzRMS™ Solution in your Hotel today!!!

Company:	Golden Blue Hospitality Enterprises
Address:	Building 1, Dubai Internet City Dubai 500069
Country:	United Arab Emirates
Contact:	Mr Najib Makhdoom
Position:	Manager Customer Services
Phone:	+971 4 391 3534
Fax:	+ 971 4 391 8925
Internet:	....
International presence:	Africa C & East Asia Europe Middle East

EzRMS™ organizes its first worldwide User Group FORUM, on the 3rd of October, in Cannes, French Riviera, at the hotel Lucien Barriere Hotel Grayd'Albion. The main issue is "Segmentation, Pricing and Distribution."

The Attendance Cost of this 2-day Forum has been fixed to the amount of 500 euro, per delegate, including two nights accommodation with breakfast, daily conference package, two dinners (the first is a GALA dinner) and access to the Casino Barriere de Cannes Croisette (with its ocean atmosphere and giant aquarium for a night of practical risk evaluation).

This forum is designed to cater for General Managers, Group Revenue Managers, Revenue Managers and Sales & Marketing Executives alike from chains as well as independent hotels currently using EzRMS™. The objective will be an interactive forum where the participants from different markets, brands and classifications have an opportunity to address these three critical challenges Segmentation, Pricing and Distribution as well as exchange ideas and thoughts with fellow EzRMS™ users.

We attached here bellow the Invitation of Philippe Coquand (Group Yield Director TOU Groupe Lucien Barriere) that describes in detail the Objectives and the Programme of this very useful interactive Forum.

For the Hotels of the Greek and Cypriot Market, we ensured special conditions, i.e. to qualify for the attendance, just a signed contract with EzRMS™ is only needed, without requirements for previous and extensive working experience in Yield Management.

I am sure that it will be an excellent opportunity to exchange ideas, thoughts, experiences and techniques with long experienced colleagues of Individual Hotels, or Chains from advanced markets of all around the World and to enhance your knowledge from their expertise.

For any further information, please contact:
Stelios G. Stylianou
Manager - Revenue Management Solutions
Goldenblue Hospitality Enterprises S.A.
Email: s.stylianou@qoldenblue.com
Tel: +30-210-3218245
Fax: +30-210-3218173

ACOM HOSPITALITY SOLUTIONS

Acom University: Accounting Solution

The Universal Accounting Solution controls disbursements and reports financial position with its three main modules: Accounts Payable, General Ledger and Financial Reporting.

Accounts Payable

Companies

- GL distributions posted in as much detail as desired;
- Accrual or cash basis accounting available;
- Inter-company AP and AR may be used.

Vendor Groups and Classes

- Controlled sharing of vendors between companies;
- Vendor info retained for to user-defined periods;
- Payment priorities for cash requirements planning.

Vendors

- All invoices for a vendor may be held;
- Discount codes indicate payment terms if a discount is taken or not;
- Government classification of vendors (such as USA 1099 types);
- Bank codes indicate the payable, the bank and the discount accounts. The currency in which the monies are to be stored and the foreign exchange clearance accounts used may also be indicated.

Invoices

- Invoice batch control supported;
- Facilities support reconciliation of trade account;
- Duplicate invoice entry is prevented;
- Invoices may be reconciled;
- Be inclusive or exclusive of Value Added Tax (VAT), Goods and Services Tax (GST), and sales tax.

Invoice Distribution

- Charge to multiple company accounts;
- Codes for commonly used GL accounts;
- Invoice information may be changed until its paid;
- A manual payment speed entry is supported;
- Goods received without invoice (GRWI) is supported.

Payments

- Can take all discounts regardless of the discount dates;
- Select invoices by due date, bank code or payment group, by vendor classes;
- A sophisticated form writer allows the user to maintain their form design as well as their electronic payment format;
- A control number for each payment form and its MICR number are maintained.

Payment Cancellation

- Payment cancellation cancels the invoice and reverses the distribution;
- A payment may be cancelled and uncancelled any number of times.

Bank Reconciliation

- Payments may be outstanding, cancelled, reconciled, stale, or held;
- Payments may be reconciled by entering each cashed payment individually, by using bank reports to quickly reconcile groups of payments, or by using bank-provided diskettes or tapes identifying cashed payments.

Inquiries

- Invoice info, including distribution, is kept online as long as the user desires;
- Vendor balances, outstanding payables and payments may be viewed;
- Invoices may be viewed using a variety of criteria, including tax codes.

Reports

- Reports suitable for all VAT, GST, sales tax and use tax reporting requirements worldwide. The system maintains separate chronological sequences for general ledger entries and for accounts payable entries by payable code.

General Ledger

Companies

- Intercompany journal vouchers supported;
- Multiple fiscal years may be simultaneously supported;
- Multiple budgets and forecasts may simultaneously exist;
- An unlimited number of previous and future years may be kept online; both period total information, and transaction details.

Chart of Accounts

- A GL account may be used for detail accounts, to store memo information, to specify a heading, or to define a total;

- The default Value Added Tax (VAT), Goods and Services Tax (GST), sales tax and other use taxes for the account are specified.

Journal Vouchers

- A list of expected JVs is kept and enforced;
- The system prevents a JV from being posted twice in the same period;
- Postings are allowed to the current and future periods;
- Repetitive entries are automated. Each repetitive entry is defined just once;
- Each posting may be charged to several periods at the same time;
- Recurring journal vouchers may be entered once;
- The invoice in a prepaid expense may be reconciled with its distribution over the course of several periods;
- Comprehensive integrated Excel interface.

Budgets

- Budgets may be entered manually or calculated using a modelling package;
- Budgets may be uploaded to the system from PC's. Information may also be downloaded to PC's.

Inquiries and Reports

- Transaction details may be kept online indefinitely;
- Transactions may be extracted using a range of criteria;
- They may also be extracted based on VAT, GST, sales, and use tax contributions.

Financial Statements

- The system may accumulate information for any period of time (monthly, weekly and daily);
- Statements may be produced for any year for which information remains online;
- Budget, forecast and historical information may be readily intermixed;
- Any sort of balance sheet oı profit and loss statement may be produced. Trends of operation, sources and uses of funds and statistical reports are also easily produced;
- Any sort of ratios may be calculated;

- Multiple currencies may be freely intermixed. Currency conversion at either book or profit and loss rates is supported;
- Statements may be viewed on screen

Account Receivable

The Universal Receivable Solution is a powerful tool for hospitality operation which effectively helps control client, guest, and member accounts. It enables the operation to track and maintain accounts on a real time basis with as much detail as required.

Invoicing/Billing

Flexible billing. Users may use the system to produce detailed invoices or simple statements, or a combination of both:

- If the invoicing feature is used for some accounts then the statement system can be useful to produce statements summarizing the invoices and sent to clients as a reminder.
- Integrated deposit management, with straightforward, user-friendly assignment of deposits to invoices.
- Option to 'retrieve' and adjust already-issued invoices, with changes automatically tracked to controlled clearance accounts.
- Full control on invoice printing, including the ability to clearly label duplicate invoices or retrieved invoices.
- An invoice 'proof' is supported and can be printed before the final invoice run, with invoice proofs clearly labelled as such.
- Multiple open invoices per customer can be allowed if desired.
- Invoices have full VAT support, including support for multiple VAT rates, and an option to identify exempt customers.
- Flexible payment posting, including allocation of payments to specific charges or across the oldest outstanding charges.
- Optional, configurable write-offs for small amounts such as caused by exchange variation.
- Ability to transfer all or part of any charge between accounts, with full audit ability.

- Support for Travel Agency customers, including deduction of commissions owed on invoices and a reflection of this on invoice journals.
- Statements are supported in both traditional 'balance forward' style, or in simple 'outstanding charges' style, the style being selectable for individual customers. Accounts with merged 'balance forward' lines maintain discrete individual transactions on account viewing, for audit ability, research, and payment allocation.
- Separate 'close' dates are supported for invoice entry versus payment entry, allowing invoicing for a particular posting date to close while clerks responsible for processing payments for that date may continue to work.
- Optional overdue messages can be generated to appear on statements, with text adjusted for the customer's language and graded by overdue severity.
- Promotional and sales messages can appear on statements, customized to the customer's language and targeted to reflect the proximity of the customer's location to the hotel.

Account Management Highlights

- Ledger inquiry system, including ability to enter and review, for any account, an unlimited history of comments on account or collection activity, and the ability to set trace dates for followup actions.
- Support for parent-child relationships between accounts, optionally reflected in invoicing, statements, and/or trial balances and aging.
- Credit limits can be established for individual customers, with appropriate warnings at posting.
- Customer accounts can be closed to new postings, while maintaining a balance and accepting payments.
- Powerful inquiry capabilities provide relevant up-to-date information. You can see a summary aging of any account, with payment, sales and payment history on one consolidated screen.
- Multiple customer home currencies supported.
- Multiple customer languages supported.
- Support for high-inflation, low value local currency – complex reports adjust to sacrifice descriptive text to show full amounts.

- Automatic write-offs for small balances, tracked in user-defined charge codes.
- Support for non-calendar-month aging reports, for 13 period sites or fiscal periods that have different number of days to calendar months.
- Aging and trial balances include two levels of subtotalling: individual account types, and account groups containing one or more account types.

Club System Highlights

- Integrated membership, club system with flexibly configured automatic dues charging.
- Support for automatic periodic charges, such as tenant rents.
- Detailed reporting on club member performance, spending patterns, and account status.
- Find out what facilities are used or not used by a club member.
- Design the Club Member report to meet your requirements without the use of a programmer or software engineer.

Mailing System Highlights

- Create separate mailing lists as required, quickly and easily.
- Receivable accounts may be included in mailings or not.
- Mail merge is supported for both promotional and collection letters.
- Powerful interface to Microsoft Word can be used to customize and automatically produce collection letters (dunning notices). The interface can also be used to produce personalized promotion letter or fliers.

General Highlights

- Automatic assignment of overdue finance charges, with the option to exempt certain customers, or only apply to certain customer types.
- Support for collecdion agency assignment and reporting.
- Produce detailed problem account reports and lists of accounts that require followup.
- Produce sales analysis reports and automatically rank accounts with respect to sales volume and payment frequency.

- Produce detailed and summary trial balances.
- Produce complete and accurate detailed and summary aging reports.
- With more than 300 parameters, you may define the operational methodology desired for the operation.
- The system is designed to operate on an international level.
- Design your invoices and statements to meet company and local regulations.
- Invoices and statements may be produced in different currencies.
- Information (such as account details, balances, etc.) may be easily exported to any ODBC (Open Database Connectivity) compliant client (such as, Microsoft Word, Excel, Access, Crystal Report Writer, etc.)

Powerful search/lookup capabilities are incorporated into almost every function. You can easily find accqunts without knowing the account number. Searches can be performed using the individual's name, the company name, the outstanding balance, the account number, and so on. Payment codes, currency codes, language codes, etc. need not be memorized. A mouse click conveniently displays all relevant information.

The Universal Inventory Solution

Acom with affiliate GoldenBlue Hospitality now offers the Universal Inventory Solution uniquely suited for your needs.

The Universal Inventory Solution allows you to minimize your investment in stock without losing revenue or efficiency. It accurately tracks all Food, Beverage, Operating Equipment, General Supplies and Engineering items and their costs:

- The Universal Inventory Solution was designed by inventory professionals and training coordinators from the hospitality industry.
- The Universal Inventory Solution tailors itself to suit specific needs by using over 200 user-defined parameters.
- The Universal Inventory Solution provides for all of your inventories – Food and Beverage, Operating Equipment, Engineering and General Storeroom.
- The Universal Inventory Solution may be used independently or may be fully integrated with our companion packages.

- The Universal Inventory Solution has total procedural and programming support provided by the software support team.
- Multiple companies may concurrently use The Universal Inventory Solution. Each company may have any number of inventories.
- Personnel are authorized to access only specific programmes. For example, the storeroom clerk may only post transactions and only the manager may close physicals.
- Inventory levels, prices, and statistics are immediately updated to provide instant, up-to-date information.
- Each location maintains, for each stock, a defined cost and/ or an average cost based on the cost of goods bought or requisitioned.
- Each location maintains restocking points and economic order quantities for each stock. The restocking algorithm and frequency of restocking is variable for each location and each stock.
- Each location maintains separate selling prices for stocks sold as is. For example, a shot of scotch may be $2.50 in a bar and $3.75 in the dining room.
- Each location maintains, for each stock, information on purchases, transfers, requisitions, sales, adjustments, shrinkage, and returns to the storeroom. Information is available on week-to-date, month-to-date, last-physical-to-date, and year-to-date bases.
- Each location maintains, for each stock, unlimited purchase history, purchase budget and consumption history.
- The details of each transaction such as quantities, units, source location, destination location, requisition number and value, may be kept for up to three years immediate retrieval. There is unlimited off-line retrieval.
- Each stock maintains ordering information—frequency, order points, tax and shipping costs, approved vendors, and levels at which to seek quotes—as well as current contracts and scheduled deliveries.
- Each stock has a standard price and allowed price variation to control purchase prices.

- Each stock has model prices to forecast the cost of future requirements.
- Purchase entry is controlled to prevent double posting of invoices or receipts.
- Purchases may be expensed to the current general ledger period or to a future general ledger period. This allows uninterrupted daily posting even if a previous general ledger period has not been closed. Such a situation regularly occurs at year-end when external auditors have not yet closed the fiscal year.
- Goods received without invoice are accepted. Estimated costs are determined and later adjusted when Accounts Payable receives the invoice.
- Direct deliveries to all locations are allowed.
- Tax, shipping costs, duty fees, etc. may be manually entered or automatically pro-rated throughout the purchasing process.
- Requisitions may be charged to the current general ledger period or to any future period.
- The name of the employee accepting a requisition is reported.
- Miscellaneous stock requests may be entered for memo purposes only.
- Information on quantities requested is kept as well as information on quantities actually received.
- The frequency of the physical count is variable from stock to stock at each location. Daily operations are in no way affected by the taking of physicals.
- Variances are reported in units, in dollars and as functions of turnovers such as covers served, room nights, or per $100 of item revenue.
- Unlimited spot-checks may be taken between full physicals to control operations. Spot-checks do not affect full physicals.
- Unlimited number of storerooms, locations, and consuming units are allowed.
- Unlimited stock groups (meats, wines, beers) and stock classes (perishable, non-consumable) are allowed.
- Unlimited stock units are allowed. Automatic conversion of units allows posting of stocks in the most convenient units at each location. The stock may be

received in cases, distributed in bottles and consumed in ounces or tenths.

- Unlimited selling prices and codes are allowed. For example, the cost of soft drinks may be raised from 45 cents to 50 cents with only one entry.
- Unlimited slow moving classifications are allowed. Meaningful slow moving and fast moving reports are produced, as slow moving criteria are selectable for each stock at each location.
- General ledger numbers to be expensed are automatically reported whether or not the companion General Ledger package is available.
- Accounts payable purchases and goods received without invoice are reported with full distributions whether or not the companion Accounts Payable package is available.
- When invoices for goods received without invoice are received, inventory costs are adjusted if the companion Accounts Payable package is available.
- Complete audit reports, with sequential page numbering between reports, provide a clear accounting trail separately for each inventory.
- All reports and updates may be scheduled to start processing at a specific time during the current day or the next day.
- All reports may be printed on any printer. They may be printed on any size paper - reducing paper costs.
- All documentation is available in computer readable format allowing the user to modify and print it on premises.

The Universal Fixed Assets Solution

The Universal Fixed Assets Solution accurately tracks all your fixed assets. It calculates depreciation using a variety of formulae. It is tightly integrated with both Accounts Payable and General Ledger.

Keeping track of your fixed assets becomes straight forward with the use of the Fixed Asset Solution. You save time and can focus your efforts on your business.

Key Benefits

- Improve the overall handling of your fixed assets.
- Improve management of fixed asset maintenance

- See an immediate overview of your fixed assets
- Select applicable depreciation formula
- Categorize (group) your assets according to your needs
- More than 300 user defined parameters make the system flexible to handle all needs irrespective of location.
- Interface to Microsoft Office products

Simple Solutions

With the Fixed Asset Solution, you no longer have to spend great amounts of time, money and effort organizing, managing and accounting for your company's fixed assets. You save time and can focus your efforts on your business.

With Fixed Asset Solution, you always know the current status on all your fixed assets. That is because Fixed Assets gives you a real-time, accurate overview of all your fixed assets. You always know your book value and your accumulated depreciation. What is more, integration to A/P and G/L means that you can easily reconcile your fixed assets to your general ledger.

Integration of fixed assets with other applications, such as General Ledger and Accounts Payable, reduces the risk of human error because you do not have to enter data in several different application areas.

You can track your fixed assets, based on a number of criteria, specified by you. For example, you can track an asset by location. This makes it easier for your auditor to verify your fixed assets. Fixed Assets can be categorized in a variety of ways within a location allowing you to be as detailed as required. Through the use of Groups, and Classes the Fixed Asset Solution makes your reporting and analysis easier and relevant.

Managing and maintaining your fixed assets does not have to cost you more time, money and effort than necessary. With Fixed Assets, when you purchase, depreciate or sell a fixed asset, the relevant application areas in your Acom solutions are updated in just one posting.

It is also easy to make different reports for different purposes. You can post fixed asset transactions and generate various reports and statistics. You save time, money and effort.

Most fixed assets depreciate in value from the day purchased. But it is often difficult to know by how much. Fixed Asset Solution gives you an overview of the accumulated depreciation on your fixed assets.

That is because the Fixed Asset Solution functionality gives you several standard depreciation methods, which are user-defined. You choose the method and the frequency according to your needs. The decision is yours.

The Universal Purchasing Solution

Acom with affiliate GoldenBlue Hospitality now offers the Universal Purchasing Solution uniquely suited for your needs.

The Universal Purchasing Solution completes the material management order cycle, exercising controls from the order point to the consumption stage. It can be configured for integrated support of both local property Purchasing Offices and centralized ones.

The Universal Purchasing Solution proves itself every day at both typical and the largest of F&B operations. We can guarantee the reliability of its data and the auditability of its results, in even the most active of environments.

The Universal Purchasing Solution automatically handles order points and finds the best prices for all Food, Beverage, Operating Equipment, General Supplies, and Engineering items. It quickly and efficiently handles the ordering of Market List items.

Purchasing Managers can override automatic ordering and enter their own manual purchase orders. With predefined market lists, the chef need only decide what changes to make each day. Variations from the best price are identified in exception reports. Powerful inquiries provide a comprehensive vendor, purchase, and quantity history at a glance in multiple levels of detail.

The Universal Purchasing Solution is bi-directionally tightly integrated with The Universal Inventory Solution and The Universal Accounting Solution's Accounts Payable and General Ledger. Data is entered once and only once, with checks and balances along the way.

As an example of the integration, The Universal Purchasing Solution checks the restocking points of items in The Universal Inventory Solution and generates purchase orders for approval based on the reorder quantities. Once approved these commitments are reflected in the General Ledger. When the goods arrive, the receipts are posted in Inventory and automatically reflected in Purchasing.

The General Ledger is automatically updated with the authorized purchase order costs, and a proforma invoice is passed to Accounts Payable. When the actual invoice arrives, Accounts Payable posts adjustments to this proforma. The Purchasing, Inventory, and General Ledger figures are automatically updated to reflect any variances between the authorized and actual costs. Should shipment or brokerage costs arrive at a later time, they are also posted in Accounts Payable, resulting in further automatic cost allocations among the items in Purchasing, Inventory, and General Ledger.

Such integration greatly reduces the clerical workload, increases the reliability of the figures, improves the auditability of the system, and improves the control of operations.

The Universal Purchasing Solution is also ideal for centralized purchasing for one city, a local region, or an area. It allows for some groups of items to be ordered locally, while others are handled regionally.

The Universal Purchasing Solution automatically integrates with the local Inventory Solutions running at each property. It supports multiple purchasing offices, multiple properties, and multiple distribution centres.

The Universal Purchasing Solution completes the material management order cycle, exercising controls from the order point to the consumption stage. It automatically handles order points and finds best prices for all Food, Beverage, Operating Equipment, General Supplies, and Engineering items. It quickly and efficiently handles the ordering of Market List items.

The Universal Purchasing Solution is also ideal for centralized purchasing for one city, a local region, or an area. It allows for some groups to be ordered locally, while others are handled regionally. It automatically integrates with the local Inventory Solutions running at each property. Purchase requests may be generated in a variety of ways: manual, blanket, market lists, par level, or reapplied purchase requests.

- The purchasing agent may enter as many quotations as desired for each item, and each quotation may have varying prices depending on the order quantity.
- The system will combine the purchase requests and quotations, select the best supplier, and produce the purchase order.
- Purchase orders may also be produced manually, and may be placed verbally or printed or both.

- When the goods are received the purchase order is automatically transformed into a receiving slip or invoice.
- Purchase orders may be displayed on a screen and the quantities entered as received.
- Data is automatically transmitted to the inventory and accounting systems.
- The general ledger will automatically be updated.
- All information is retained: all purchase order details, vendor performance statistics, and comparative quotation information.
- Par level analysis and order frequency statistics are provided.

The Universal Menu Engineering Solution

Acom with affiliate GoldenBlue Hospitality now offers the Universal Menu Engineering Solution uniquely suited for your needs.

The Universal Menu Engineering Solution does more than exploding menu items to their ingredients and determining the potential cost of sales. It serves as an invaluable tool for food and beverage management in analyzing and evaluating menus and their performance.

- The recipe subsystem allows detailed recipe and preparation information to be entered, produced as recipe cards, cataloged and costed based on the costs in The Universal Inventory Solution.
- Sales data may be automatically extracted from various types of point of sale systems, along with financial settlement information. The sales may be exploded back to the recipe ingredients.
- Thorough analysis is available, including comparison of actual vs. potential costs, profitability of items, turnover rate of items, the Donald Smith and Michael Kasavana analysis (plowhorses, stars, puzzles and dogs), the Miller analysis (winners, marginals and losers), the Pavesic analysis (standard, sleeper and problem), and the Hayes analysis (above and below goal).

The Universal Menu Engineering Solution, used in conjunction with the MICROS system, produces Menu Analysis based on various formulas and generates requisitions, sales, transfers and production requests in the Inventory system in order to reflect the sales and decrease the physical inventory of all ingredients used.

The Universal Menu Engineering Solution can also be used by manually entering actual sales or sales forecast. This feature is useful when designing new menu lists.

The use of the Universal Menu Engineering Solution makes menu analysis a straight forward and easy task. Compare sales volumes to contribution margin; or sales volume to food cost percentage; or weighted contribution margin to food cost percentage simply by pressing a function key or a click of the mouse.

You have many tools available to determine a menus strengths and weaknesses, to maximize your profit and minimize your costs. The Universal Menu Engineering Solution is an integral part of this process, providing up-to-date and accurate information to ensure your analysis is relevant and accurate.

PM HOSPITALITY

PM Hospitality Strategies

About The Company

PM Hospitality Strategies, Inc. [pmHS] is dedicated to managing assets in a manner which will optimize durable financial returns. Its hands-on founders oversee all aspects of the day-to-day operations emphasizing marketing, employee development, and cost effective operations for each hotel.

pmHS was launched in 1995 providing pre-opening management services for a 131-room middle-market hotel in Fairfax County, Virginia. In addition to consulting/technical services, the principals of pmHS acted as the General Contractor during construction. Following on the heels of its successful completion, pmHS retained the on-going management function and immediately launched its second pre-opening project for a 140-suite hotel in Anne Arundel County, Maryland (between Baltimore and Annapolis). This successful project was immediately followed by a third management contract for a to-be-renovated/ repositioned hotel project located on Washington DC's beltway.

Management Capabilities

Overview

As a relative new comer to the professional hotel management scene, pmHS has already demonstrated its ability to successfully add value to the assets it oversees. That success is a direct result of the experience of its founders and senior officers.

- Organizations and Certifications
- Key Players
- Well Managed Projects
- Value Added Features
- Proprietary Systems
- Tactics/Methods

Organizations and Certifications

As a relative new comer to the professional hotel management scene, pmHS has already demonstrated its ability to successfully add value to the assets it oversees. That success is a direct result of the experience of its founders and senior officers. The following is a list of industry professional memberships, degrees and certifications attained by pmHS professionals.

Professional Memberships

- Cornell Society of Hotelmen
- Hospitality Financial and Technology Professionals
- Hotel Sales and Marketing Association International
- Virginia Hospitality and Travel Association
- Maryland Hotel and Motel Association
- Maryland Tourism Council
- Baltimore CVA
- Fairfax County CVB
- Prince William County CVB
- National Tour Association

Key Players

With 20 years already dedicated to the industry, COO Greg Miller's credentials, exposure and experience proves effective in directing the pmHS team of professionals. Greg's background encompasses serving on the management team for two of this country's finest resorts, Camelback Inn - Scottsdale, AZ and Arizona Biltmore - Phoenix, AZ, both long-standing winners of the coveted Mobil 5-star award; managing two Travel Holiday Award winning restaurant operations; consulting on over 200 hotel development, acquisition and management projects with a combined valued at over one billion dollars, and hotel developer for the world's largest hotel company - Bass Hotels & Resorts.

With 28 years of management experience, Director of Facilities Jim Lowe capably implements the engineering, maintenance, security and life-safety programmes. Having built an illustrious career with Nordstrom, his exposure to customer service philosophies and the "Nordstrom Experience" blends very favourably to the principals.

Well-Managed Projects

In the short period of time since its inception, PMHS has organized and staffed several newly built hotels, reorganized a hotel that was not operating successfully and renovated / repositioned a hotel in a good market with a sub-standard product.

We evaluate the success upon the following criteria:

Administration

- labour / staffing controls in place... emphasis on productivity improvements
- implementing effective job descriptions, policies and procedure manuals
- using technology to the best advantage

Marketing

- identifying target market and competition
- positioning product and develop strategies
- developing a plan to maximize near-term penetration
- putting in-place accountability to hit sales targets
- generating same store profit increases

Value Added Features

We provide our clients with carefully developed systems and quality products throughout the Mid-Atlantic Region.

- Marketing
- Sales
- Accounting
- Case Study
- Financial Modelling
- Employee Leasing
- Insurance

Marketing

Assisted by the Regional Revenue Manager, the Managing Director is responsible for allocating the marketing dollars, analyzing the tracking reports with sales, implementing promotional programmes, placing publication listings, coordinating all the collateral material, writing and reviewing the marketing plans, submitting press releases, and placing cost-effective advertising.

Our marketing effort engages us in a constant research process leading to strategic marketing plans that are put in place for each property in the portfolio. Our effort does not conclude, however, with simply uncovering trends and creating plans. Too often hotel companies do not react to opportunities because they cannot implement and/or are unable to mobilize into action. At pmHS, we quickly seize on the opportunity. Every good campaign responds to customers needs/wants and then is executed with passion.

Sales

The sales department works locally, regionally and nationally. A major emphasis is placed on identifying and working hard to make a difference during slower periods. In order to further promote sales for our properties, we send our Regional Sales Manager to major national conventions such as HSMAI, NTA and ABA regularly.

Accounting

At PMHS, we find that a coordinated, centralized accounting effort results in more accurate, informative and timely financial information. You will appreciate the lower administrative payroll costs from our centralized accounting services.

The central accounting office closely monitors daily accounting reports, supervises payroll processing, prepares monthly bank reconciliations, files sales and use tax returns, pays all invoices and manages hotel cash.

To assure both a high degree of operating efficiency and administrative accuracy, audits are regularly conducted. Every week, our controller reviews the accuracy of daily reports, an accounting of payables and receivables. At least once each month, a thorough inspection of the physical property along with a complete examination of the hotel's cash handling and reporting methods is accomplished. Twice each year, a check of all employment records and a detailed analysis of all front office and administrative procedures is completed.

Both monthly and quarterly reports are prepared for ownership. These reports are an analysis of past and projected performance. The monthly financial statements include balance sheets, cash flow statements and income statements.

A quarterly "Feedback Review and Update" report is prepared to show and explain deviations in the income statement from the budget, personnel changes, market conditions, sales updates and capital improvement expenditures.

Financial Modelling

1. Use zero-based budgeting effectively.
2. Identify and allocate hidden costs.
3. Use information from marketing research to provide sales volume.
4. Estimate revenue and expenses for full year.
5. Fixed variable
6. Manage inventory receivables and fixed assets.
7. Troubleshoot with ratio analysis.

Employee Leasing

Through an important new relationship with a professional employment organization (PEO), pmHS has obtained significant labour cost savings while simultaneously providing Fortune 500 benefits to its associates. Under a PEO agreement, a hotel is able to enlist a team of professionals to assist in human resource responsibilities while retaining full operational control over its employees.

Most notable in cost reduction is extremely competitive pricing in the workers compensation and group health insurance areas. By combining the employees of hundreds of smaller companies in a region under a single umbrella organization, the PEO is able to generate significant savings on workers compensation and group health costs. Through its PEO, pmHS can offer a comprehensive package of employee benefits and still deliver a guaranteed savings of 20 per cent of workers compensation costs to its hotel clients.

Insurance

By signing a management agreement with pmHS, a hotel becomes eligible to participate in the Group's property and casualty insurance programme and the savings can be significant. Through pmHS's programme, annual insurance costs can be dramatically trimmed while improving the overall coverage. Very competitive rates are available to new hotel clients that do not possess unusual risk characteristics.

Proprietary Systems

Three Essential Goals of pmHS Include

- Manage assets in a manner which will optimize durable financial returns.
- Cultivate a dedicated team of skilled employees taking pride in their work and who are aware of the importance of repeat customers.
- Perpetuate a virtuous cycle wherein satisfied employees contribute to employee retention which delivers customer loyalty and enhances each hotel's profitability.

Satisfied and Motivated Employees

Our philosophy as it relates to people is that of helping them to be all that they can be. We understand that our employees must believe in themselves and in the product and service that we provide. Once this is accomplished, the rest is easy. Make no mistake, however, getting employees to believe in themselves and in our systems takes work—constantly addressing their motivation, soliciting feedback, and implementing new techniques/strategies that result in performance improvement.

GLOBAL HOSPITALITY RESOURCES, INC.

Established in 1986, Global Hospitality Resources®, Inc. (GHR), is a leading, international hospitality research and publishing firm headquartered in San Diego, CA. GHR is a pioneer and leader in Internet-based publishing and marketing. The firm created and publishes the industry-acclaimed, Internet delivered GlobalHotelNetwork.com e-Newsletter and the research-based "market intelligence focused" GlobalHotelNetwork.com Web Site. Global Hotel Network® Sponsors include over 25 leading tourism organizations and academic institutions from every region of the world. GHR is a Sponsor, Supporter, and Allied Partner of many industry conferences around the world, and is a member of the WTO Panel of Tourism Experts.

Donald E. Stephenson is an international hotelier with more than 35 years experience. Prior to co-founding Global Hospitality Resources®, Inc., he was Executive Vice President and a member of the Board of Directors of ITT Sheraton Corporation. Stephenson holds a B.S. in business administration and a law degree from the University of Kansas.

Robert G. Harp, CCIM, has specialized in the hospitality industry since 1987. He serves on the Programme Steering Committee for the Americas Lodging Investment Summit (ALIS) and the Hotel Investment Conference Asia Pacific (HICAP). Harp is Programme Chair for the annual San Diego Hospitality Industry Outlook and a member of the San Diego Civic Solutions Committee. He also serves as an article reviewer for the Cornell Quarterly. Harp is a Certified Commercial Investment Member (CCIM) and a past president of the San Diego CCIM Chapter. He is a founder and past president of the Commercial Realtors Association, San Diego County. Harp holds a B.A. in economics from Wheaton College (IL), a M.A. in communications from Wheaton Graduate School (IL), & a Th.M. degree from DTS (TX).

The Firm

Global Hospitality Resources, Inc.

- Publishes the fee-based GlobalHotelNetwork.com e-Newsletter, the #1 e-Newsletter in the global hospitality industry;
- Publishes the GlobalHotelNetwork.com website, one of the industry's best research-based websites;
- Conducts hospitality industry studies relating to the growth and development objectives of global and regional hotel chains - for every region of the world;
- Tracks hotel sales, mergers and acquisitions worldwide;
- Conducts Global Hotel Network® Custom Research.

Global Hotel Network® Sponsors Include

- ABIH Nacional—Brazilian Hotel Association
- American Hotel and Lodging Association (AH&LA)
- American Resort Development Association (ARDA)
- Asian American Hotel Owners Association (AAHOA)
- British Hospitality Association (BHA)
- Caribbean Hotel Association (CHA)

- Conrad N. Hilton College of Hotel and Restaurant Management at the University of Houston
- Cornell's Centre for Hospitality Research (Cornell)
- Embratur
- Federation of Hotel and Restaurant Associations of India
- Hong Kong Hotels Association
- Hospitality Financial and Technology Professionals (HFTP)
- Hospitality Sales and Marketing Association International (HSMAI)
- Hotel Association of Canada (HAC)
- Hotel Association of India (HAI)
- International Association of Convention and Visitor Bureaus (IACVB)
- International Congress and Convention Association (ICCA)
- International Hotel and Restaurant Association (IH&RA)
- International Society of Hospitality Consultants (ISHC)
- Johnson and Wales University (J&W)
- Mexico Tourism Board
- New York University's (NYU's) Preston Robert Tisch Centre for Hospitality, Tourism and Sports Management
- Pacific Asia Travel Association (PATA)
- Travel Business Roundtable (TBR)
- Travel Industry Association of America (TIA)
- World Tourism Organization (WTO)
- World Travel and Tourism Council (WTTC)

Global Hospitality Resources®, Inc., serves as a Sponsor, Supporter, and Allied Partner of many industry conferences around the world. The firm is a Sponsor of such conferences as: Americas Lodging Investment Summit (ALIS), the Hotel Investment Conference Asia Pacific (HICAP), the Caribbean Hotel and Tourism Investment Conference (CHTIC), Arabian Hotel Investment Conference (AHIC), The Lodging Conference (Phoenix), Euromoney's European Hotel Finance and Investment Summit (London), Meet the Money (Los Angeles), The International Hotel Conference (Monaco), International Hotel and Resort Investment Seminar (Brazil), IH&RA's annual Congress, and a Supporter of WTTC's Global Travel and Tourism Summit. The firm is also an Allied Partner of HITEC, hosted by the

Hospitality Financial and Technology Professionals (HFTP), and serves on the WTO Panel of Tourism Experts.

In addition to its research and publishing activities, Global Hospitality Resources®, Inc., co-founded in 1994 and annually organizes the San Diego Hospitality Industry Outlook which is hosted by the San Diego CCIM Chapter and annually sponsored by the San Diego Convention and Visitors Bureau, the San Diego Daily Transcript and Global Hospitality Resources®, Inc.

Global Hotel Network Market Intelligence Library

The Member Section of the research-based www.GlobalHotelNetwork.com website houses the Global Hotel Network® Market Intelligence Library featuring:

- Global Hotel Network® CITY REPORTS: The GHN City Report provides insight into hospitality market conditions for a selected city around the world. Each report is written by an advisor with expertise of that region.
- Global Hotel Network® SPECIAL REPORTS: The GHN Special Report analyzes specific industry issues or presents insights on regional market conditions.
- Global Hotel Network® EXECUTIVE PROFILES: The GHN Executive Profile features an executive's perspective on industry issues/corporate plans
- Global Hotel Network® TRANSACTION REPORT: The GHN Transaction Report summarizes selected mergers, acquisitions, and hotel transactions from around the world—as reported by leading industry sources.
- Global Hotel Network® NEWS DESK: The GHN News Desk features important news stories in the World of Global Hospitality®.

Global Hotel Network® #1 e-Newsletter

Global Hospitality Resources®, Inc., provides decision makers in the hospitality industry with important news and market intelligence via the industry-acclaimed. Internet delivered GlobalHotelNetwork.com e-Newsletter and the research-based, "market intelligence" focused, GlobalHotelNetwork.com website.

The firm specializes in tracking hotel markets worldwide, profiling chief executives and companies, and reporting on hotel sales, development news, and selected industry trends.

The GlobalHotelNetwork.com e-Newsletter is the #1 e-Newsletter in the global hospitality industry, designed exclusively for:

- Executives of hotel management, franchise, referral, reservation and time share companies;
- Hotel and resort owners, investors, developers, financiers;
- Hospitality advisors, brokers, analysts, attorneys;
- Officers of tourism associations and government offices;
- Service providers to the hospitality and travel industry;
- Restaurateurs, food, beverage and equipment suppliers;
- Airlines, travel agencies, industry suppliers, architects, credit card issuers, technology companies;
- Public relations and advertising agencies;
- Global, regional and local media sources;
- Academic institutions.

THE CENTRE FOR HOSPITALITY RESEARCH

For over 70 years the School of Hotel Administration at Cornell University has served the hospitality industry through its commitment to timely research. In 1992 the Hotel School embarked on a new chapter of this tradition by creating The Centre for Hospitality Research (CHR). The Centre was designed as a forum in which scholars and industry professionals can work together in pursuit of common research goals.

Tools for the Hospitality Industry

The CHR plans to release a variety of tools for use by the hospitality industry. All of these tools may be used without charge for a 90-day period. Should you wish to use a tool for more than 90 days, there is a modest charge, which varies by tool. We expect to release a new tool approximately every two months, so check back often.

Emergency Preparedness Essentials

Developed by Professor Robert Kwortnik.

This tool provides a checklist to help hotel managers prepare for the loss of electrical power, whether in a natural disaster or by failure of the power grid.

Mega Tips: Scientifically Tested Techniques to Increase Your Tips

Developed by Professor Michael Lynn

This booklet for servers provides instruction in the psychology of tipping as well as specific techniques that can be used to earn larger tips. All the suggested techniques have been scientifically tested and the evidence of their effectiveness is described along with the techniques. Using even a few of these techniques should increase servers' tips by 10 to 30 per cent.

Managers are free to download the file, print out the manual, make hard copies of it, and either post it on employee bulletin boards or distribute copies directly to their servers.

Managers who distribute the manual to their servers should benefit from:

1. Increased sales
2. Greater Customer Satisfaction
3. Lower labour costs due to reduced server turnover

Turnover Cost Evaluator [Web Application]

Developed by Professors Tim Hinkin and Bruce Tracey

This tool, a web application, is an excellent tool for understanding the direct and indirect costs associated with turnover. This tool allows users to identify how much they are spending to replace line, managerial, and executive staff. If the costs of turnover are better-understood, then more effective strategies can be developed to reverse the negative effects of this endemic problem.

Hospitality Valuation Software

Developed by Stephen Rushmore, CRE, MAI, CHA and Jan deRoos, Ph.D. Stephen Rushmore is Founder and President of HVS International, a corporate partner of the CHR. Jan deRoos is HVS International Professor of Hotel Finance and Real Estate in the School of Hotel Administration at Cornell University. This tool is provided through the generosity of HVS International.

The Hospitality Valuation Software is the only non-proprietary computer software designed specifically to assist in the preparation of market studies, forecasts of income and expense, and valuations for lodging property. The software provides an accurate, consistent, and cost-effective way for hospitality professionals to forecast occupancy, revenues and expenses and to perform hotel valuations. Using established methodology, the Hospitality Valuation Software is a sophisticated tool for lodging professionals. The tool consists of three separate software programmes written as Microsoft Excel files and a software users' guide. The three programmes are:

Room Night Analysis

- Enables the appraiser to evaluate the various competitive factors such as occupancy, average room rate, and market segmentation of all hotels in a local market.
- Calculates the area-wide occupancy and average room rate, as well as the competitive market mix.
- Produce a forecast of occupancy for each existing hotel or proposed hotel in a local market. The programme incorporates such factors as competitive occupancies, market segmentation, unaccommodated demand, latent demand, growth of demand, and the relative competitiveness of each property in the local market. The programme output is a ten-year projection of occupancy.

Fixed and Variable Revenue and Expense Analysis

- The key to any market study and valuation is a supportable forecast of revenues and expenses. Hotel revenue and expenses are comprised of many different components that display certain fixed and variable relationships to each other. This programme enables the appraiser to input comparable financial operating data and forecast a complete 11-year income and expense statement by defining a small set of inputs.
- The expected future occupancy levels for the subject hotel.
- Base year operating data for the subject hotel.
- Expected inflation rates for revenues and expenses.

Hotel Capitalization Software

- A discounted cash flow valuation model utilizing the mortgage-equity technique forms the basis for this programme. Values are produced under two different binding constraints:
  - A loan-to-value ratio, in which the size of the mortgage is based on property value.

   - A debt coverage ratio (also known as a debt-service coverage ratio), in which the size of the mortgage is based on property level cash flow.
- By entering the terms of typical lodging financing, along with the ten-year forecast of revenue and expense, the programme determines the value that provides the stated returns to the mortgage and equity components.

HOSPITALITY ACCOUNTING SERVICES, INC.

Hospitality Accounting Services is a multi-faceted company that provides , data archiving and report automation systems and hotel information systems consulting. It is Hospitality Accounting Services's goal to provide services that enhance the accuracy and efficiency of hospitality information systems and will create a positive, long-term financial impact. The accounting, bookkeeping, internal control auditing, contracted controller solutions, and Expert Witnessing. Our consulting services provide experienced hospitality specialists who will add value to your accounting process with revenue enhancement and cost containment recommendations.

Outsourcing hotel accounting functions has been a standard practice with the evolution external companies processing hotel payrolls. Today, the advantages with outsourcing hotel accounting functions are becoming more apparent. Hospitality Accounting Services, Inc's clients range from International full-service hotels, resorts, as well limited-service hotel management companies. We are able to customize our services to meet your needs. We specialize in the hotel internal audit process and adding expertise and value to the accounting process.

Hospitality Accounting Services, Inc. takes pride in our mission statement that "Hospitality Accounting Services, Inc. provides professional hotel accounting services that increase expertise and value to our clients' accounting process and is the hotel industry's premier accounting service."

- Our services provide the hospitality accounting expertise to perform hotel accounting and internal control audits.
- Consulting services providing expertise to maximize hotel business systems efficiency and effectiveness.
- Consulting services to assist in fraud and embezzlement situations.

- Consulting services to determine revenue enhancements and cost containment opportunities.
- Software systems consulting ranging from cost effective archiving (storage) of data, report automation, report data mining capabilities, and business intelligence systems.

Hospitality Accounting Services, Inc. presents attractive alternatives to hotel owners and hotel management companies. We believe, our hotel accounting staff combined with today's technology offers reliable expertise and cost savings opportunities. Today, technology advances have successfully afforded other businesses an opportunity to concentrate on their core services. The hospitality industry trends are similiar. Hotels are automating or outsourcing administrative tasks and focusing on their major areas of concern: service, product, and guest satisfaction. The opportunity to gain expertise in the accounting process and minimize the software, hardware, and staffing costs make our accounting options a "win-win" solution for the hotel industry.

The goal of Hospitality Accounting Services, Inc. is to be the premier accounting service provider in the hospitality industry. The accounting services that we provide will be both cost effective and offer a level of expertise that will add value to your accounting process.

Please allow us to provide positive alternatives for your future accounting and business systems needs.

Services: Audit Outline

1. Executive review
2. Cash - general ledger
3. Accounts receivable
4. Other assets
5. Accounts payable
6. Tax liabilities
7. Payroll liabilities
8. Auditing
9. Purchasing
10. Receiving
11. Storeroom
12. Payroll

13. Security
14. General comments

Systems

Hospitality Accounting Services, Inc. would like to share several systems links that specialize in accounting and hospitality services respectively. We would encourage you to use this site as a systems resource link to research the options presently available.

- Accounting Systems - AccountingNet
- Accounting Systems - Excelco
- Archiving and Report Automation Systems (R.A.S.) - DB Technology, Inc.
- Data Mining Siftware - KD Nuggets
- Hospitality Systems - Hospitality Index
- Intelligence Systems - G6G Directory of Intelligent Software
- OLAP SYSTEMS- Alta Plana
- Hardware, Software, and Operating Systems -The Ultimate Industry Connection - James Lumber and Ace Hardware
- Hardware Systems - Tom's Hardware Guide
- Software Systems - Accounting Top 100 Software Products-1998-Accounting Today
- Year 2000 Systems - Year 2000 Info Centre

Professional/Consulting Services: Hotel Accounting, Internal Control Auditing, and Business Information Systems

The archiving and report automation system services offer cost effective approaches leading to business intelligence systems that strategically utilizes archived information. The archiving system, Report Automation System (R.A.S.), provides a short-term pay back period with future annual savings. In addition, R.A.S. software provides the unique technology enabling a host computer to archive information from different hotel systems (i.e. PMS, POS, Payroll, Catering & Sales, Human Resources, Telephone, Engineering, and back office Accounting) and reformat new reports from the archived data. These newly formatted reports would be automated and could be sent to remote sites via e-mail, internet, or company WAN. R.A.S. can be upgraded to interface with multi-dimensional tools to create an Business Intelligence System. Overall, the R.A.S. technology allows a hotel or hotel company to cost justify upgrading their information systems by investing in a cost saving strategy that offers a "win-win" opportunity.

Accounting Services

- Our services provide the hospitality accounting expertise to perform accounting and internal control audits.

Consulting Services

- Consulting services providing expertise to maximize hotel business systems efficiency and effectiveness.
- Consulting services to minimize fraud, theft, or embezzlement of funds.
- Consulting services to determine revenue enhancements and cost containment opportunities.
- Software systems consulting ranging from cost effective archiving (storage) of data, report automation, report data mining capabilities, and business intelligence systems.

C.P.A. firms have demonstrated over the years that their main focus is auditing financial statements. The financial audits or reviews are necessary but expensive. Also, the level of the auditors' hospitality experience is limited and offers little practical knowledge of internal controls. The trend is to reduce the auditing scope and rely on other alternatives.

Regional Controllers and internal audit teams have been very cost efficient alternatives. The growth of our industry has increased the Regional Controller's job scope and responsibilities. The internal audit team can be a costly approach if turnover or the lack of hospitality experience minimize the potential problem-solving benefits an audit can provide. Last, but not least, it has been shown that the integrity of an in-house team performing audits has the potential of being compromised.

The goal of Hospitality Accounting Services is to be the premier accounting service provider in the hospitality industry. The auditing service that we provide will be both cost effective and offer a level of expertise that will add value to your auditing process.

WORLD OF HOSPITALITY.NET

WorldofHospitality.net aims to provide links to relevant information for event industry professionals, educators, students and researchers.

Within the Links Directory you will find a range of information, including careers, recruitment agencies, links to education programmes and a suppliers directory. For job vacancies and other career related resources, please visit the Careers/Employment section.

We have completely redesigned the site to improve the look and feel and to make it much easier to contribute links and other resources (including the ability to indicate country specific links/ resources).

WorldofHospitality.net has also moved to a new hosting company to increase the speed and performance and allow a range of new features that will be introduced over the coming months.

Please register and contribute to the development of this resource by submitting links, articles (copyright cleared of course!) and other resources.

Hotel Software

miHotel Manager is a Windows® based Hospitality Software designed for hotels/motels. It is an extensive software package specially designed to help you manage your hotel. This type of application is sometimes referred as Property Management System in the hospitality industry. The many features includes: Hotel Guest Management, Hotel Reservation Management, Hotel Front Desk and Hotel Accounting. User friendly interface, high speed and stability, client-server architecture, all these characteristics allow you to easily manage all the tasks for your hotel/motel. User Defined Fields for high flexibility, high-quality graphical representation of your rooms, real-time statistics, ... all these will help you to perform your duties faster, and with less effort.

Online Booking Manager (OBM)

The http://www.onlinebookingmanager.com">Online Booking Manager (http://www.onlinebookingmanager.com) is a unique multilingual system and a highly cost-effective method for promoting your accommodation services online. Hotels, motels, B&B, etc., who cannot afford large complex reservations systems can now successfully offer online bookings with the Online Booking Manager a low cost high performance solution for all hotels, motels, B&B owners.

Increase Bar Revenues: Probar

There are many ways for a bartender to increase revenues for his/her establishment and for him/her self. Get to know your regulars. Introduce yourself and ask them their names. If you have a hard time remembering names create a visual memory trick that will help you remember both their name and their favorite drink. I use very stark tricks connecting a name with the first letter of an animal and a visual of the animal with its drink, (i.e. Robert/Red Robin/Scarlet Ohara (Southern Comfort/Cranberry Juice -R for the first name and animal/Red for the drink color) When the customer enters ask them immediately if they would like their regular drink. They will enjoy that. Suggest some food that compliments the drink. If the drink is not top shelf suggest a more expensive top shelf substitute. Once you are a little comfortable with the customer, suggest they bring a friend. With liquor and food prices commanding excellent margins you have just created some real revenues and profits. Once your regular customer brings a friend to the bar they will stay longer and eat and drink more. Your bar is livelier and more inviting to still more customers. On top of that you are enjoying yourself more while making more money!

CADENZA HOSPITALITY GROUP

Hospitality is a Wonderful Activity. A Pity About the Rewards

One positive answer - operating a quality business involved in comfort, enjoyment and sustained customer satisfaction. Without consistent business quality, a hospitality venture will struggle to survive in the longer term, irrespective of all other considerations

AON HOSPITALITY

Making sure our hospitality clients receive quality insurance products.

Signature Service

Background

Aon Hospitality's commitment to quality service is embodied in

our Signature Service programme. A client-focused approach to our brokerage activities, Signature Service provides the internal direction to insure top quality service is provided to our clients and that office procedures are consistent with the high expectations of the corporate culture.

Signature Service Entails

Quality Professional Services (QPS)

- Formal corporate quality control programme.
- Development of underwriting specifications.
- Market analysis and presentation.
- Policy review and transmittal.
- Schedules of insurance.
- Administration of programmes.
- Review of exposures.

Client-Focused Approach

- Total quality management.
- Quality awareness training.
- Client surveys.
- Management level awareness.

Aon Hospitality Services include:

- Account Management
- Marketing
- Loss Control
- Claims Department
- Workers' Compensation Services

Aon Hospitality is dedicated to making sure our hospitality clients receive quality insurance products, risk management, and financial services. We accomplish our mission through a highly-trained and motivated professional staff which is committed to always providing client-focused quality services.

Account Management

Background

Aon Hospitality account managers are highly trained professionals with extensive experience in the insurance industry. They have authority, responsibility, and accountability for delivery of all services to our clients. Assisted by an experienced technical services team, the account manager not only coordinates services but also will assist the client in negotiating and designing insurance and risk management programmes.

Capabilities

The primary function of the account manager is to coordinate:

Services

- Work for the client's benefit.
- Foster long-term relationships.
- Coordinate and monitor all account team activities.

Stewardship Review

- What have we done over the past year?
- What will we do in the future?

Signature Service (Total Quality Management)

- Formal corporate quality control programme.

Team Approach-Coordinate with the risk management service groups, which include:

- Casualty loss control and employee safety.
- Workers' compensation.
- Property loss control.
- Marketing.
- Claims.
- Surety bonds.

Liaison with Senior Management.

Marketing

Background

Aon Hospitality has full-time marketing specialists. We are part of an organization that has a global presence and worldwide relationships which provide:

- Worldwide marketing capabilities.
- Placement with top-rated insurance companies.
- Specifications which are detailed, accurate, and attractive to the market place.

Capabilities

Our marketing specialists are an integral part of our account management team, and have experienced backgrounds in underwriting to provide the following services:

- Aggressive negotiations to find the most favourable terms and conditions and the best possible price.
- Strong and long-term relationships with markets.
- Monitoring trends in the marketplace.
- Creative marketing to develop and deliver innovative new solutions.

Loss Control

Background

The Loss Control Department of Aon Hospitality has consultants who work directly with the account manager and the client, addressing their needs in the following areas:

- Property
- Casualty
- Workers' Compensation

Capabilities

- Develop policies and programmes for loss recognition, and control.
- Create training, audits, and documentation to support targeted programmes.
- Review historical and/or recent loss data in order to identify client! industry loss trends and to create control activities to prevent reoccurrences.
- Gather information on regulatory and industry loss control standards impacting the present business environment.
- Coordinate the insurance carrier(s) service schedule to maximize management/staff time commitments in addressing company goals and objectives.
- Review and plan capital expenditures associated with long-term loss control objectives.
- Document progress on general loss issues and targeted objectives through written and graphic presentation materials.

Claims Department

Background

Aon Hospitality has a full-time claims staff with specialists devoted specifically to the discipline of property and casualty. Our knowledgeable and experienced staff has over 15 years experience in handling claims. This experience and knowledge is essential in our role as facilitator, expeditor, and mediator in the management of our clients' claims.

Capabilities

- Assist the policyholder in all aspects of the claims process, from the initial loss to the final settlement.
- Establish a claims file for every policyholder loss, notify the proper carriers, and monitor the adjustment process.
- Act as a liaison between the policyholder and carrier while evaluating the coverage issues and possible liability exposures.
- Prepare loss runs for policyholders to include claims status and reserves.
- Submit timely reports and analyze coverage when policyholders are served with lawsuits.
- On large losses, Aon Hospitality personnel visit the loss site to work with the policyholder and insurance adjustor in determining the scope of damage, repairs, possible business interruptions, and resolve any coverage issues.
- Assist in bringing all first-party and third-party claims to a timely settlement.
- The claims department works closely with our engineering and safety consultants in a claims situation where loss investigation and analysis are important to the negotiations with insurers and to the development of future loss prevention programmes.

Workers' Compensation Services

Background

Workers' Compensation at Aon Hospitality is one of our greatest strengths. Our account executives and consultants are highly trained in a wide variety of industry segments specializing solely in workers' compensation coverage. With the help of well-trained technical support, we have been able to customize programmes for clients throughout the United States.

Capabilities

An account executive, claims consultant, and loss control consultant are assigned to each account to provide the following services:

- Insurance marketing to obtain the most cost-effective programme.
- Evaluation and analysis of competitive plans.
- Review of policy and experience ratings to ensure accuracy.
- Analysis and premium projection for budgetary planning.
- Future cost projections for retrospective rating plans.
- Review of audits and retro adjustments.
- Monitoring and analysis of loss reports.
- Claims reviews with the insurance company to fit your objectives.
- Assisting in mediating claims disputes.
- Conduct a unit review prior to submission for rating and retro purposes.
- Project new experience modification.
- Monitoring of legislative developments.
- Monitoring of legal decisions affecting benefits and coverage.
- Assist in the development of a programme to meet each company's workers' compensation objectives.

HOSPITALITY SAFEGUARDS, INC.

About Us

Earl J. Bleser, CFE, established HOSPITALITY SAFEGUARDS, INC. in 1988 to assist and guide industry professionals in solving accounting, operational and loss prevention problems. Mr. Bleser's 30 years experience in the hospitality industry began with Howard Johnson's Corporation as Director of Loss Prevention followed by Marriott Family Restaurants. Prior to entering the hospitality field, he became an expert polygraph examiner as an Investigator with the New York State Police Department and Bureau of Criminal Investigation, specializing in white-collar crime.

David M. Bleser, Vice President of Operations, is a graduate of the University of South Carolina with a bachelor's degree in Hotel Management. David is a former Assistant Manager for Cracker Barrel Restaurants and a former Food and Beverage Director for Servico and Starwood Hotels and Resorts. As a member of the American Hotel and Lodging Association, he is currently Vice Chairman of the Loss Prevention Committee. He is also a member of the Association of Certified Fraud Examiners, The Institute of Internal Auditors and the American Society for Industrial Security. For over 8 years David has participated as well as managed the Internal Auditing and Loss Prevention projects conducted by HOSPITALITY SAFEGUARDS, INC. He has extensive knowledge in operational policies and procedures and has written several articles for special fraud publications.

HOSPITALITY SAFEGUARDS, INC. is a respected firm that employs experienced hospitality professionals exclusively, including former Hotel General Managers, Corporate Staff Accountants, as well as Senior Hotel and Restaurant Management. These professionals provide objective evaluation, critical analysis, and detailed reports to assist hospitality management with managing quality of service and product. We can offer help in all areas in the hospitality industry including task force personnel when needed.

Our objective is to protect our clients and their assets through comprehensive, customized programmes. In addition, it is our responsibility to offer suggestions on reducing overhead, improving efficiency and implementing policies and procedures.

Accounting Resources

The newest programme offered by HOSPITALITY SAFEGUARDS, INC. is Accounting Resources. This programme is designed to eliminate one or more accounting positions in the corporate and/or property capacity. Hospitality Accounting Centre located in Orlando, Florida has the ability to successfully provide management of the entire Accounting function including, but not limited to, Accounts Receivable, Accounts Payable, Income Reporting and Financial Statements. With the support of one individual at the property, Orlando Accounting Centre can provide owners and General Managers with an invaluable tool to assist in reducing overhead and increasing the bottom line. In most cases they are able to reduce accounting expenses by up to 50 per cent.

The majority of these savings are derived from the elimination of at least one accounting position.

How it Works

The designated individual at the location records the income, makes the deposit and prepares a daily report. The daily report along with the validated deposit slip is faxed to the Accounting Centre each morning. The daily support documentation is gathered and forwarded to us twice weekly.

We collect and process Accounts Receivable and Accounts Payable weekly and completely manage both on a daily basis. All bank deposits are verified daily as well.

At the end of the accounting period, they prepare all necessary financial reports and bank reconciliations. If needed, assistance with budget preparation and cash flow projections are available.

They employ only qualified personnel, and Hospitality Task Force is available.

Investigation

In the ever changing field of financial investigations, the investigator must be familiar with the laws that govern financial crimes and be able to adapt their investigations skills to keep up with the changing times. The passing of the Sarbanes - Oxley Act is a prime example.

Through our internal investigations and forensic accounting reviews, Hospitality Safeguards, Inc. has been able to uncover and help in the successful prosecution of individuals and the recovery of millions of dollars in internal fraud committed within the hospitality industry.

Investigations are conducted with respect and dignity for both the client and the associate. Associates are interviewed, not interrogated. Both company and individual rights are proctected at all times.

A successful conclusion is always the primary goal of every inquiry. Detailed reports are prepared for possible restitution, presentation towards law enforcement or insurance claim recovery.

Civil investigations and complaints are conducted in the same manner. The emphasis is placed on protecting the assets of the client. In many cases expert testimony can be provided.

Internal Auditing

When you walk through your hotel or restaurant everything looks just fine, does not it? The employees are attentive, the different areas are operating efficiently, and the revenue is recorded properly. But, what goes on when you are not around? You cannot be everywhere, or at every property. You need to know that your business is running properly and that the revenue and expenses are recorded properly.

Hospitality Safeguards, Inc.'s operational audits are invaluable tools for management to analyze the efficiency, integrity and competency of its operations. These audits are customized to our clients' needs.

Hospitality Safeguards, Inc. operational internal auditing rating form has become an accepted industry standard for judging performance and covers all aspects of hotel and restaurant operations.

Included in the audit reviews are:

- Cash Verification
- Bank Account City Ledger
- Guest Ledger
- Advance Deposits
- Accounts Payable
- Daily and Monthly Revenue
- Food and Beverage Operations
- Safety/Security
- Human Resources/Payroll

How it Works

A hospitality professional internal auditor is assigned to your account. The average hotel is audited annually or semiannually.

The audit process is completed in one to five days with emphasis on five selected days and a six month operating period. The topics covered in the audit are selected by the client and expanded by the auditor if deficiencies are noted.

The auditor will make specific requests for five to seven days' audit packs and will verify all transactions and adjustments for that period. A review will be made for the prior six months' records on a monthly basis. All unusual and excessive transactions or adjustments are reviewed and the necessary supporting documentation noted.

In addition to the financial records, a complete review of other hotel functions such as housekeeping and maintenance, are reviewed for OSHA, safety, and loss prevention requirements.

A complete review and audit of all food and beverage procedures and operations are included in each audit. This includes revenue, inventory and food handling procedures as established by the client.

Every category is assigned a value and at the completion of the audit, a grade is determined. The audit is then reviewed with the General Manager and Controller. The final audit is prepared and sent to the client within one week of completion.

Operational Analysis

Operational and Hotel analysis are an invaluable tools for analyzing and rating the level of service and integrity of the employees in all areas of your establishment. These programmes have become an industry standard, conducted by the industry leader. We give you a professional review of your operation from the guests' point of view. Depending upon your company's needs, these reviews include all or some of the following aspects of your operation:

Rooms

- Reservations
- Check-in/Check-out
- Guest Services
- Guest Room Appearance
- Lobby

Food/Beverage

- Greeting
- Food Preparation/Presentation/Temperature
- Room Service
- Quality of Food
- Outlet Appearance

Other

- Landscaping
- Parking
- Corridors
- Security
- Overall Appearance

All Areas

- Friendliness
- Employee Appearance
- Cleanliness
- Management Visibility
- Overall Experience.

How it Works

A team of our professional shoppers visit your establishment just like a regular customer. They zero in on the areas you are particularly concerned with. For example, the area where receipts have been dropping off while volume appears to remain consistent, or fast food service, or retail shop where inventory statistics indicate a loss is occurring.

Immediately after our team leaves the unit we send you a comprehensive, detailed narrative report of the team's findings. These reports include check numbers and amounts, descriptions of employees as well as name plate identifications.

Numerous cash and integrity tests are conducted during each visit. Great emphasis is placed on those little details that you know can make such a difference. For example,

Is service acceptable?

Are employees neat in appearance?

Was the customer treated courteously?

Their associates will match your usual customer profile. In every way they will look just like your typical patron. Investigators are experts at blending in.

Risk Management

With our law enforcement and loss prevention background, HOSPITALITY SAFEGUARDS, INC. has the ability and experience to offer many services in the risk management areas.

- Workshops and seminars can be conducted relating to any area of concern.
- Expert witnesses are available with extensive law enforcement knowledge and experience.
- Location investigations can be performed.
- Reports can be prepared for legal presentation and insurance claims.

- Utilization of our computer network permits us to resolve outstanding issues.
- Access to Fraudline and Background checks are available.
- Surveillance equipment can be installed and observed if needed.
- Consultation and recommendations are provided as needed.

A properly performed risk analysis has many benefits. The following are some of the benefits:

- The analysis will show the current security profile of the organization
- It will highlight areas where greater or lesser security is needed
- It will help to assemble some of the facts needed for the developement and justification of cost effective safeguards.
- It will serve to increase awareness by assessing the strengths and weaknesses of the organizations levels of security.

The success of any risk analysis is strongly contingent upon the role upper management takes in the project.

Preferred Vendors

Hospitality Safeguards, Inc. has used these vendors and have referred them to dozens of our clients with excellent results. They personally recommend them, however these recommendations are based on past history. If you have problems or complaints about anyone on this list, they should appreciate a detailed account of the problem. Upon hearing of your complaint, they will contact the vendor directly. If the situation warrants it, they will remove the vendor from the list.

Fraud Aware/Hospitality

Fraud Aware/Hospitality is the first online course designed to meet the growing demand from security and financial managers for a cost effective training tool to equip employees with the knowledge to detect, prevent and report fraudulent schemes that increasingly threaten hotels, resorts and restaurants worldwide. Fraud Aware/ Hospitality supports corporate ethics and governance initiatives by enlisting everyone in the organization to root out embezzlement, credit card scams, acceptance of counterfeit checks, internet fraud, and a host of other fast growing monetary crimes against the hospitality industry.

Hospitality Risk Controls Inc.

Hospitality Risk Controls/Security Litigation Group is a nationwide company established in 1990 that provides safety and security services to major hotel companies across the United States. Hospitality Risk Controls specializes in assisting clients in making informed business decisions, reducing insurance costs and security risks, as well as managing liability exposure and workers' compensation costs. Other services performed by Hospitality Risk Controls include writing corporate security, safety and Occupational Safety and Health Administration (OSHA) manuals; conducting safety, security and OSHA evaluations of properties; leading seminars covering a wide range of topics; responding to major incidents occurring at properties in preparation of litigation and foreseeability issues; and performing pre-acquisition site surveys. The Security Litigation Group provides case evaluation services and expert testimony in premises security cases nationwide.

Safety Source

Safety Source offers a vast library of safety training videos to meet the training needs of almost any industry or job description. We also offer a full line of videos tailored specifically to the Hospitality Industry. Our videos comply with the latest regulations and are presented in a way that is both effective and easy to understand. They have been used by thousands of companies to train millions of workers worldwide. Our videos are priced much lower than our competitors which allows any company, regardless of size or budget to have their own "in-house video library." We also offer a free 5 day preview on any title.

Clients

Below is a list of our current and former clients along with how some of them feel about them.

All Florida Hotels and Resorts	Lend Lease
Boykin Lodging Company	Lodgian Hotel

Criimi Mae Food Services	Morrison
Driftwood Hospitality	Prism Hotels
E-Brands	Pinnacle
Hyatt Hotels Procaccianti Group	The
Inverness Partners Inc.	Park Place
Hospitality Linchris Hotel Corporation	Richfield
Hospitality (SWAN)	
Hospitality Management Corporation	

"We have found that since using Hospitality Safeguards our internal controls and bottom line have drastically improved. The professionalism and service we receive from them is unnmatched and we consider them a true 'partner' in driving profitablity, and maximizing return for our owners."

— Chris *Russell*
Executive V.P/C.O.O
Prism Hotels

"Over the last 30 years, I have had the opportunity to operate a broad spectrum of hotels througout the United States, as a Unit Manager, Regional Vice President, and Owner/Operator of several hotel companies. During most of that time, I have also had the pleasure of knowing Earl and David Bleser and their company, Hospitality Safeguards, Inc.

I can unequivocally say that Hospitality Safeguards is not only an extremely qualified and results oriented organization, but is immediately responsive to the needs and situations that may suddenly arise in the Hospitality Industry. From time to time I have used many of their services, including monthly accounting, periodic field audits, investigations, prosecution assistance, development of safety and security systems, background checks, and more. In several instances, I replaced internal departments with the outsourced services of Hospitality Safeguards. That action not only saved substantial overhead dollars but brought a significant higher level of experience, professionalism and results, to those disciplines.

Hospitality Safeguards remains a valued associate of Pinnacle Hotel Management."

—Al Baerenklau
President
Pinnacle Hotel Management

"I have depended on the internal audits and investigations provided by Hospitality Safeguards for over 10 years. We believe that the internal audits to be an effective training tool. Their proactive approach and attention to detail is unmatched in the hospitality industry."

—David Buddemeyer
President Driftwood

Case Studies

Identity Theft

Idenity theft is on the rise within the hospitality industry. We have handled more cases of it in 2004 than we have in the previous four years combined. Contrary to popular belief it does cost a hotel revenue. Recently we had one client who had 6 cases of identity theft at one convention centre hotel. One of the individuals whose identity was stolen was a meeting planner. I am convinced the next time that individual is looking to book an event, she will think twice about booking it at that hotel. As a result, the hotel has lost thousands of dollars in potential revenue.

There are things that the hotels can do to minimize their and the guests exposure.

First, if your Franchisor allows online check-in, make sure your front desk clerks ask to see the guest's I.D. and ensure it matches the name on the registration card before a key is handed out. We suggest that you do this for every guest that stays at your hotel regardless if they check-in online or not. The government allows online check-in for flights but they still require proof of identification prior to the issuance of a ticket. We see no reason as to why the hotel industry should not do the same. If the guest inquires as to why, simply explain to them you are trying to prevent someone else from using their credit card. Immediately the hotel has established goodwill with the guest. An informal survey conducted in 2003 indicates that people would not mind providing their I.D. if they knew it was to reduce the potential of identity theft.

Second, review all documentation that is printed by the front desk and ensure that only the last 4 numbers of an individuals credit card number appears the folios, receipts or other reports that are created by the property management system. This should be done for your point of sale system as well.

Third, review your Banquet Event Orders. We have seen an increasingly amount of B.E.O's that show the entire credit card number. Train your staff to put the number of the Group Master/ House Account number in the method of payment field instead of the credit card number. The only person that should see the entire credit card number is the accounting representative who is pre-authorizing the card for the estimated charges of the function.

Fourth, if your establishment is still using the manual credit card imprint forms, instruct your staff to shred the carbon paper.

Fifth, purchase a shredder for your administrative offices. All documents that contain guest information or hotel information should be shredded.

Ultimately, the hotel should conduct a thorough review of all documents to ensure that the exposure to entire credit card numbers is severely limited. Of course, a review should also be done on the I.T. side as well.

Holiday Parties

Holiday parties are just around the corner. Now is a good time to review your alcohol policies and procedures. Most importantly ensure that the proper individuals have been TIPS Certified or other alcohol certification. The following individuals should be certified:

- All Managers
- All Food and Beverage Associates.
- Bellman/Valet
- Depending on the location of the lounge, night time front desk clerks
- Security guards

In addition make sure your associates know the number of a local taxi company.

Alcohol liability lawsuits are on the rise. A couple of dollars spent on certification can save a hotel thousands of dollars.

Case File/Home

In God we Trust, Everyone Else we Monitor

When you walk through your hotel or restaurant everything looks fine, does not it? The employees are attentive, the different areas are operating efficiently, and the revenue is being recorded properly. But, what goes on when you are not around? You cannot be everywhere, or at every property. You need to know that the revenue and expenses are being recorded properly.

Hospitality Safeguards, Inc. is a firm that specializes in Internal Auditing, Internal Investigations, Accounting Resources, Operational Hotel Analysis, and Loss Prevention for the hospitality industry. Our primary goal is to protect your company's physical and financial assets.

Other services offered by Hospitality Safeguards, Inc. include Fraud Investigations, Task Force Personnel, Expert Witnesses, Anti-Fraud Hotline, and Hospitality Fraud Seminars.

HOSPCON

On stage you will see a successful restaurant concept or a smooth and efficient hotel operation, behind the scenes lies a superb expertise of a dynamic company. This dynamic company consists of a group experienced specialists with a rich, global background in the fast pasted hospitality and leisure industry. Today's drive for efficiency, flexibility and "thinking outside the box" has created a need for specialist assistance in order to create a better understanding or simply assist management teams to reach their goals. The global experience of HospCon results in an increase of efficiency for existing hospitality operations, successful and cost effective start for new hospitality operations and cost savings for owners by combining the resources of the designers, other consultants and management companies. In addition to the above, we have a passion for details and to do things right straight away! Professional expertise in the hospitality consulting is crucial to quality and a profitable operation which requires thorough knowledge and skills in combination with dedication to the clients expectations and vision. Hospitality Operations are an expertise on their own, Architects, Interior Designers and Project Management cannot be expected to provide answers and solutions to operational matters, it is not their field of expertise! Therefore HospCon is the solution where clients are looking for. We will function as a third party and will identify issues related to the problem in a more detached and less emotional manner. Our services should not be considered as an added expense or a quick fix solution, but rather a future investment for a long term strategy.

5

International Hotel and Guest Management Enterprises

SYNXIS

At SynXis, we provide the best reservation services in the industry.

That is our mission.

Because we know that our customers can not afford to miss a single booking.

Central Reservation Management System:

- Voice Reservations
- Web Booking Engine
- Global Distribution System (GDS)
- Internet Distribution System (IDS)

Solutions

The SynXis Difference: At SynXis, we know that you can not afford to miss a single booking! Our reservation management system maintains a single, real-time representation of property inventory that is accessible by all booking channels including GDS, IDS, a hotel's Website, and direct voice reservations. Without such a product, a truly effective system of yield management is difficult, if not impossible, to implement.

SynXis engineers worked closely with the hospitality industry to develop a low-cost, highly functional, and scalable hotel reservation system. The result is the SynXis Reservation Management System, which leverages years of research and development and opens the door for an unparalleled leap forward in the profitability of hotels and chains.

The SynXis Difference:

Market-Driven Technology

- World-class reservation system with connectivity to all distribution channels
- Easy-to-use Control Centre for managing occupancy and rates
- Interfaces to other best-of-breed applications

Results-Driven Service

- Dedicated Account Managers
- Practical revenue management guidance
- Online and personal training programmes
- Tiered levels of support to meet your property's needs

Company

Our Mission: With our reservation system as a keystone, SynXis® will become the preferred hospitality industry partner for optimizing room distribution.

Corporate Overview: Founded in 1996, SynXis Corporation delivers proven reservation management and distribution systems to more than 6,000 hotels, resorts and casinos worldwide. Through a suite of Internet-based applications, SynXis empowers hotel operators with the ability to consolidate and control hotel inventory from all sources, while maintaining a single guest record. It also provides money-saving direct access to the major GDSs and helps build hotel revenue by enabling consumers to conveniently book hotel reservations online through the hotel's Website.

Among SynXis's customers are some of the industry's leading hotels, including MGM-Mirage, Interstate Hotels & Resorts, Harrah's Entertainment, CHIP Hospitality, Jumeirah Hotels, Candlewood Suites and VIP International. The company has 60 employees. It is headquartered in McLean, VA, with development centres in Boston and Denver and an international office in Amsterdam, The Netherlands.

Services

SynXis offers a variety of services to help you streamline operations, increase revenue, and gain maximum exposure for your property or group of properties.

- Customer Support

- Training
- Account and Revenue Management
- RFP and Consortia
- Travel Agent Commission Processing
- Additional Marketing Services

THETA

Introduction

The tourism, hospitality and sport sector has the potential to be South Africa's largest employment sector, largest foreign exchange earning sector and largest economic sector in terms of GDP. In addition to the potential for tourism to increase foreign exchange earnings, it is a multiplier domestic industry. That is, domestic tourism and hospitality operations create economic activity and employment also.

The tourism, hospitality, sport and conservation industries are diverse, complex and large, and the sector overlaps many other industry sectors such as transport, arts, culture, entertainment, business and retail.

Chambers that fall within THETA's scope include:

- Hospitality
- Gambling and Lotteries
- Tourism and Travel Services
- Conservation and Tourist Guiding
- Sport, Recreation and Fitness

It has been estimated that up to 80 per cent of all businesses in the sector are small, micro and medium-sized enterprises, and more than 80 per cent are located in urban settings. If true, this reflects industry's desire to access the domestic as well as the international market in order to smooth out as far as possible the peaks and troughs of demand; and it also reflects the availability of services and infrastructure. In addition, a substantial part of the sector is primarily involved in food preparation, food and beverage service and catering – for the general population, not only for tourists – so they are located where their markets are concentrated.

Employment within these chambers is characterised by it being labour intensive; many occupations are operational and require low to intermediate skills; and a relatively high proportion of jobs are part-time and casual. In the Sport and Recreation sub-sector in particular, large numbers of workers are voluntary, unpaid people.

Much of the sector operates 24 hours per day, year-round, but is subject to significant seasonal fluctuation. The sector's clients are both domestic and international, and they seek both natural and built attractions and services. Customer service and ambience are fundamental to the quality of a tourist's or patron's experience, and to the likelihood of return business.

The broad tourism sector and all its five chambers cover a range of enterprises, skills and occupational categories. Listed below are the standard industrial classification (SIC) codes, covered by sector as well as the terms of reference of the chamber committees, their members as well as the THETA travel policy applicable to Chambers and their operations. They comprise:

Standard Industrial Classification Codes

Group	SIC Code	Standard Category
Hospitality		
	64101	Hotels, motels, boatels and inns not registered
	64104	Hotels, motels, boatels and inns registered
	64102	Caravan parks and camping sites
	64103	Guesthouses and guest farms
	64105	Bed and breakfast
	64106	Management and operation of game lodges
	64201	Restaurant or tearoom with liquor license
	64202	Restaurant or tearoom without liquor license
	64203	
	64205	
	64206	Take-away counters; take-away restaurants; fast food establishments
	64204	Caterers (including private clinics)
	64207	Other catering services n.e.c. including pubs, taverns, night clubs
	84111	Timesharing (including resorts and parks; self-catering apartments/cottages)
	88994	Bioscope cafes
	91308	Control of undertaking that sells liquor to the public
	9130A	Licensing and control of undertakings that sell food to the public
	96195	Operation and management of convention centres

Gambling & Lotteries		
	96494	Gambling, licensed casinos and the national lottery (including bookmakers, totalisators, casinos, bingo operators)
Tourism & Travel Services		
	71214	Tour operators (inbound and outbound tour operators)
	71223	Safaris and sightseeing trip operators
	73002	Inbound international flights
	74140	Travel agency and related activities
	85111	Renting of land transport equipment including car rentals
	96336	Tourist info centres
	99048	Tourism authorities including but not limited to tourism marketing, tourist information centres, publicity associations
	99028	Car hire
Sport, Recreation & Fitness		
	93195	Operation and management of health and well-being centres including but not limited to hydros, spas, fitness centres etc.
	96000	Recreational, cultural and sporting activities
	96002	Recreational, leisure and outdoor adventure activities including management and operation of facilities, government departments
	96191	Beaches and amusement facilities and fairs
	96196	Amusement parks
	96410	Sporting activities
	96411	Operation and management of sporting facilities and clubs
	96412	Operation and management of sport academies
	96413	Promotion and management of sporting events and activities
	96415	Management and operation of non-motorized sporting activities
	96416	Operation and management of recreation parks and beaches, fairs and shows and recreational transport activities
	96417	Sporting activities including but not limited to sport federations etc.
	96418	Management and operation of motorized sporting activities

	96419	Operation and management of horse racing events and clubs and academies
Conservation & Tourism Guiding		
	96320	Museum activities and preservation of historical sites and buildings
	96322	Provision for management and operation of monuments, historical sites and buildings
	96323	Management and operation of museum, cultural and heritage activities
	96333	Game parks, reserves including but not limited to wildlife, parks, zoological or animal parks and botanical gardens
	96334	Activities of conservation bodies
	96335	Wildlife conservation including wildlife, game, parks, game reserves, zoological establishments, botanical gardens etc
	11520	Hunting and trapping including related services
	99049	Guides including tourist river, mountain etc.

Theta Chamber Committee Terms of Reference Index

1. Introduction

This Terms of Reference are intended to clearly explain the specific roles and responsibilities of the Chamber Committees as set out in the THETA Constitution. In constituting SETA's, the Skills Development Act of 1998 recommends the constitution of sectoral committees to allow broad participation in implementing the Skills Development Strategy.

The contents of this Terms of Reference are to be read and interpreted in conjunction with the constitution of THETA. In the case of any dispute related to the interpretation of the Terms of Reference, the Constitution of THETA shall take precedence.

2. Purpose

- The Chamber Committee shall be responsible for representing the views, interests and expertise of the major sub-sectors that fall within THETA's scope.
- Provide expert advice and strategic information to THETA through the Operations Committee.
- Enable appropriate recognition of the sub-sectors education and training needs in the sector skills plan,

business plan and budget, learnerships, quality assurance and such other activities as are undertaken by THETA

- The Chamber Committee shall exercise such further powers and functions as may be entrusted or delegated to it by THETA.

3. Approval

The Terms of Reference of the Chamber Committee shall be approved by THETA and shall be reviewed, and if required, revised annually.

4. Structure

4.1 Composition of Chamber Committee's

4.1.1 Chambers must be established for the following sub-sectors:

- Hospitality
- Gaming and Lotteries
- Sport, Recreation and Fitness
- Travel and Tourism Services
- Conservation and Tourist Guiding

The minimum membership of the 'THETA Chamber Committee' shall be as outlined in Table 1: Composition of the Chamber Committee

Table 1: Composition of the Chamber Committee

Appointee	*Representation*
1. Representing Employer Interests	3
2. Representing Employee Interests	3
3. Representing Interest Groups • Government Agency • Statutory Body • Industry Association, etc.	1
4. Representing SMME's and previously disadvantaged stakeholders	3
5. Theta Chamber Co-ordinator	1
Total	11

- THETA Chamber Co-ordinators shall serve as Executive Officers and Secretariat of the Chamber Committees.
- THETA shall have the power to constitute and dissolve the Chamber Committee.
- The Chairman, deputy Chairman and a Sector Skills Plan representative shall be elected by the members of the Chamber Committee.
- The Chamber Committee shall not have the power to co-opt additional Members.

4.2 Establishment and Terms of Office of the Chamber Committees.

- Chambers may be established on authority of THETA after consultation with the stakeholders in the sub-sectors.
- The term of office of each Chamber Committee Member shall be for a period of not more than two years from date of election.
- The Chamber Co-ordinator shall be Executive Officer, including Secretariat function of the Chamber and shall have voting rights.

4.3 Meetings

- Chambers shall hold no fewer that two meetings each year or as often as necessary for the proper performance of their duties and functions.
- Special meetings of the Chamber Committee may be convened as required.
- Any voting member of the Chamber Committee may request the Executive Officer to call a special meeting, if necessary.
- Committee members residing outside of Gauteng will be provided with flights bookings, transport to and from the airport and to meetings, accommodation and other associated travel costs (within set limitations) as prescribed by THETA.
- A quorum shall be fifty per cent + one of the voting Members.

4.4 Notice of Meetings

- Notice shall be given in writing to all Members of the Chamber Committee of each meeting to be held, at least fourteen (14) days prior to the date on which such meeting is to be held.

- The Agenda of the meeting shall be prepared and distributed at least seven (7) days prior to the meeting. Any person attending the meeting may add items to the Agenda up until five (5) days before the said meeting. Such items are to be provided to the Secretariat of the Chamber Committee.
- The proceedings of all meetings will be documented in the form of minutes and these shall be kept by the Secretariat.
- The Secretariat shall distribute DRAFT minutes of any and all meetings, within two weeks of the date of the said meetings, for review and action by Chamber Committee Members.
- The Secretariat shall include the minutes with the Agenda of the following Chamber Committee meeting.

4.5 Reporting

- The Chamber Committee shall be responsible to and shall report to the Operations Committee of the THETA Board of Directors.
- The Chairperson of the Chamber Committee shall report to the Executive Officer on all significant issues that may indicate the presence or possibility of a contingent liability.

Travel for Theta Stakeholders

THETA upon formal invitation to stakeholders will pay the following travel and subsistence costs.

All travel arrangements will be made by THETA.

Accomodation

THETA makes use of the City Lodge Group as per corporate agreement. If accommodation is unavailable in this regard the following terms and conditions will apply:

Any accommodation facility may be used to the value of R 350.00 night including dinner, bed and breakfast.

Stakeholders/travellers who elect to be accommodated by friends, family, colleagues or other individuals will not be recompensed any amount toward accommodation or breakfast cost in that environment.

The following expenses are for the personal account of the traveller:

- Accommodation facility telephone bill
- Laundry and dry cleaning
- Additional beverages to standard meal packages
- Movies
- Videos
- Gifts
- Tips
- Room service, over and above the meal limitation

THETA will provide all other meals (if overnight stay is necessary) at a rate of R 65.00 per night.

Stakeholders/travelers staying with friends, family, colleagues or other individuals are authorised to claim up to a maximum of R 65.00 for dinner (including drinks)/night provided the original invoices are submitted together with an original THETA Expense Claim Form in the prescribed manner.

Accommodation and travel arrangements must be made through THETA offices.

Any alternative arrangements made and all expenses incurred will be at the expense of the traveller.

Travel

Air Travel

All local air travel must be undertaken in economy class. Any upgrades or alternative arrangements are for the expense of the traveller.

Train or Bus

THETA will make travel arrangements for Train and Bus service utilization where needed.

International Travel

THETA does not envisage involving stakeholders in international ventures.

Vehicle Rental

All vehicle hire arrangements are to be made via THETA offices.

For all bookings the following table will apply:

Category	*Vehicle Group*	*Make of Vehicle*
Stakeholders	A	1.3 or similar
Stakeholders	B	1.6 or similar
People with disabilities only able to drive automatic vehicles	D	1.6 or similar
People with disabilities and are unable to drive	Chauffer drive	1.6 or similar
A group of 5 or more stakeholders	L	Microbus or similar

The decision to utilize an A class vehicle rental as opposed to a B class vehicle rental will be at THETA's discretion based on the following criteria:

Weather

Distance

Claim Procedure

Attain and complete an 'Expense Claim Form' from THETA.

Attach supportive original invoices to claim form.

Attach invitation to travel at THETA's request.

No faxed copies will be accepted, only original copies.

Please ensure that all claims reach THETA no later than 7 days after the meeting.

Use of Personal Motor Vehicles

Stakeholders may use their personal vehicles when attending THETA meetings and claim accordingly.

This is not applicable to employees or representatives of all Government Departments, Parastatals and all other statutory stakeholders, who are using Government vehicles and who have been provided with travel allowances from their departments/organizations.

THETA will only reimburse an amount of R 2.07 per kilometre travelled.

Petrol Claim Procedures

A petrol claim form needs to be attained from THETA.

Follow claim procedure in attaching supportive documentation.

THETA reserves the right not to hire vehicles as a resident THETA driver may be available to provide a chauffer service.

SSP (Sector Skills Plan)

Overview

THETA is responsible for developing a Sector Skills Plan, which is a four-year strategic document. The SSP represents the implementation framework for achieving the objectives and targets set out in the National Skills Development Strategy. The first Sector Skills Plans were for the period 2000 – 2004. Currently THETA has begun a process of developing the SSP document for the Period 2005 – 2009, this SSP document will be aligned to the National Skills Development Objectives and Targets, which is under review.

The Sector Skills Plan is a strategic vision of the SETA for the skills development in the sector to be based on an assessment of the economic and development trends, and associated skills requirements.

Avenues for compiling data:

- SETA commissioned research
- Ongoing research and surveys conducted by sub-sectors
- Department of Labour research and other government research institutes
- Focus groups from the sector
- Department of Labour Employment Services
- Information from Labour Brokers and Recruitment Agencies
- Analysis of WSP and Implementation Reports

The expected date of Submission of the SSP 2005 – 2009 to the Department of Labour is the 30 June 2004. When the Department of Labour has approved the THETA SSP document, then THETA will make it available to all stakeholders, through its Website, Call Centre and on request by stakeholders.

2005 - 2009

- Dates for the SSP Research and Development
- Sector Skills Plan Working group
- Sector Skills Plan Focus Groups Schedule

Constitution

March 2000

Chapter 1 Name and legal status
Chapter 2 Interpretation
Chapter 3 Object, functions and duties
Chapter 4 Composition of THETA
Chapter 5 Meetings of THETA
Chapter 6 Office Bearing of THETA
Chapter 7 Standing Committees
Chapter 8 Executive Committee
Chapter 9 Resource Committee
Chapter 10 Planning Committee
Chapter 11 Quality Committee
Chapter 12 Learnership Committee
Chapter 13 Chambers
Chapter 14 The Chief Executive
Chapter 15 Final Provisions
Chapter 16 Conduct of Members
Chapter 17 Terms of Office
Chapter 18 Amendment of this Constitution
Chapter 19 Dispute Procedure
Schedule 1 List of organizations consulted during the process of the formation of THETA.
Schedule 2 Organization agreed by constituent organizations to appoint Members to THETA

July 2003

The Revised Constitution

Acts

- Skills Development Act 1998
- Skills Development Levies Act 1999
- Skills Development Act Amendment 2003
- SAQA Act 58 of 1995
- FET Act 98 of 1998

Functions of the Department

The skills development department is responsible for:

- Collecting and disbursing skills development levies;
- Developing and implementing the Sector Skills Plan;

- Facilitating Chamber Committee operations;
- Implementing the National Skills Development Strategy
- Liaising with the sector
- Monitoring and auditing skills development implementation

The Levies and Grants Section is responsible for:

- Receiving levies from the Department of Labour
- Administering the grant disbursement schedules
- Receiving the Workplace Skills Plans (WSP) and Implementation Reports (IR)
- Conducting administrative validation of the WSP and IR
- Facilitating reallocation of any misallocated employers
- Administering Change of Jurisdiction applications
- Compiling a Skills Development Facilitators database
- Preparing Grant Disbursement Schedules for qualifying employer organizations
- Capturing WSP, IR, and other grants as required by THETA
- Administering queries on levies and grants

The Chamber Co-ordinators are responsible for:

- Sector liaison on skill development in the respective sectors.
- Providing necessary strategic information to Chamber Committees and facilitating implementation of Chamber initiatives.
- Supporting development of sub-sector capacity building in implementing the National Skills Development Strategy.
- Monitoring and auditing implementation of Skills Development initiatives by employers in the respective THETA sub-sectors.
- Participating in THETA committees as required by THETA management.
- Validating WSP and Implementation Reports from the respective sub-sectors.
- Developing stakeholder databases.

THETA is responsible for developing a Sector Skills Plan (SSP), which is a four-year strategic document. The SSP represents the implementation framework for achieving the objectives and targets as set out in the National Skills Development Strategy. The first Sector Skills Plans were developed for the period 2000–2004. Currently THETA has begun a process of developing a SSP document for the period 2005 – 2009, this document will be aligned to the National Skills Development Objectives and Targets, which are under review.

The Sector Skills Plan is a strategic vision of the SETA for implementation of skills development in the sector, to be based on an assessment of economic and development trends, and associated skills requirements.

Avenues for compiling data include:

- SETA commissioned research
- Ongoing research and surveys conducted by sub-sectors
- Department of Labour research and other government research institutes
- Focus groups from the sector
- Analysis of Workplace Skills Plan and Implementation Reports from employers

NSDS Implementation

There are specific NSDS objectives that the Skills Development Department is directly responsible for implementing and the balance are implemented in conjunction with other THETA core departments and projects.

The Skills Development Department is directly responsible for:

- Fostering skills development in the formal economy for productivity and employment growth (Administering Levies and Grants).

Monitoring

Through the Skills Development Act of 1998 and the Skills Development Levies Act of 1999 SETAs are required to monitor, audit and inspect employer organization, in implementing the Skills Development Strategy. In a bid to implement and meet the NSDS targets, monitoring plays a crucial role in ensuring quality management. This is achieved through the process of verification of the implementation of the Workplace Skills Plan and putting developmental programme where required.

In a bid to implement and meet the NSDS targets, monitoring plays a crucial role in ensuring quality management. This is achieved through the process of verification of the implementation of the Workplace Skills Plan's and putting developmental programmes in place where required.

Organogram

Executive Manager

Acting Skills Development Manager: William Chuene

Operations

Levies and Grants Co-ordinator: Abigail Shabangu – abigail@theta.org.za

Hospitality and Gaming Co-ordinator: Jinty Ainsworth – jinty@theta.org.za

Sport, Recreation, Fitness and Lotteries Co-ordinator: William Chuene – william@theta.org.za

Tourism and Travel Services Co-ordinator: Muzi Mwandla - muzi@theta.org.za

Conservation and Guiding Co-ordinator: Patrick Duigan - patrick@theta.org.za

Administrative Support

PA: Martha Lubasi – martha@theta.org.za

Levies and Grants Administrator: Nomhle Shabangu – nomhle@theta.org.za

Levies and Grants Administration: Bernita Sithole-bernita@theta.org.za

Grants Administration: Issac Matse - isaac@theta.org.za

UNICA

Hospitality Enterprise Marketing Management

Delivering a superb customer experience is paramount to the world's leading hospitality organizations that are looking to strengthen customer relationships through multi-channel, real-time marketing. In today's environment, delivering a consistent customer experience across multiple brands spanning geographic regions is critical to retaining valuable customers. Many of these hospitality leaders are leveraging marketing technology to not only target customers with pre-season and in-season promotions and manage loyalty programme communications, but also to analyze customer behaviour over time to optimize targeted promotions.

Unica's Affinium Suite is used by leading hospitality companies to drive more customer-centric programmes, use better targeting methodologies, and increase customer spend for higher retention and profitability.

Affinium SUITE

Unica's award-winning Enterprise Marketing Management (EMM) solutions help hospitality organizations:

- Increase acquisition and renewal rates.
- Identify most valuable customers and those most likely to churn.
- Better service preferred guests by providing targeted cross-sell and up-sell offers.
- Coordinate marketing efforts across brands and leverage customer data stored throughout the organization.
- Build customer loyalty by identifying opportunities in real time and reacting more quickly to events such as a change in travel stays.

Deriving the most value from your existing customer data and implementing effective acquisition and retention campaigns takes deep customer understanding. But how do you analyze information stored across multiple brands and in real time to develop more sophisticated promotions and deliver more superior customer service?

Unica's Affinium Model provides award-winning data mining and predictive modelling software, integrates segmentation and profiling, valuation, response modelling and cross selling features to solve specific marketing problems throughout the complete customer life cycle.

LEISURE

Experts in Hospitality

Leisure is a group of hospitality companies each offering specialized services, operated by experienced and dedicated experts in their field. From hospitality management to development and construction services to commercial brokerage, we provide owners and investors the services needed to succeed.

Latest News

12/13/2004 - Leisure Hotels to Manage weldon, Missouri Wingate Hotel

Quick Links

Leisure Home

Hospitality Management

- Finance & Administration
- Marketing & E-Commerce
- Management Services

Development

- Development Services
- Construction Management
- Purchasing

Commercial Brokerage

Careers

Press & Media

Links

Contact Us

Services

Hospitality Management

The hospitality management division of Leisure Group of Companies, Leisure Hotels L.L.C., offers a full menu of services encompassing all aspects of operations in the hospitality industry. From pre-opening planning and marketing to day to day operation and asset repositioning, Leisure Hotels offers the flexibility and ease where you need us, when you need us.

Development Services

Leisure Development is aimed toward achieving the primary objectives for each client and each project: profitability, occupancy, quality, and property sales.

Development services include not only development, but construction management and purchasing services as well.

Brokerage Services

Leisure Real Estate Advisors was created to fill an important niche in the lodging industry—a results oriented hotel brokerage service.

Recognizing this need, Leisure Hotel Corporation has integrated a multi-talented team of experienced knowledgeable and highly successful hotel brokers.

Leisure Hotels and Resorts represents many hotel locations throughout the Midwest and United States.

Hospitality Management

Acheiving results through determination, motivation and innoration

At Leisure Hotels and Resorts, our focus is on superior customer service, quality facilities and providing beneficial financial results to the owner. That is why we have received not only the accolades from our guests, but from our hotel owners as well.

Successes

If you market it, they will come

Using E-commerce Marketing that has made Leisure well-known in the industry, we have been able to increase the reservation traffic for one small independent hotel by 75 per cent in just one month and $75,000 in two months.

Cost Controls and Quality Assurance

Leisure Hotels and Resorts was asked to assume management of a mid-sized full service hotel near a major metropolitan area. Our management team analyzed the hotels staffing situation and by implementing our cost control methods and our unique management support, we were able to cut labour costs by over $120,000 the first year.

At the same time, our service level continued to rise and the Franchise scores increased due to our close relationship with the hotels and corporate management.

Management Services

Management

Leisure Hotels and Resorts is a leader in the hospitality management industry. Our knowledgeable and experienced staff work with each hotel as if we were owners and guests. Our goal is to provide quality service, maintain impeccable facilities, revenues and expenses. We do this with years of experience.

Finance and Administration

Our Finance and Administration group uses new technology and tools to help retrieve and analyze the properties financial performance. Our efforts provide up to date business intelligence to the property management and corporate staff, allowing them to anticipate trends and respond accordingly.

Marketing and E-Commerce

The Internet is the fastest growing resource for travel and hotel resellers. Leisure has been at the forefront in embracing the Internet and E-Commerce to promote hotels more effectively and efficiently. We provide hotels with channels to increase distribution possibilities reaching more customers.

Leisure Hotels and Resorts represents many hotel locations throughout the Midwest and United States.

BRITISH ASSOCIATION OF HOSPITALITY ACCOUNTANTS (BAHA)

The British Association of Hospitality Accountants (BAHA) was formed in 1969 with the aim of bringing together those professionals who were involved in financial management and control within the hotel industry. Since inception the membership has expanded to include systems specialists, hospitality consultants and accountants, bankers, investment analysts, property professionals, academics and others who retain an interest in the hotel, catering and leisure sectors.

BAHA has become recognised over the years as an authoritative voice in the hotel, catering and leisure industry on financial management, technical accounting issues, taxation, hotel valuation and other related aspects.

Members come from both large and small companies and all share a desire to see the hospitality industry progress through ensuring a high standard of financial management at all levels.

BAHA hold many regular meetings both in London and the Regions. We also arrange Conferences and Social Events throughout the year. We provide access to industry specific publications and manage ongoing vocational training.

HOSPITALITY SALES AND MARKETING ASSOCIATION INTERNATIONAL (HSMAI FOUNDATION)

Established in 1983 to serve as the research and educational arm of the Hospitality Sales and Marketing Association International. Its mission is to expand and enhance the educational opportunities available to hospitality sales and marketing executives and to increase the amount of in-depth research conducted on behalf of the profession. Today, and in the years ahead, the HSMAI Foundation plans to accelerate its research and publishing activities to contribute even more to the continuing education of those engaged in this fast-paced, increasingly demanding profession.

Audience

The HSMAI Foundation's research projects have resulted in cutting-edge publications and other educational materials that contain invaluable insights and information of importance to hospitality marketers, salespeople and practitioners.

The work of the HSMAI Foundation depends entirely on the voluntary financial support it receives from individuals and organizations. Those who underwrite a particular project by awarding the Foundation a full or partial grant are recognized on the title page of the resulting publication or in the credits of a film or audio or video cassette. Since the Foundation is tax-exempt under the provisions of Section 501 (c) (3) of the IRS code, monetary contributions and donations of goods and services are tax deductible as the law allows.

Work

The HSMAI Foundation can help you to grow as a hospitality sales and marketing executive by providing you with the information that you must have to be effective in an increasingly demanding profession. Because the members of the Foundation's Board of Trustees are your peers, they understand what you must know toe productive in your organization and successful in your career. Foundation projects, therefore, are designed to help you develop practical skills that you can apply on a day-to-day basis. In addition, the Foundation strives to make available reliable facts and figures that will increase your ability to deal with the problems and manage the opportunities in today's competitive hospitality industry. Look at the descriptions of the publications that the Foundation has produced since 1983 and you will appreciate the range and depth of the work that has been accomplished.

In the future, the Foundation will accelerate its research, book publication, and creation of pertinent course material in order to contribute even more to the education of hospitality sales and marketing executives. What can the HSMAI Foundation do for you? Quite simply, it can give you the tools, and therefore the edge, you need to move ahead in your profession and in your career.

Favour

Because you are committed to the advancement of the hospitality sales and marketing profession, please consider making a contribution to the HSMAI Foundation. The work of the Foundation depends entirely on the financial support it receives from voluntary gifts and grants from individuals and organizations. All contributions are tax deductible under the current provisions of Section 501 (c) (3) of the IRS code. HSMAI chapters and other organizations that underwrite a particular project by awarding the Foundation a full or partial grant are recognized on the title page of the resulting publication or tin the credits of a film or audio or video cassette. Please make an investment in your profession and in your future by sending your gift to.

Education and Events

HSMAI offers educational opportunities for all levels of sales and marketing professional through programmes sponsored by the national office, European division and individual chapters. These programmes range from networking and panel discussions on business trends at the local level to conferences and seminars that touch on international travel and hospitality issues. HSMAI also offers educational opportunities and business-building opportunities specifically for meeting planners at our HSMAI Affordable Meetings and HSMAI Meetings Quest events across the country. To search for HSMAI events that may be taking place in your region or are geared toward specific subjects, you can use the search function on this page.

RSI INTERNATIONAL, INC.

RSI International is a world-leader in web-based reservation and property management systems with integrated real-time room reservation capabilities. By increasing revenue and reducing expenses, our products have proven time and time again that they boost the profitability of our hotel and resort industry customers.

Key benefits of our systems and model:

- Cost efficiency
- *"Any Time Any Where"* access
- Short lead time to deployment
- End to End solution provider

SIEMENS

Germany-based Siemens AG, with 430.000 employees and subsidiaries in 190 countries, established its Global Centre of Competence (CoC) for hospitality solutions in Dubai, offering in-depth expertise, consulting and support as well as a complete product and solution portfolio to the hotel industry. The pool of industry experts with global headquarter functions bundle all Siemens activities towards hotels, cruise ships and wellness clinics. The CoC is a global contact points for hotel chains, with a special focus to cater the local market in Dubai. The Siemens hospitality units boasts Global Marketing, Product Management, Sales, Sales Support and Back Level Support as well as a fully equipped showroom, displaying hospitality solutions from IT, telecommunications, building technologies, and in-room entertainment like video streaming solutions.

Siemens Hospitality Services is a system integrator and turnkey solution provider for the planning, implementation and management of all information and communications equipment for hotels, cruise ships and wellness clinics. Siemens is a leading player in Real Time Communications and has developed a comprehensive portfolio of converged and native IP platforms plus an unmatched application and service portfolio. Siemens has a global footprint with Sales and Service subsidiaries in over 190 countries, and ample hotel project experience with more than 2800 hotel installations all over the globe. For more information, please visit www.siemens.com/hotel.

Hospitality Trend Window

The competitive hospitality industry is continuously challenged to keep in step with the needs of today's demanding corporate and leisure travellers. Travellers expect impeccable, fast and reliable guest services. Savvy, time-pressed business travellers expect leading-edge communications services in their rooms, conference facilities and public areas such as lobbies and lounges.

Hotel Operation Challenges

The global hotel market is being driven by consolidation, expansion and unprecedented takeovers. A softening global economy, safety concerns about terrorism and a cutback in corporate sponsored events has reduced hotel occupancy. Most importantly, hoteliers are fighting diminishing brand loyalty. The international hotelier is striving to establish and grow a consistent global brand positioning, which is crucial in achieving a rewarding brand value. Not only due to the ongoing chain takeovers and market consolidation, hotels are often faced with local variations in the technology that is available in different markets around the world, making it difficult to implement consistent service levels and workflow processes. Hotels are faced with improving efficiency, integrating new technology in current infrastructure, and improving customer service in an environment in which budgets are shrinking. The challenge is now to define brand- and segment-specific service levels that reflect the increasing demand for services by the hotel guest but also the need for global availability, reliability and consistency.

Strategic Portfolio Analysis

In high-level workshops with experts from the hotel industry and hotel chains, the following model of a "magic triangle" was developed. Moving away from the traditional PBX model, technologies on the move are ASP solutions, converging solutions and, most importantly, solutions for Customer Relationship Management (CRM). Hotel chains will invest in converging technology if such a platform provides CRM-relevant improvements and centralized hosting of real-time applications (ASP).

Guest Services

Guests now have increasingly high expectations of service levels. Standardized services are expected across locations. As guests get used to technology at work and home, they are coming to expect it in their hotel rooms as well. Since high-tech equipment in the guest rooms is fast becoming a prerequisite, this does not produce a tangible competitive edge on its own. What provides competitive advantages today are superior guest services, efficiently managed by the appropriate technology. The centralization and integration of workflows to cut costs and real-time hotel management tools are key challenges.

Technology Investment

Today, the hospitality industry is changing its IT investment model from CAPEX (capital expenditures, up-front investments) to OPEX (operational expenditures, running costs), which focuses on centralized Shared Service Centres for voice and data hosting. This approach will significantly change the value chain for hotels and IT solution vendors. Therefore the following layers will gain key importance:

- Organization model and supply chain integration (local processes vs. central processes, central monitoring and controlling, outsourcing and outtasking, redefinition of so-called key performance indicators)
- New business intelligence tools that track, analyze and present previously defined KPIs
- Technical Infrastructure (interfaces, data security, accessibility, network redundancy, quality of service. bandwidth availability, managed services, load balancing)
- Choice of partners (ASP models, global footprint, financial strengths, strategic alliances)
- Commercial model (revenue generators, cost cutting, internal accounting transformation)

Technology Trend Window

Seamless and cost effective solutions that are easy to manage are the great goal for communication services in the hospitality industry. Hoteliers seek for innovative technologies and reliable partners in a fast changing market.

2nd Generation IP

The stated real-time communications strategy for many hotels is to lower capital, operational and management expenses by at least 20 per cent. This will only be accomplished by implementing a bundle of measures, such as commercial consolidation of carrier and maintenance contracts, a global help desk, network consolidation and introduction of Voice over IP. Cost reductions are substantial if voice communications services are managed in the same way as data applications. Voice over IP, as it is implemented today, follows the PBX model. However, this model has led us to the current model of Enterprise Telephony Networks with all its deficiencies. Premise-based decentralization, proprietary protocols and endpoints with little interoperability between different vendors' products have made it impossible to build seamless solutions that are easy to manage. The fragmentation of the different communications services adds to the complexity and makes matters even worse.

Second generation IP systems will change the traditional communications model in every respect and leverage the inherent advantages of IP available in Next Generation of Networks. The deployment of communications services will follow the data model. Communications services will become data applications. Cost savings in operation and maintenance and the availability of new services and hospitality applications will be the first tangible results that are achieved with hosted real-time communications solutions. Siemens has a well-defined strategy to provide cost-effective bridges, ensuring that the transition to highly scalable IP communications focuses on making a positive and significant impact on the bottom line.

Upcoming Hotel Solutions

(a) Guest Rooms

Logically interdependent devices will enable the connection of IP phones with PC-based systems and displays. The following easy-to-use in-room applications are expected to be available in the near future, providing considerable productivity enhancements:

- Mobile VoIP phones, which work in a WLAN environment and provide unified messaging services on premises

- Integration of room-based multimedia PCs for IP workflows (unified messaging, guided conference calls. Internet access, content management)
- Multiple display access (phones, PCs, plasma screen, etc.)
- "At your service" workflows, which track and control all guest-related service bundles
- Centralized room control based on IP, access via integrated displays
- Centrally hosted interactive multimedia content, which can be streamed and broadcast from external sources.

(b) Public Areas

Hotels are increasingly becoming hotspots for WLAN roaming, which enables guests to connect to their network provider from various locations around the globe. The new generation of mobile phones will be able to connect to both UMTS networks and, when moving onto the hotel grounds, the available WLAN network. In the public hotel areas, such as the lobby or even in the spa, a major role will be played by security enhancements for data networks through new encryption methods. New communications services will soon be available, since bandwidth has increased 10-fold thanks to new technology standards. As a means of regaining brand loyalty, profiled guest portals with different Internet access rates due to certain membership status (platinum member, etc.) are applications of importance in the CRM context.

(c) Conference Area

In the hotel conference area, up-front booking systems of communications services including multimedia conferencing is becoming more and more a prerequisite to organize events and meetings without the necessity of technical staff. New technologies will support fully managed multimedia conferencing. After conferences, temporary virtual private networks will make presentations and other event materials available. Participants will be able to log on to the network from their room and download files of their interest.

(d) Administration/Back Office

- *Converged switches and platforms*: Communication systems have evolved in recent years from traditional closed TDM models to converged switches for both voice and data. Secondary IP softswitches for premises networks based on VoIP emerged, which are now being followed by the latest second generation IP (so-called 2gIP) central softswitches over public networks with centralized application hosting. Like other vertical industries, hospitality is jumping from analog technologies straight to IP telephony based on SIP protocols.

- *Workflow centralization*: In order to centralize key processes, especially those related to satisfying guests, hotels are looking for centrally managed Guest Service Centres, which can retain the human touch for the guest while also providing intelligent service tracking software that helps to monitor guest requests from order to completion. Additionally, embedded intelligent software tools are needed to track, store, analyze and display data that was previously generated in IT and telephony systems.
- *Management tools*: The above-mentioned data will be made available to the local hotel property management (Management Information Systems) or to headquarters management of the hotel chain (Executive Information Systems). Tools to measure the quality of service delivered as well as a wide range of information and statistics about guest data and service calls will prove very helpful, for example to track brand value-related indices (guest satisfaction index, retention rates, etc.) or to deploy hotel service personnel efficiently on the basis of statistics about peak times and staff productivity.

Our Strategy

Siemens Hospitality Services is a system integrator and turnkey solution provider for the planning, implementation and management of all IT and communications equipment in the hotel environment. We support Siemens' sales units in 190 countries by providing a global point of contact for major hotel chains in the world. The combination of our in-depth hotel industry know-how, a complete product and service portfolio as well as extensive system integration capabilities allows us to provide consistent turnkey solutions on a global basis.

HiPath Hospitality Solution Portfolio

(a) HiPath Hospitality

Intelligent solutions with your guests' comfort and satisfaction in mind. The Siemens HiPath Hospitality solution is a powerful hospitality offering that combines the advanced Real Time Communications features of the HiPath IP system with a hotel services application package that can interface with leading third-party Property Management Systems (PMS).

(b) Applications

- *HiPath Hospitality Service Centre*: In anticipating the demand for intelligent CRM solutions, Siemens developed a completely new software application – the HiPath Hospitality Service Centre. The goal was to create a client/server application that optimizes telephony at the hotel workstation while also making use of excellent integration capabilities to leverage the benefits of central data resources. The HiPath Hospitality Service Centre integrates a guest call centre with an intelligent service tracking module and a powerful data mining system that allows for productivity control, staff resource planning and management scorecards.
- *Conference solution*: Our conference solution software makes it possible to reserve selected communications and data services for a planned conference or meeting. All voice and data services are made available at any time without need for technical staff. Both short-term and long-term reservations are possible. The organizer enjoys unlimited configuration freedom when choosing analog, ISDN, high-speed Internet, LAN and WAN structures as well as bandwidths and fixed IP addresses.
- *Security solutions*: Siemens offers comprehensive security solutions from consulting to implementation of physical and logical access control as well as network security solutions. These ensure that our hotel customers and their guests can operate their business in a secure manner. We provide the advantages of a complete security solution as a one-stop-shop.

(c) Services

- *HiPath Professional Services*: Complete voice and IT consulting, assessment and customization services including hotel needs analysis and workflow assessment, hospitality application design, configuration and implementation, project management and systems integration as well as training, e.g. for service centre agents.
- *HiPath Managed Services*: Wide-ranging outsourcing and outtasking services, including managed voice and data services, and 24/7 help desk support.

Siemens provides you with and end-to-end solution

- Most comprehensive communications solution portfolio in the hospitality market
- Turnkey solution in the areas of information technology, communication and building technologies
- Complete and integrated services from a single source
- Seamless integration of third-party products

Quality guest services

- Individualized and profiled communications services
- Fast and reliable services through service tracking
- A perfectly organized IT infrastructure creates the latitude for personalized guest services and the human touch
- Impeccable services help retain customers and win new ones
- Greater guest loyalty leads to increased hotel brand value

Better cost position

- Improved operational efficiency assists your business in capitalizing on the benefits of the Internet and IP
- The possibility of centralization (shared service) is an important cost-sharing aspect for hotel chains with various properties in a city or region.
- IT cost savings on property through converged networks, connection to host systems, ASP models, and modular upgradeable suites.

- *HiPath Lifecycle Services*: Comprehensive implementation and support services for hospitality solutions, including design, installation, upgrades, repair, and preventive maintenance.

(d) Internet Access

- *Wireless hot spots*: Siemens can help you build and brand your own wireless hot spots using the latest wireless technology with tight integration to your front-office billing systems.
- *High-speed Internet access (HSIA)*: Complete solution for delivering high speed Web access and Internet-based services to the guest and conference rooms.

(e) Communications Platforms

- HiPath 3000 is the Real Time IP System for small and medium-sized hotels.
- HiPath 4000 is the IP Convergence platform for medium-sized and large hotels. It combines the benefits of IP networking with the rich features, applications and availability of a circuit-switched system.
- HiPath 5000 is a native IP communications system that works in packet-switched and circuit-switched environments.
- HiPath 8000 is a central second generation IP softswitch, which enables the connection of various hotel properties, dispersed across a city, country or region, with only one host system (voice/data).

The availability of centrally hosted hospitality services and applications will be the first tangible result.

(f) Phones and Devices

Our range of devices includes analog, digital, IP and SIP phones, softclients, cordless DECT phones, as well as special devices such as PDAs and Tablet PCs.

(g) LAN Components

We provide assessments, validation, network planning, administration and a complete set of active LAN components for secure networks, including routers, cabling, and switches.

(h) System Integration

Siemens HiPath Hospitality's open architecture supports leading third-party solutions for call accounting, property management, and guest room devices. Our innovative applications unfold their full performance under any network structure. In close cooperation with Siemens Building Technologies, we integrate:

- Security and access control
- Fire protection
- Energy control
- Thermal comfort
- Hotel room management systems.

About Siemens Hospitality Services

We are a vertically specialized Line of Business (LoB) within the Siemens Group Information and Communication Networks. Siemens is a leading player in Real Time Communications and has developed a comprehensive portfolio of converged and native IP platforms as well as an unmatched application and service portfolio.

Siemens Partnership

A basic principle of our business is to establish strong, sustainable partnerships with our customers based on trust, reliability and in-depth industry knowledge. More than a strategic partnership, we believe in Customer Centric Leadership (CCL) that comprises solution development and a proven CRM platform with executive workshops, training, joint market communications, strategic pilot projects and travel management.

We establish sustainable partnerships with our hotel customers:

- We are a trusted partner with longstanding customer relationships
- We understand the business processes of our customers ("people business")
- We are as global as our customers
- We tailor the right IT strategy to our customers' business strategy

Siemens Information and Communication Networks is a leading supplier of networks and real-time applications for enterprises and network operators. Over one million customers in more than 160 countries trust our solutions. Our global footprint and our expertise in voice and IP communication enable us to deliver turnkey network solutions of any scale and complexity throughout the world.

(a) Life Works

With Life Works, the communication of the future starts today. Innovative applications can be delivered over any network and to any communication device in a user-friendly and efficient way. Life Works leverages the potential of Next Generation Networks for network operators, companies and users.

(b) Next Generation Networks

Next Generation Networks deliver voice, data and video applications over one network. Network operators can now increase profitability by generating new revenue streams at a lower cost. Enterprises are able to boost productivity by integrating our communication solutions into their business processes. End users enjoy the benefits of new voice/data applications.

Siemens Information and Communication Networks supplies everything you need for a smooth and profitable migration from existing networks to Next Generation Networks:

- Real Time Communications
- Next Generation Switching
- Next Generation Access
- Next Generation Optics

(c) Comprehensive Services

We offer our customers comprehensive services for the whole value chain. Our worldwide presence also allows us to address customers' needs at a local level.

(d) Your Partner for Profitable Networks

Siemens Information and Communication Networks has extensive knowledge in the areas of carrier and enterprise networks. We exploit this expertise to further realize our vision of a seamless network extending from the global carrier down to the individual customer. As your partner, we offer innovative solutions that deliver fast return on investment, boost productivity, and help you explore new business opportunities. Your continuing success is our priority.

Our Strengths – Your Gain

HiPath Hospitality solutions offer in right innovative communication solution for every need. Intelligent functions and modules improve quality of guest services and optimize the working processes to ensure greater customer satisfaction, while at the same time reducing costs. Our intelligent solutions have your guests' comfort and satisfaction in mind.

Hospitality Industry

Hospitality Market Challenges

The entire travel industry has been under tremendous pressure over the last two and a half years. A softening global economy, safety and security concern over terrorism, the threat of SARS and a cutback in corporate sponsored events has reduced U.S. hotel occupancy to 60 per cent of capacity. Additionally the hotel industry is challenged to maintain established revenue sources. Income from guest phone calls, for example, has declined substantially as more travellers use personal cellular phones.

Hoteliers are responding to these challenges by reducing staff, canceling hotel development plans, consolidating administrative facilities and exiting non-profitable brands. In addition to these efforts they are actively marketing themselves to increase occupancy rates and seeking alternative revenue sources that include expanding guest services.

Key Challenges

- Hoteliers are constantly searching for the perfect balance between guest satisfaction and profitability. In today's environment of continuous change, hotels must have a communications system that is flexible, efficient, secure and reliable.
- Hotels are faced with improving efficiency, integrating new technology with current infrastructure, and improving customer service in an atmosphere where budgets and workforce are shrinking.
- Hospitality businesses are constrained on their ability to apply traditional IT-enabled money saving business solutions due to their round-the-clock, highly mobile operations and multiple locations, widely scattered across the United States and around the world.

Siemens Solution

With our, global experience, life-cycle services and turnkey hospitality solutions, Siemens can help.

Siemens has everything from real-time communications systems, customized voice mail and attendant consoles, to IP-based networks, distributed management tools and a variety of analog, digital and soft client telephones.

As a turnkey solution partner we can help you:

- Get more out of your existing infrastructures
- Increase operational efficiencies
- Generate new revenue while increasing customer service

Providing the Ultimate Lux in Hotel Services

Large or small, every hotel is faced with the same challenges: how to respond to ever increasing guest demands for convenience, and personalized service. Hotel services should be available quickly and smoothly – perfect all-round care is regarded as a matter of course. In this environment, reception is the pivotal point of every hotel. This is where visitors become guests, where inquiries are made, information provided, and action taken. Friendly, competent, and caring guest service is the visiting card of the establishment.

With Siemens HiPath Hospitality solution, you can:

- View the guests name allowing personalized greetings and efficient call handling
- Control call flow via a PC screen with the same efficiency as a typical Call Centre agent, optimizing guest service
- Allow operators to satisfy guest's needs within seconds with a programmable one-touch buttons that automates guest service functions.

Key Solutions

HiPath Hospitality

Siemens HiPath Hospitality solution includes the industry's most robust, specialized Hospitality Attendant Console (HAC) - a PC-based Client/Server application designed specifically for the hospitality market.

GUEST SERVICES, INC.

Guest Services, Inc. is dedicated to providing excellence in food service and hospitality management for hotel, recreation and retail, resort and Business and Industry venues since 1917. Guest Services has a rich history of delivering a broad range of quality food service and other hospitality services including; restaurants, cafeterias, food courts, full service hotels, resorts, conference centres and recreational and retail facilities. Our group dining outlets are located in some of the most prestigious government buildings and most popular museums in Washington, DC.

Among our other food service activities, we are proud to offer a variety of group dining choices ranging from boxed lunches to full service catering at Washington's most prestigious cafeterias, food courts, cafes and restaurants. Personalized food service arrangements are available for groups of 20 or more. Guest Services has developed discounted group menus to make your itinerary planning easier. We offer vouchers upon request and most locations honour the standard complimentary policy. Our food service management efforts will be tailored to meet the needs of your park, hotel, resort, stadium, museum, art gallery, government, business office or retail space.

Environmental Management Programme

"Conservation means development as much as it does protection. I recognize the right and duty of this generation to develop and use the natural resources of our land: but I do not recognize the right to waste them, or to rob, by wasteful use, the generations that come after us." *—Teddy Roosevelt, August 31, 1910*

Mission

Guest Services is dedicated to conducting our business in the most environmentally friendly manner practicable. To accomplish this, we have selected leaders from around the company to continually investigate and recommend better ways of managing our businesses to protect the environment, educate our employees, and reach out to our customers and communities on these important issues.

Guest Services

Guest Services has a rich and proud history of offering management services [including fully integrated hospitality management services] to our clients. The following services are a sampling of what we have to offer. We provide signature services tailored to the individual client's needs.

Marketing

As a centralized resource for marketing and advertising expertise, the Marketing Department is available to assertively and effectively promote the public restaurants, resorts, hotels, and recreation to the tourism industry and the staff restaurants to employees. A comprehensive programme of trade shows, promotional events and advertisements directed at tourism professionals is currently being implemented to increase business in our facilities. This programme will be continually updated to achieve maximum results.

Human Resources

The Human Resources Department manages the Guest Services "SPECTRUM" programme of employee benefits and labour relations issues. They take the lead in maintaining the company's comprehensive and extremely effective Affirmative Action Plan. Human Resources also plays an advocacy role in dealing with critical concerns affecting employee/management relations and maintains open lines of communication with all levels of management for speedy handling of benefit questions and quick resolution of grievances. This department ensures compliance with employment laws and governmental reporting requirements.

Employee and Management Training Programme

Guest Services has a strong, long-standing corporate commitment to training. In our state-of-the-art Training Centre, we develop and implement custom seminars and training programmes to assure quality service and cuisine to our customers. Our programmes use externally and internally produced audio visual media, a wide selection of "in-service" training modules, and interactive role play to instill new concepts in Total Quality Management, employee empowerment, managing diversity, safety and sanitation, business relationships and job skills training. In addition, managers frequently attend seminars and college level training courses to better prepare them for their assignments. On-the-job mentoring is also a very strong element of our training processes.

Health and Sanitation

Our corporate Environmental Health Specialist regularly monitors sanitation at the operational unit level. He teaches the Food Service

Sanitation Course (required by Federal and D.C. law for at least one food service manager on-site at each facility) and certifies new managers in safe food handling procedures and re-certifies managers at three year intervals. Most of our hourly employees currently working have also been certified in safe food handling procedures.

Procurement

Through our corporate Director of Procurement, Guest Services operates a procurement programme aimed at obtaining a high quality product at the best cost. By means of corporate and local product research, the monitoring of all purchasing activities, field testing, competitive bidding, frequent vendor evaluation and qualification, we are able to achieve this goal. All food products purchased conform to published quality standards and specifications.

Quality Assurance

Guest Services is dedicated to the principles of continuous improvement in the quality of products and services we provide our customers and clients.

The Quality Assurance Department, headquartered in the Corporate Office, has the directive to evaluate, measure and encourage the highest quality standards for each of our businesses. Comprehensive Quality Assurance reviews are conducted of each business. Reviews include checking for adherence to company policies as well as customer service, detailed sanitation inspections, equipment inspections, and merchandising reviews. Special emphasis is placed on food quality reviews and food production systems in food service businesses. Safety, adherence to company policies, housekeeping and repair and maintenance are also evaluated and scored. The results are reviewed with the managers, District Manager and Division Head. Summary reports are sent to the President, COO. The Quality Assurance team is available to assist in developing corrective actions to solve any problems noted. In food service businesses quality Assurance provides coordinating assistance with menu cycle and recipe development, organizes equipment research and testing, arranges for (and provides certain) on-the-job training services and troubleshoots quality, cost and service problems.

In addition to the Division of Quality Assurance, an ad hoc Quality Assurance committee participates as needed in the various tasks of the new department. This committee consists of the Corporate Chef, the Director of Training, the Director of Purchasing, the Sanitarian and representatives from the Human Resources Department and the finance Division. Others are called upon as needed from time to time.

The Quality Assurance Department plays a pivotal role in new business openings and assists when new concepts are being introduced or extraordinary changes are made to an account.

The Quality Assurance Department of Guest Services will help ensure continued excellence into the new millennium.

Test Kitchen

Our state-of-the-art test kitchen facilitates product testing, recipe development and menu planning under the direction of our Executive Chef. Menus and recipes are tailored to reflect standards of the highest quality, artfully presented.

Safety and Security

Guest Services has comprehensive procedures for safety, security, and loss prevention. These subjects are stressed in employee orientation, and managers and hourly employees take part in almost continuous training through seminars and "in-service" training. Safety of guests, safe work practices, safety inspections conducted by an effective corporate and operations level Safety Committee Programme receive strong emphasis at Guest Services. The protection of supplies and equipment and the personal possessions of guests, our employees and our client is assured by an effective loss control programme headed by our Director of Security in coordination with our Internal Audit Department.

Maintenance and Construction Support

Our experienced staff provides quick response to HVAC, refrigeration, general maintenance and construction issues. We have on-call resources available day or night, seven days a week to serve our clients needs.

Management Information Systems Department

Guest Services operates a central computer at its headquarters for our corporate accounting including General Ledger, Accounts

Payable, Accounts Receivable, and Fixed Assets. The computer is also used for our human resources and payroll functions. Point-of-Sale systems are customized to our different locations and are networked to, and supported by, a personal computer located at the manager's desk. The Point-of-Sale system handles both cash and credit card transactions and provides detailed and summary information on sales and inventory at the item and department level. Menus and pricing are easily changed by the manager. The manager can also easily set up and track various promotions and discounts.

Choice Cuising

Guest Services provides you with a "choice of culinary concepts." Not only in the beginning, but concepts can be changed with minima! time and investment.

Our selection of branded concepts is developed in our test kitchen by a team of chefs and quality assurance experts. New recipes are constantly being created.

Call us today for a fresh perspective on your food and beverage needs.

Recreation

Guest Services manages recreational facilities for the National Park Service in the Washington DC area, as well as in Washington State (*Mt* Rainier) and for the state of West Virginia (Canaan Valley Resort).

Biking

Whether you are interested in hiking along the Potomac River or mountain hiking in West Virginia, Guest Services can put you on the trail.

Bike rentals are available at Thompson Centre and Washington Sailing Marina. Bike paths take you to the monuments in DC or along the river to Mt. Vernon, home of George Washington.

Canaan Valley Resort, located a three and one half hour car trip from DC, has mountain bike rentals available for use in the state park.

Boating

The Washington Sailing Marina (at Daingerfield Island - one mile south of National Airport) offers sailing and sail board lessons and rents Sun Fish, Flying Scots and bicycles. It has a full ship's store and gift shop (Spinnaker 'N Spoke), a galley (Afterdeck Cafe), launch ramp, boat storage and yearly slips.

Columbia Island Marina (George Washington Parkway between 14th Street and Memorial bridges) offers slip rental for power boats, launch ramp, fuel, and a cafe renowned for its pork barbecue.

The Thompson Boat Centre (2900 Virginia Avenue across from the Watergate in Georgetown) specializes in people-powered boating. There are rental bikes, canoes, kayaks and rowing shells/ single sculls. Our professionals at Thompson offer rowing classes in single and sweep.

The Tidal Basin peddle boats offer an afternoon family outing or a romantic early evening date. While enjoying the sun and exercise, you will view the Jefferson Memorial and the Washington Monument.

Tennis

As a concessionaire for the National Park Service, Guest Services operates three tennis centres.

Rock Creek Tennis Centre (16th & Kennedy, DC) has indoor and outdoor courts, a tennis stadium, ample free parking, snack bar and pro shop. We host the Legg Mason Tennis Classic every August. The facility is adjacent to the Cartre Barron amphitheatre.

East Potomac Tennis (1090 Ohio Drive SW, Haines Point DC) has indoor and outdoor courts, seasonal membership or walk-in court rental, tennis lessons and racquet stringing.

Pierce Mill is a small centre in beautiful Rock Creek Park which offers clay courts.

Skating

Guest Services operates three ice skating rinks:

The Sculpture Garden Ice Rink, located across from the West entrance of the National Gallery at 7th and Constitution, Washington, D.C. provides the visitor with an extraordinary view of the art sculptures in meticulously landscaped gardens. Throughout the winter months (November-March) you can relax and watch skaters on the ice skating rink while enjoying a cup of hot chocolate or your favourite cappuccino or join in the fun! Indoor and outdoor seating is provided. Groups are welcome.

The Pavilion Cafe, found amidst the casual elegance of the National Gallery of Art Sculpture Garden, offers a tempting array of soups, salads, sandwiches and gourmet pizzas year-round.

Pershing Park Ice Rink, located at 14th Street and Pennsylvania Avenue, NW, Washington, DC. Outdoor skating mid-December-March (weather permitting). The snack bar has plenty of hot chocolate to warm those frosty fingers!

Canaan Valley Resort also offers ice skating in the winter.

Horseback Riding

View Beautiful Rock Creek Park by Horseback - DC's only full-service equestrian facility. www.rockcreekhor secenter.com.

Retail

Gifts & Memorabilia

- *Washington, DC Visitor's Information Centre*: Make your first stop in Washington the Washington, DC Visitor's Information Centre located inside the Ronald Reagan International Trade Centre Building. Our friendly staff provides information, brochures, and tour services to visitors of our Nation's Capital. The Centre also provides interactive kiosks, Discover Channel film. Ticket Master outlet, tour sales, hotel and restaurant reservations. Shop in the Centre's gift shop or online and purchase unique souvenirs and memorabilia reflective of the city's rich and colourful history.
- *The National Aquarium*: Visit DC's underwater adventure. The country's oldest aquarium is located inside the Department of Commerce Building. Over 1,000 specimens of aquatic life and 200 species of fish are represented.
- *The Indian Craft Shop*: Located inside the Department of the Interior, the Indian Craft Shop has been providing authentic American Indian arts and crafts since 1938. This nationally recognized store is known for quality in arts and crafts, educational programmes, and exhibits spanning 45 tribes within the United States.
- *White House Easter Egg*: The White House will not be authorizing the sale of the 2002/2003 Easter Egg. A limited number of 1999 and 2000 eggs are still available by ordering through Guest Services online at www.white houseeasteregg.com. To order 2003 eggs.call

Resorts/Hotels

Canaan Valley Resort

A Four Seasons Mountain Resort. If you can not relax here, you can not relax anywhere!

Located in Davis, West Virginia, Canaan Valley Resort: Skiing, boating, camping, tennis and fishing are available for your family, tour group or corporate retreat. Enjoy the scenic outdoors with nature walks, hiking, miniature golf and a par-72 championship golf course.

Mt. Rainier National Park

Breathtaking vistas. Lush alpine flowers. But Mount Rainier National Park is more than a sanctuary for natural beauty, it is also a natural playground. Which means there is as much for you to do up here as there is to see.

Doubletree Guest Suites

Congratulations to Vikki Fritz, General Manager of the Doubletree Guest Suites Naples, Barry Trice, Assistant Vice President, Hospitality-South and their superb staff for again winning; for the third time in tour years, the "Connie" award at Hilton Hotels' Full Service Brand Conference last week. They also won the Doubetree Pride Award and the 2004 CARE Cup Annual Award.

We are very proud of our Doubletree staff for taking service and hospitality to such a notable level.

Located in Naples, Florida, The Doubletree Guest Suites presents guests with an array of features to accommodate their stay on the Gulf Coast. This all-suite hotel sits on a peninsula on the Cocahatchee River overlooking a wildlife preserve and offers these advantages:

- Minutes from the beach
- Close to shopping
- Golf privileges at some of Naples' finest courses
- 30 minutes from the Fort Myers Airport
- 45 minutes from the Everglades
- Minutes from Old Naples
- Minutes from a wide variety of restaurants

The Marbella

The Marbella at Pelican Bay, a luxurious residential tower in Naples, Florida. 7425 Pelican Bay Blvd., Naples, FL 34108

Tour Groups

Make your first stop in Washington the Washington, DC Visitor Information Centre located inside the Ronald Reagan International Trade Centre Building. Our friendly staff provides information, brochures, and tour services to visitors of our Nation's Capital. The Centre also provides interactive kiosks, Discover Channel film. Ticket Master outlet, tour sales, hotel and restaurant reservations. Shop in the Centre's gift shop and purchase unique souvenirs and memorabilia reflective of the city's rich and colorful history.

Guest Services is particularly interested in making tour groups visiting our Nation's Capital and the surrounding areas feel welcome. Senior and student groups travelling by motor coach, convention, associations and corporate groups in town on business—all are treated to the same warm and friendly food and service which has made us famous.

Planning Services

Our commitment to the group tour industry is strong and we are happy to offer:

- Discounted group vouchers for dining
- Complimentary meals
- Gift shops and free parking in some locations
- Picnic box lunches

Sightseeing

Our restaurants are located in some of the most visited museums in the city and include:

- The Cafe des Artistes in the Corcoran Gallery of Art
- The Hillwood Cafe in the Hillwood Museum (home of the late Marjorie Merriweather Post)
- The Museum Cafe in The United States Holocaust Memorial Museum
- Potowmack Landing Restaurant at the Washington Sailing Marina on historic Daingerfield Island

For fun times before or after your group meals, a stop at some of our recreation facilities will provide a memorable addition to any itinerary:

- Pedal Boats at the Tidal Basin across from the Jefferson Memorial
- Ice Skating on the National Mall
- Sailboard, bike and boat rentals at the Washington Sailing Marina and Thompson Boat Centre
- Volleyball and croquet along with an outdoor barbecue at the Columbia Island Marina
- A unique tour on the DC Ducks, refurbished World War II land and water boats, followed by lunch or dinner in a waterside setting.

Staying Connected During an Emergency

Unit(s) in Lock-Down	Evacuated Unit(s)
None at this time	None at this time

ERNST & YOUNG

Ernst & Young launches its Regional Hospitality, Tourism and Leisure Advisory Services from Dubai.

Ernst & Young, the Middle East's largest assurance and business advisory firm, has launched their Middle East Hospitality and Leisure Advisory Service to an expectant market.

Through its Dubai based Advisory Services, Ernst & Young is now assisting regional organizations in the tourism and hospitality sector improve and control the way they manage their investments and operations in real estate assets throughout the entire lifecycle of their property portfolio.

Ernst & Young's range of services will include strategic tourism enhancement planning, hotel operational reviews, positioning analyses, asset management, management company selection/ negotiations, capital sourcing, benchmarking, valuations, mergers and acquisitions due diligence, and market driven feasibility studies for a variety of asset types. These include mixed-use resort developments, large hotel portfolios, traditional hotels, golf courses and clubs, theme parks, vacation ownership, condominium-hotels, cruise ships, airlines, retail, office, marinas and residential developments.

"Given the anticipated growth in the construction industry in the Middle East over the next five years, coupled with the number of hospitality and leisure-related projects currently under development, there is a strong need for a trusted business advisor who can provide specialized resources, industry expertise and innovative solutions," said Mohammed Dahmash, Regional Practice Leader and Partner of the Ernst & Young's Middle East Hospitality and Leisure Advisory Services. "Today's hospitality and leisure executives around the globe face a set of business challenges that place unprecedented pressure on management. Real estate, operations, marketing, and financing functions must be synchronized to maintain a competitive edge. Quality of service is paramount," Dahmash continued.

The services will also provide Ernst & Young's clients with effective strategies to minimize risk, as well as control expenses, and generally improve overall performance, which in turn can accelerate the creation of bottom line value for any company or organization in the hospitality and leisure sectors.

The new service has already been extremely well received and Ernst & Young are advising various regional government departments on tourism development issues and tourism master planning. Other projects also include feasibility studies for large-scale development projects in the region for both private and public sector investors.

"Our experience in advising clients, combined with our knowledge and expertise in Middle East and African hospitality and leisure markets, is unmatched. We offer a full scope of services, including acquisitions, development, strategy, operations and diagnostic reviews, for every real estate industry segment, not just hotels." said Dahmash.

Dahmash has many years experience in the industry and has put together a strong and sophisticated global team of professionals who all have extensive real estate and hospitality operations and advisory experience. Dahmash and his team had been instrumental in the development for many prestigious projects in the Middle East and Africa.

The Middle East practice of Ernst & Young is an independent professional firm and a full member firm of Ernst & Young Global. Since the firm's establishment 80 years ago, the Middle East firm has evolved to provide a full range of assurance and business advisory services to meet all legal and commercial developments within the region, and today the firm's more than 10,000 clients are serviced by over 1,800 staff operating from 16 offices in 12 Arab countries.

Ernst & Young, a global leader in professional services, offers clients the right tools and advice in order to meet the demands of an ever changing and dynamic business world. Ernst & Young has the industry and financial experience to provide fresh perspectives on operating successfully in the new economy. Ernst & Young provides a range of assurance and business advisory services including corporate finance, risk management, tax, technology, business valuation and hospitality and leisure services.

4HOTELIERS

4Hoteliers is the online hotel news division of Lifestyle Concepts Limited and was launched in early 2002 by a group of hoteliers and industry consultants who had been searching for a quality industry website where global hoteliers and trade executives could source information, related articles and investigate trends as well as to meet others to exchange ideas and thoughts. As a result we created this unique portal which has quickly risen though the ranks to become the news and information website for international hoteliers. It serves a worldwide audience of hospitality and travel trade executives and professionals, providing content and featured articles updated on a daily basis. The site offers the latest industry news and trends together with press releases from the main hotel chains, industry related technology, as well as career and industry resource centres. Each and every member of the 4Hoteliers News and Research Team has an extensive hospitality background, representing the many different divisions of hospitality businesses. As a result our multi-skilled team has the ability to present you a rich, in-depth understanding of our industry. We supplement this with a number of freelance journalists who contribute content from related and non-related industries. We actively encourage and welcome your involvement and participation, be this through submitting content for publication to promoting your company or services, or telling us about an upcoming event. In addition to 4Hoteliers offers several different types of advertising options each designed to reach a targeted audience of global hoteliers and related professionals.

NBTA

Mission

The Hotel Committee's Mission is to provide strategic direction on business travel issues to the hotel industry. The committee provides leadership to members and the global business travel community through education, strategic direction and universal standards, as it relates to the hotel industry.

Objectives

- To improve the understanding and professional relationships between corporate travel managers, procurement professionals, business travellers, and related hotel industry suppliers
- To engage in projects that will assist NBTA members in developing, implementing, and marketing corporate hotel programmes
- Act as a resource for NBTA members seeking information on the hotel industry; publish hotel committee standard documents and research material
- Provide strategic direction to streamline contracting, communication, and other process efficiencies.

KABA

Kaba Lodging Systems, www.kabalodging.com, is pleased to sponsor the Global Hotel Network® Executive Profile featuring Monty Bennett, President and CEO, Ashford Hospitality Trust.

Thanks to its expertise in access control, its high-quality products and its excellent worldwide reputation, Kaba Lodging Systems has recently become an Ashford Hospitality Trust partner through Remington Hotel Corporation.

Kaba is proud of this alliance with the "premier capital provider to the hospitality industry" and shares the values of long-term vision and flexibility with Ashford Hospitality Trust. The association between these two hospitality specialists who understand the value and opportunity of hotel assets is unique and extremely valuable for the industry. In today's world, investors, developers and hotel owners are looking for experienced, reliable and innovative partners. In business since 1862, the Kaba Group, who acquired IIco Unican (now Kaba Lodging Systems) is a "Total Access" solutions provider.

Kaba is a worldwide leader and innovator in electronic access control solutions for the lodging industry. After decades of innovative research and development, Kaba can proudly claim that it has a solution for most access control applications or security needs. The company's many successes derive from its commitment and understanding of the needs of the lodging industry and satisfying those needs by designing unparalleled access control systems with state-of-the-art electronic locks. This commitment has earned Kaba the reputation for being the reliable choice for electronic access control. Kaba's solutions range from a stand alone Front Desk Unit (FDU) to ATLAS, a PC-based system, Erased system. The new Generation E-760 and Solitaire 710-11 locks function with both of these systems. Kaba Lodging Systems also offers a world-class client programme with a customer service department dedicated to answering the needs of clients live, 24/7. This unsurpassed after sales-service and local technical support ensure Kaba Lodging Systems' customers Peace of Mind.

PRESERVED TREESCAPE INTERNATIONAL

Freshen up your properties, and update your landscaping by incorporating some realistic replica, preserved or custom trees and plants. Your property will look completely new. Let us give you a custom quote. You will be amazed at how much money Preserved TreeScapes can save you with a quick makeover or renovation. Find out what we have done for over 6,000 installations worldwide; visit our Website: www.treescapes.com

In "Photo Gallery" you will view exquisitely majestic and astonishingly realistic, yet wonderfully practical and cost-effective (no light, no water, no bugs, no fires, no worries), preserved and replica trees and plants. All created and manufactured to your unique landscape needs.

Interior and exterior tree and plant creations from Preserved TreeScapes International can be seen in prestigious hotels, restaurants, casinos, resorts and spas, shopping centres, amusement parks, regional mails, corporate headquarters, and many historic buildings around the world. Many have won prestigious awards, hopefully, you will see one of yours Contact us and see what Preserved TreeScapes International can do for you.

CNN INTERNATIONAL

CNN International, the world's leading global 24-hour news network, is available to more than 160 million households and more than two and a half million hotel rooms worldwide. According to the latest survey results, CNN is the undisputed news leader and the channel of choice for frequent business travellers.

The CNN Hotel Partnership Programme is a comprehensive, strategic marketing programme that combines the licensed signal to distribute CNN International in hotel rooms with high exposure and multimedia coverage for hotel properties – online, on-air and in-print.

CNN Partner Hotels are pronto to more than 500 million potential hotel quests, including frequent travellers, business decision maker and affluent, adults who prefer CNN International over any other cable or satellite channel in Asia Pacific.

In a world that never sleeps, immediate access to the latest information on global events has never been more important to people on the move Your guests expect 5 star service – give them one more reason to stay at your hotel with CNN International For more information on the CNN Hotel Partnership Programme, email: partner.hotelsgturner.com or log on to CNN's exclusive partner hotel website www.cnnpartners.com

AMERICAN EXPRESS

American Express is a diversified worldwide travel, financial and network services company. Founded in 1850, it is a world leader in charge and credit cards, Travellers Cheques, travel, financial planning, investment products, insurance and international banking. For more information, please visit the company on the Internet at www.americanexpress.com

The American Express Latin America/Caribbean Business Travel Monitor, produced by the American Express Business Intelligence team, provides strategic, innovative and value-added travel expense management solutions including: Information Systems Management, Purchasing Management, Process and Policy Management, and Research and Publications.

RESORT DATA PROCESSING, INC.

Resort Data Processing, Inc. (RDP) was founded in 1981 and is headquartered in Vail, Colorado. We develop, install, and provide 24-hour support for Hotels, Vacation Rentals, Condo-Hotels, and Timeshare management systems worldwide with over 1,000 installations.

- Hotels and Resorts
- Vacation Rental/Condo Hotels
- Timeshare/Interval Ownership
- More about RDP
- Customer Conference 9/19/2005

Why buy from RDP?

- RDP support answers the phone immediately, without wading through endless prompts.
- RDP helps you generate significantly more revenue.
- Our software adapts to the needs of the customer, not vice-versa.
- RDP provides personal service and direct contact with management
- We will add custom features to meets your requirements.

RDP offers a complete Windows based system that includes a wide variety of interfaces. The links below describe our features for Hotels and Resorts.

- Hotels and Resorts start here
- Sample Screens
- Sample Reports
- Reservations
- Yield Management
- Internet Reservations
- Packages
- Front Desk and Night Audit
- E-Mail Marketing
- Groups and Conferences
- Travel Agents/Wholesalers
- Guest Relationship Management
- Guest Itinerary and Concierge
- Housekeeping Scheduling
- Wait List/Denial Tracking/Quotes

- Integrated General Ledger
- Activity Scheduling (rentals, etc.)
- Work Orders and Asset Management
- Booking Pace and Forecasting
- Messaging/To-Do List
- Installation and Training
- Crystal Reports
- Hardware Requirements
- RDPWin Technology Overview
- Software Features
- Internet Reservations
- Global Distribution System (GDS)
- Interfaces Available
- Fast Credit Card Processing
- Virtual Store on Internet
- Crystal Reports
- Email Marketing
- Wireless Internet Access Interface
- Pervasive.SQL Database
- New Modules Available
- Sample Screens

RDP also offers solutions for Vacation Rentals, Condominium Hotels, Campgrounds and Timeshare Resorts, which include all Hotel/Resort features.

- Vacation Rentals start here
- Timeshare Resort Overview
- Campground Overview
- RDP Replaces First Resorts
- Reservation Board (Tape Chart)
- Owner Direct Access with Internet
- Email Integration for Owners
- Short Term/Long Term Rentals
- Manage Units not in Rental Pool
- Unlimited Charges Per Owner
- Month-to-Date and Year-to-Date totals
- Fast Creation of Owner Statements
- Work Orders Integrated to Owners
- Housekeeping Billing to Owners
- IRS 1099 Year-End Reports
- Room moves pay correct owner

- Trust Accounting and Owner History
- Interface to General Ledger
- Print Checks to Owners
- Reprint Statements Forever
- Accounts Receivable and Aging
- Extensive Custom Reporting
- Support Home Page
- 24-Hour Support
- Installation and Training
- Downloads and Documents
- Software Updates
- RDP Headquarters in Vail
- Customer List
- Quotes from Customers
- RDP Partners
- Frequently Asked Questions
- RDP Forms Available
- Enhancement Requests
- Refer a Prospect for $$CASH$$
- Additional Links - Site Map

Why Buy From RDP?

A Message from Barry Biegler

President and Founder, Resort Data Processing, Inc.

Why should you buy property management software from Resort Data Processing? This website is filled with many potential reasons, but here are five of the most important:

1. RDP helps you generate significantly more revenue.
2. Our software adapts to the needs of the customer, not vice-versa.
3. RDP support personnel answer the phone immediately, without the customer entering "voice mail hell".
4. We are a small company that provides personal service and direct contact with top management to get things done quickly.
5. RDP has been in business over 20 years. We know what we are doing. We are a very solid company financially, so we will be here in the future to support and improve the system.

Each of these points is explained in more detail below.

More About RDP

- Hotels and Resorts
- Vacation Rentals
- Condominium Hotels
- Timeshare
- Campgrounds
- Customer Quotes
- RDP Facility
- Directions to RDP
- Why Buy From RDP?
- Refer a prospect for cash
- Link to RDP
- News
- RDPWin
- RDP Hiring New Employees

Generate Customer Profits

Most property management software companies talk about cutting expenses via "ease-of-use," or saving employee time. While we believe cutting expenses is important, and our software can help in this area, we would rather focus our efforts on generating significant additional income for our customers. Some of the revenue generating tools that are part of RDP:

- With detailed documentation on how to implement. Our average customer has increased revenue by over $200,000 per year.
- Our Internet Reservation Module allows guests to make reservations over the Internet, 24 hours a day, 365 days a year, directly into the RDP system, without paying reservation commissions. We also provide extensive training on how to make your website more "findable" on the Internet.
- We have various marketing tools, such as integrated E-Mail to guests, groups, travel agents, wholesalers, etc.
- Our RDPConnect programme provides low-cost connectivity to the Global Distribution System (GDS), so your property will receive its share of reservations from travel agents and thousands of websites such as www.Travelocity.com. We also provide no-cost consulting on how to maximize your GDS exposure and revenue.

- Our annual customer conference in Vail, Colorado, brings together hundreds of companies similar to yours. While providing in-depth training, the focus of the conference is to brainstorm with our customers to determine what else we can do to help them make money. Most of the best features in our system have come from customers.
- Our research and development, documentation, and training are all focused on increasing customer profit. Our competition often worries about implementing new technology just because it is new. At RDP, we focus on only implementing whatever technology we need to help you make money. And our track record shows we have been very good at it over the years. Take a look at our new Windows-based software, RDPWin.

RDP Adapts to the Customer

At RDP, we believe software should adapt to the needs of the individual customer, instead of forcing the customer to adapt to the software. While this seems like a self-evident truth, you may find that many of our competitors believe otherwise and have a "take it or leave it attitude." i.e., you either use the software the way it is, or you do not use it at all.

Your business is important to us. If this means we have to change our software to get the deal, we will. Over half of our 1000 customers have a unique feature that we added just for them. To avoid confusion, we add these features with "switches," so that the feature is only active for specific customers.

Our software is designed so that you can configure it to operate the way your business does. If you cannot, we will change it so you can.

RDP Answers the Phone Directly

Have you ever tried to call almost any large software company to buy something or ask for help? Usually, you cannot even find phone numbers on their websites. If you do find a number, a machine will most likely greet your call. May be, after about 10 different voice messages, you may get into a holding queue for a human. Then, after about another 30 minutes, someone will finally answer the phone that has been employed by the company for about three days. This is the pattern when you are trying to buy something from their sales department. Support is even worse. It can take days to get a human on the phone that has a clue what you are talking about.

At RDP, our support and sales teams answer the phone directly and provide quality help immediately. "Directly" means without a machine, without a secretary. When you call RDP Support, a support technician answers the phone and says, "Hi, how can I help you?"

The trend in the industry is "automated help" with website support, E-Mail support, online help systems, etc. While we have these tools at RDP, we find most customers would rather just pick up the phone and call us. We are unique in the industry in this area. All of our support employees answer the phone directly; even our senior employees. No machines. No voicemail. Just help, immediately.

Our system is designed to help you make more money. A critical element of this goal is to make sure we have a qualified person immediately answer the phone when you call!

Customers Stay in Direct Contact with Top Management

While RDP has been in business for more than 20 years, we have not allowed the company to grow into a bureaucratic nightmare. We are still a small company with direct contact between top management and customers.

We have become friends with our customers over the years. Our annual customer conference in Vail, Colorado, has the feeling of a family gathering: not a corporate function. This is a very important element of who we are; as it is always much more fun to help a "friend" with a problem than a "customer."

With most companies, it is almost impossible to find someone who is in charge and actually able to make a decision. There are legions of people who screen calls and redirect customers. At RDP, everyone answers their own phone, so if you ever have a problem with my company or need something, just give me a call.

Company Stability - Over 20+ Years & Solid Financial Position

If the company you purchase software from goes out of business, the software becomes effectively worthless. This is because the software is only 15 per cent of the solution. The other 85 per cent is technical support, product updates, onsite training, etc. RDP has been in business over 20 years. We are very solid financially, with no company debt. We have sold over 1,000 systems, which provides an installed base of support contracts to insure we will be in business for many years to come.

Summary – Why Buy From RDP

When you purchase a Property Management System (PMS), we believe it is more important to look at the character of the company who creates the software than the technical system details.

All of the major PMS vendors handle the basics: reservations, check-in, check-out, night audit, etc. The key to a PMS purchase is to understand that the software is only the beginning of a partnership between two companies. Many of our competitors believe it is all about the software. Nothing could be farther from the truth. It is all about the people. The software is just one of our tools.

A software vendor can tell you anything in a brochure or in a demo; so please, check out our story with our customers. Ask them if our support people actually answer the phone immediately. Find out if our Yield Management and Internet Reservation Module are making them money. Ask our customers if the system is flexible enough for them, and adapts to their needs.

RDP truly is a different company. We have been in business for over 20 years, with many of the same customers and employees. If you ever need anything from RDP, help is just a phone call away.

To learn more about RDP and our product line, please use the links below.

Hotel/Resort Software Overview

Resort Data Processing (RDP) software has been installed since 1981 at over 1000 locations worldwide (see customer list). Please use the links below to learn more about RDP software for Hotels and Resorts. If you are renting homes or condominiums short term please start with Vacation Rental Overview and timeshare properties should see Timeshare Resort Overview. Our Campground management system is also available. Our systems are fully integrated, so that all features in our hotel system are available for Vacation Rentals and Timeshare resorts, and vice versa.

Core RDP Modules

- Technology Overview - RDPWIN
- Sample Screens

- Sample Reports
- Reservations
- Rates and Yield Management
- Packages
- Front Desk and Night Audit
- Groups and Conferences
- Travel Agents/Wholesalers
- Guest History and Marketing
- Housekeeping Scheduling
- Integrated General Ledger
- E-Mail Marketing
- Crystal Reports
- Installation and Training
- Hardware Requirements
- Internet Reservation Module (IRM)
- Vacation Rentals (Condo Accounting)
- Timeshare and Interval Ownership
- Campground Management
- Guest Itinerary and Concierge
- Activity Scheduling (bike rentals, etc.)
- Wait List/Denial Tracking/Res Quotes
- Frequent Guest/Rewards
- Work Orders and Asset Management
- Booking Pace and Forecasting
- Virtual Store on Internet
- Messaging/To-Do List
- Change Tracking
- 24-Hour Support
- Customer List
- RDP Headquarters in Vail

Interfaces

- Overview of All Interfaces
- Global Distribution System (GDS)
- Central Reservations
- SDC Credit Card Interface
- High Speed Credit Card Authorization
- In-Room Video Checkout
- Call Accounting
- Phone Actuator (On/Off)
- Point of Sale

- Voicemail
- Maid-Phone (Housekeeping)
- Environmental
- Back-Office Accounting
- Nomadix Wireless Internet Billing
- Room Key (Ving Card, etc.)
- RDP Partners and Alliances

Vacation Rental and Condo-Hotel Features and Links

- Powerful Reservation Board (Tape Chart)
- Data Flow From Reservation to Owner Statement
- Mix of Rental Types - Condos, Houses, Hotels, Timeshare
- Internet Reservations with Unit Pictures and Virtual Tours
- Live Demonstration of Internet Reservations
- E-mail Integration for Guests, Owners, etc.
- Short Term and/or Long Term Rental
- Lock-Off Units Allowed
- Manage Units Not in the Rental Pool
- Extensive Custom Reporting with Crystal Reports
- Work Orders and Asset Management
- Housekeeping Forecast, Schedule, and History
- Reservation Quotes, Wait List, and Denial Tracking
- Customer Relationship Management (CRM)
- Travel Agent Commissions Deducted
- Unlimited Charges Per Owner
- Owner Recurring Charges
- Various Billing Cycles - Monthly, Quarterly, etc.
- Split Revenue Across Billing Period
- Fast Production of Owner Statements
- Month-to-Date and Year-to-Date Totals Per Owner
- Statements Can Be Reprinted Forever
- Print Checks to Owners
- Trust Accounting and Owner History
- Automatic Interface to General Ledger (Back Office)
- Integration to GDS, POS, Credit Cards, etc.
- Accounts Receivable with Aging
- Print or E-mail Overdue Notices Automatically
- IRS 1099 Year-End Reports
- Room Moves Pay Correct Owner
- Yield Management Integrated
- Sharewith Folios or One Guest with Multiple Folios

- Taxes Adjusted for Length of Stay and Location
- Timeshare and Interval Ownership Allowed
- All RDP Hotel Features Available for Owner Systems
- Resort Data Processing Home Page

See: Hotel and Resort Overview
See: Vacation Rentals and Condo-Hotel Overview
See: Timeshare/Interval Ownership Overview

Other Links in http://www.resortdata.com/

RDP Overview Topics

- Software Overview
- Why Buy from RDP?
- Frequent Questions (FAQ)
- RDP Partners
- RDPWin Technology Overview
- Referral Programme (Earn Cash)
- Download Documentation List
- RDP Customer List
- New RDP Modules
- RDP Corporate Office
- RDP News
- RDP Contact Information

Internet Reservations (IRM)

- Internet Reservations Overview
- Condominium IRM Demo
- Hotel IRM Demo
- IRM Customer Sites
- IRM Customer Quotes
- Optimizing the IRM
- New Features
- IRM Hardware Requirements
- IRM Knowledge Base
- Installation Checklist
- Bridge Server Installation
- E-Mail Marketing

General

- Support Home Page
- Installation and Training

- Anti-Virus Installation Issues
- 2005 Customer Conference
- Pervasive Software
- Global Distribution System
- New Preprinted Forms
- RDP Partners and Alliances
- Hardware Requirements
- High-Speed Credit Card Processing
- RDP Interfaces Available
- Submit Product Enhancement

Bibliography

Archer, B. and Cooper, C., (1998), The positive and negative impacts of tourism. In: Theobald, W.F. (ed.) *Global Tourism: the Second Decade,* 2nd edn. Butterworth-Heinemann, Oxford, pp. 63-81.

Archer, B.H. & Fletcher, J.E., (1990), Tourism: Its economic significance. In M. Quest (ed.), Horwath Book of Tourism (pp. 10-25). London: The MacMillan Press.

Archer, B.H., (1995), The impact of international tourism on the economy of Bermuda. *Journal of Travel Research,* 34(2), 27-30.

Armington, Stan, (1976), Trekking in the Himalayas, Lonely Planet Publications, Victoria.

Ashley, Caroline, (1998), 'Tourism, communities and national policy: Namibia's experience.' *Development Policy Review* 16(4): 323-352.

Ashley, Caroline, (2000), *The Impact of Tourism on Rural Livelihoods: Namibia's Experience.* ODI Working Paper no. 128. London, ODI.

Belk. R.W. and Costa. J.A., (1995), International tourism an assessment and overview. *Journal of Macromarketing* 15(2), 33-48.

Belsky, Jill, (1999) 'Misrepresenting communities: the politics of community-based rural ecotourism in dales Point Manatee, Belize.' *Rural Sociology* 64 (4): 641-666.

Benjamin, Medea, and Andrea Freedman. *Bridging the Global Gap.* Cabin John, MD: Seven Locks Press, 1988.

Bennett, O., Roe, D. and Ashley, C., (1999), Sustainable Tourism and Poverty Elimination Study: A report to the Department for International Development, April http://www.propoortourism.org.uk/dfidr_eport.pdf

Berger D.J., (1996), The challenge of integrating Maasai tradition with tourism, in M.F. Price (ed.) *People and Tourism in Fragile Environment.* John Wiley & Sons, Chichester, 175-198.

Blanchard, K., (1994), Culture and seabird conservation: the North Shore of the Gulf of St. Lawrence, Canada in D. Nettleship. J. Burger and M.Gochfeld (eds) *Seabirds on Islands Threats. Case Studies and Action Plans,* Birdlife International Conservation, Cambridge, England, 294-310.

Blank, U. and Perkovich, M., (1987), Research on urban tourism destinations, in J.R.B. Ritchie and C.R. Goeldner *(eds) Travel, Tourism and Hospitality Research,* John Wiley & Sons, New York, 165-177.

Blazey, M., (1992), Travel and Retirement Status. *Annals of Tourism Research* 19(4), 771-783.

Blunden, G., Cocklin, C. and Davis, P., (1995), Land based production in Northland, Occasional Paper 30, Department of Geography, Auckland University, Auckland. Beo E. (1990) *Ecotourism: The Potentials and Pitfalls* 2 vols. World Wildlife Fund, Washington.

Boissevien, Jeremy, (ed.), (1996), *Coping with Tourists: European Reactions to Mass Tourism.* Oxford Bergham Books.

Boniface, B.G. and Cooper, C.P., (1994), *The Geography of Travel and Tourism,* 2nd eds., Butterworth-Heinemann, Oxford.

Britton, S.G., (1991), Tourism, capital and place: towards a critical geography of tourism, *Environment and Planning D: Society and Space* 9, 451-478.

Brohman, J., (1996), New directions in tourism for Third World development, *Annals of Tourism Research* 23(1), 48-70.

Brohman, John, (1996), 'New directions in tourism for Third World development.' *Annals of Tourism Research* 23(I): 48-70.

Canadian Environmental Assessment Research Council (CEARC) (1988), *The Assessment of Cumulative Effects: A Research Prospectus,* CEARC, Ottawa.

Carey, A. and Jones, L. (eds), (1993), *The Buzzworm Magazine Guide to Ecotrav*-Buzzworm Books, Boulder.

Carey, J., (1993), *Review of Management of Impacts of Commercial Tourism and Private Recreation in the Great Barrier Reef Marine Park.* Report to the Great Barrier Reef Marine Park Authority, Townsville.

Cavanagh, James E., (1993), et al., "Ocean Energy Systems". In *Renewable Energy: Sources for Fuels and Electricity.* Ed. Thomas B. Johansson, et al. Washington D.C.: Island Press.

Ceballos-Lascarain, Hector, (1996), *Tourism, Ecotourism, and Protected Areas: The State of Nature based Tourism Around the World and Guidelines for Its Development.* North Bennington, VT: The World Conservation Union and Ecotourism Society.

Center for Responsible Tourism, PO Box 827, San Anselmo, CA 94979; (415) 258-6594, fax (415) 454-2493. Publications, reports, newsletter, advocacy.

Center for the Advancement of Responsible Travel (CART) 70 Dry Hill Park Road. Tonbridge, Kent TN10 3 BX UK. Center for information on responsible tourism in Europe.

Central Television Enterprises, Hesketh House, 43-45 Portman Square, London W1H 9FG. Tourism films include *Thailand for Sale,* produced by David Jay and coproduced by Small World Productions.

Centres for Disease Control, (1994), *Health Information for International Travel.* Atlanta: Centers for Disease Control.

Cerovsky, J., (1990), IUCN and Eastern Europe, *IUCN Bulletin,* 21(4), 1-4.

Cerovksy. J. and Podhaiska. Z., 1990, Czechoslovakia, in IUCN, *Environmental Status Reports 1988-1989,* Vol. 1. IUCN-EEP, Cambridge, 3-53.

Danaher, Kevin, Beyond Safaris, (1991), A *Guide to Building People-on-People Ties with Africa,* Trenton, NJ: Africa World Press.

Daniels, A., (1995), Ahousat band's ecological walk business booms, *Vancouver Sun,* 27 January.

Dartmoor National Park Authority, (1994), *Traffic Management Strategy,* Devon County Council and Dartmoor National Park Authority, Bovey Tracey.

Davies E., (1987), Planning in the New Zealand National Parks. *New Zealand Geographer* 43(2), 73-78.

Davison, R., Vogel, D., Gricar, J., Harris, R. and Sorrentmo, M., (2003), Electronic Commerce on the New Silk Road: Rejuvenating a Historical Trade Network, The European Conference on Information Systems June 19-21 Naples, Italy.

Ecumenical Coalition on Third World Tourism (ECTWT), (1992), *Caught in Modern Slavery.* Bangkok: ECTWT.

Edgell, D.L., (1999), *Tourism Policy: The Next Millennium.* Advances in Tourism Applications Series, Sagamore Publishing.

Edmonton Journal, (1991), Neighbours demand silence from fort, *Edmonton Journal,* 22, August, B2.

Edwards, F. (ed), (1988), *Environmentally Sound Tourism in the Caribbean,* The University of Calgary Press, Calgary.

Eight Northern Indian Pueblos Council, (1996), *8 Northern Indian Pueblos 1996 Visitors Guide,* Eight Northern Indian Pueblos Council, New Mexico.

Fairchils, H.N., (1928), *The Noble Savage: A Study in Romantic Naturalism.* Columbia University Press, New York.

Foghorn Press, 555 De Haro Street, The Boiler Room #220, San Francisco, CA 94107; (415) 241-9550, fax (415) 241-9648. Outdoor and recreation books.

Forbes, B., (1993), *Tourism Development Plan, 1993-1998,* Brooking-Harbor Chamber of Commerce, Brookings.

Foresta, R.A., (1984), *America's National Parks and Their Keepers*, Resources for the Future, Washington.

Goodwin, M. and Painter, J. (1996), Local governance, the crises or Fordism and the changing geographies of regulation, *Transactions of the Institute of British Geographers* 21(4), 635-648.

Goodwin, N., (1987), A *Complete Guide to Travel Agency*, Albanj, Dalmer.

Goodwin. P., Hallet, S., Kenny, F. and Stokes, G., (1991), *Transport: The New Realism*. Transport Studies Unit, University of Oxford, Oxford.

Graefe., A.R. Kuss, F.R. and Vske, J.J., (1900), *Visitor Impact Management*, 2 vols., National Parks and Conservation Association, Washington.

Graham, Scott., (1992), *Handle with Care: A Guide to Responsible Travel in Developing Counties*. Chicago: Noble Press.

Hall, C.M. and Johnston, M. (eds), (1995), *Polar Tourism: Tourism in the Arctic and Antarctic Regions*, John Wiley, Chichester.

Hall, C.M. and Wouters, M.M., (1994), Managing nature tourism in the sub-Antarctic islands, *Annals of Tourism Research* 21, 355-374.

Hall, C.M. Mitchell, L. and Keelan N., (1992), Maori cultural heritage and tourism in New Zealand, *Journal of Cultural Geography* 12(2), 115-128.

Hall, C.M., (1992a), *Wasteland to World Heritage: Preserving Australia's Wilderness*, Mellboutne University Press, Carlton.

Hayden, T., (1999), Tuberculosis is making a comeback *Newsweek 8* November, p. 77.

Hayes, John L., (1976), Trekking North of Kathmandu, Peter Purna Banks Avalok, Kathmandu.

Hays, S.P., (1957), *The Response to Industrialism*, 1885-1914, University of Chicago Press, Chicago.

Jones, P., (1993), Wildlife viewing in Atlantic Canada: A case study of constraints and opportunities, unpublished Master's project, Simon Fraser University, Burnaby.

Jones, S.B., (1933), Mining tourist towns in the Canadian Rockies, *Economic Geography* 9, 368-378.

Kaiser, C. Jr. and Helber, L.E., (1978), Tourism: Planning and Development, Mass CBI Publishing, Boston.

Kalisch, Angela, (2000), *The GATS and Fair Trade in Tourism: Briefing Paper*. Paper presented at the fair Trade in Tourism Forum, London, 20 November 2000.

Kay, J. and Schncider, E., (1994), Embracing complexity: the challenge of the ecosystem approach, *Alternatives* 20(3); 32-39.

Keelan, N., (1996), Maori heritage: visitor management and interpretation, in G.M. Hall and S. McArthur (eds) *Heritage*

Management in Australia and New Zealand: The Human Dimension, Oxford University Press, Melbourne, 195-201.

Lawson, F., and M. Baud-Bovy (1977), *Tourism and Recreation Development,* London: Architectural Press.

Lea, John, (1988), *Tourism and Development in the Third World.* London: Routledge.

Leheny, D., (1995), A political economy of Asian sex tourism. *Annals of Tourism Research* 22(2), 367-384.

Leininger, A., *(1993), Algunos aspectos de la geograia touristica y su application en Costa Rica, Escuela de Ciensias Geograficas.* Universidad National Costa Rica, Heredia, unpublished.

Leiper, N., (1990), Tourist attraction systems, *Annals of Tourism Research* 17(3), 367-384.

Lemons, J. and Brown, D.A., (1995), *Sustainable Development, Science, Ethics and Public Policy,* Kluwer Academic Publishers, London.

Maderey, John, (1995), *Foreign Exploits, Transnationals and Tourism.* London. Catholic Institute for International Relations.

MAFF, (1991), *Success with Sporting Entreprises on Farms: A Guide to Farmers and Landowners,* Ministry of Agriculture, Fisheries and Food, London.

Maiden, A.N., (1995), Exploring the Maori experience, *The Independent Monthly,* July, 74-81.

Mak, A., (1981), The Montagnais. In *The Lower North Shore.* Ministere des Affaires Culturelles du Quebec, Quebec, 86-99.

Mallari, A.A. and Enote, J.A., (1996), Maintaining control: culture and tourism in the Pueblo of Zuni, New Mexico, in M.F. Price (ed.) *People and Tourism in Fragile Environments,* John Wiley & Sons, Chichester, 19-31.

Mander, Jerry, and Edward Goldsmith, (eds.), (1996) *The Case Against the Global Economy.* San Francisco: Sierra Club Books.

Manidis Roberts Consultants, (1995), *Determining an Environmental and Social Carrying Capacity for Jenolan Caves Reserve,* Manidis Roberts, Sydney.

Meadows, D.H., Meadows, D.L. Randers, J. and Behrens, W.W., (1972), *Limits to Growth,* Universal Books, New York.

Medlik, R., (1988), 'What is Tourism? Teaching Tourism into the 1990s. Published in the Proceedings of International Conference. *Tourism Educators,* July, 1988, University of Surry, Guildford, U.K.

Nadler L., (1980), "Defining the field—is it HRD or O.D. or.......". *Training and Development Journal,* published by ASTC 34, No. 12, p. 66.

Olindo, Perez, (1991-1997), The old man of nature tourism: Kenya.' Reprinted in Lesley France (Ed.). *The Earthscan Reader in Sustainable Tourism*, pp. 90-97. London, Earthscan.

Olmsted, F.L. and Wharton, W.P., (1932), The Florida Everglades: where the mangrove forces meet the storm waves of a thousand miles of water, *American Forests* 38 (March), 142-147, 192.

Olwig R, and Olwig, K. (1979), Underdevelopment and the development of 'natural' parks ideology *Antipode* II (2), 16-25.

Partners for Livable Places, (1981), *Tourism and Communities: Process, Problems, and Solutions*, Washington, DC: Partners for Livable Places.

Pattullo, Polly, (1996), *Last Resorts: The Cost of Tourism in the Caribbean*. London: Cassell.

Patty, A., (1999), Australian sex tourists find their laws back home don't take a vacation. *The World Paper* January-February, p. 16.

Pearce, D. (1981), *Tourist Development*, London: Longman.

Pearce, D., (1989), *Tourism Development (Second Edition), John Wiley*, New York.

Prior, D., (1996), 'Working the network': local authority strategy in the reticulated local state. *Local Government Studies* 22(2), 92-104.

Rames, K.T., (1995), *Structural Adjustment, World Trade and Third World Tourism: An Introduction to the Issues*. Bangkok: ECTWT. Ramsar, (1992), New opportunities for cooperation in Europe, *Ramsar Newsletter*, 13. 2-7.

Rao, T.V. and Pereira, (1986), *Recent Experiences in Human Resource Development*, Oxford Publications, New Delhi.

RDC, (1997), *The Economic Impact of Recreation and Tourism in the English Countryside. Rural Development Commission and Countryside Commission*, London.

Redclift, M. and Benton, T., (1994), *Social Theory and the Global Environment*, Routledge, London.

Redclift, M., (1987), Sustainable Development and the market a framework for analysis *Futures* 20(6), 638.

Reed, D., (1990), *The European Bank for Reconstruction and Development: an Environmental Opportunity*, World Wide Fund for Nature, Washington.

Reed, Ralph Thomas, (1952), *American Express: Its Origin and Growth*. New York: Newcomen Society in North America.

Sindiga, Isaac, (1996), "Domestic tourism in Kenya.' *Annals of Tourism Research* 23 (I): 19-31.

Singh, Shalini, (1997), "Developing Human Resources for the Tourism Industry in India." *Journal of Travel and Tourism,* IITTM Vol. 1, No. I, Gwalior.

Singh, Tej Vir, H. Leon Theuns, and Frank M. Co. (1989), *Towards Appropriate Tourism: The Case of Developing Countries.* New York: Peter Lang.

Smith, S.L., (1989), *Tourism Analyses,* Longman, Harlow.

Smith, S.L.J., (1988), Defining Tourism, a supply side view, *Annals of Tourism Research,* 15 (2), Pergamon, London.

Smith, Stephen L.J., (1995), *Tourism Analysis. A Handbook.* Essex: Longman Scientific & Technical.

Smith, V. (ed.), (1977), *Hosts and Guests: The Anthropology of Tourism,* University of Pennsylvania Press, Philadelphia.

Smith, V., (1989), Eskime tourism micro-models and marginal men, in V.I., Smith (ed.) *Hosts and Guests: The Anthropology of Tourism,* 2nd edn., University of Pennsylvania Press, Philadelphia, 55-82.

Smith. V., (1996), The Inuit as hosts: heritage and wilderness tourism in Nunavut, in M.F. Price (ed.) *People and Tourism in Fragile Environments,* John Wiley, Chichester, 33-50.

Sofield, T., (1991), Sustainable ethnic tourism in the South Pacific: some principles, *Journal of Tourism Studies,* 2. 56-72.

Sofield, T.H.B., (1996), Anuha Island Resort, Solomon Islands: a case study of failure in R. Butler and T. Hinch (eds) *Tourism and Indigenous Peoples:* International Thomson Business Press, London, 176-202.

Sooacmalelagi, L., Hunter, S. and Brown. S., (1996), Alternate tourism development in Western Samoa. Paper presented at 3rd Pacific Indigenous Business Conference 11-13 December 1996 Oxford Koala Hotel, Sydney.

Spaho, E., (1992), Tourism: promising contracts, *Albanian Economic Tribune,* 6(10). 17-19.

Spaho, E., (1993), Personal interview. Deputy Minister of Tourism, Tirana, 27 March.

Taylot, G. (1995), The community approach: does it really work: *Tourism Management* 16(7), 487-489.

Turnock, D., (1979), Water management resources in Romania, *GeoJournal,* 3, 609-622.

Underhill, Geoffrey R.D., (1994), 'Introduction: conceptualising the changing global order.' In Richard Stubbs and Geoffrey R.D. Underhill (eds.), *Political Economy and the Changing Global Order,* pp. 17-44. London, MacMillan.

Urquico, C., (1998), Community Based Sustainable Tourism: A Handbook, ASSET. Philippines.

Wheeller, Brian, (1991/1997), "Tourism's troubled times: responsible tourism is not the answer." Reprinted in Lesley France (Ed.), *The Earthscan Reader in Sustainable Tourism*, pp. 61-67. London, Earthscan.

Wilkinson, P.P., (1989), "Strategies for future development in island microstates", *Annuals of Tourism Research* 16(2): 156-177.

Williams, P., (1990), "Tourism Technology and Environment", *Journal of Travel Research*, Vol. XXIX, No. 2, pp. 55-56.

Williams, P.W., and A. Gill, (1991), *Carrying Capacity Management in Tourism Settings: A Tourism Growth Management Process.* Centre for Tourism Policy and Research, Simon Freser University, Burnaby, British Columbia.

Wood, M.E., (1993), 'Costa Rican parks threatened by tourism boom: Society launches letter-writing campaign'. *The Ecotourism Society Newsletter.* 3(1), pp. 1-2.

Wood. M.E., (1993), Costa Rican parks threatened by tourism boom: society launches letter-writing campaign. *The Ecotourism Society Newsletter*, 3(1), 1-2.

Index